Atlantic Currents

Atlantic Currents

Connecting Cork and Lowell

EDITED BY

PAUL MARION
TINA NEYLON
JOHN WOODING

LP

Loom Press
Lowell, Massachusetts
2020

Published in the United States of America
First edition

The stories and parts of novels as well as certain poems in this collection are works of fiction whose names, characters, places, and incidents are products of the respective author's imagination. Any resemblance to actual persons, living or dead, or to real entities or locales is coincidental.

A grant from the Human Services Corp. Endowment of the Greater Lowell Community Foundation provided funding for this project. Thanks also to the UMass Lowell Center for Irish Partnerships. Proceeds will benefit Cork Learning City in Cork, Ireland, and Lowell: City of Learning in Lowell, Massachusetts. For more information: **corklearningcity.ie** and **lowellcityoflearning.org**

Atlantic Currents is supported by the Creative Ireland Programme, an all-of-Government five-year initiative, from 2017 to 2022, which places creativity at the centre of public policy. For more information: **creative.ireland.ie** and **ireland.ie**

Loom Press P.O. Box 1394 Lowell, MA 01853
www.loompress.com info@loompress.com

Design: Victoria Weinreb and Hernan Florez
Printing: King Printing Co., Inc. Lowell, Mass.
Typefaces: Adobe Caslon Pro, Atrament, Bebas Kai, and Bodoni 72

To the people who live, love, learn, work,
and pursue happiness in Cork and Lowell,
and to all those in time who have done the same.

Contents

Lowell

This anthology of writing emerged, in part, from a passing comment. A participant at an international conference on sustainability in Lowell in the fall of 2016 mentioned that Cork (where he was from) had become a successful UNESCO Learning City and that Lowell seemed like a perfect candidate to do the same. (UNESCO is the United Nations Educational, Scientific, and Cultural Organization.) That comment led to a group from Lowell traveling to Cork to attend its Festival of Lifelong Learning and to building connections between the two cities and between the University of Massachusetts, Lowell, and University College Cork. This, in turn, sparked an initiative in Lowell to follow Cork's lead, and we began the process of designating and framing Lowell as a learning city.

Like Cork, Lowell had much to build on. In Europe and in North America, many cities' and towns' glory days as centers of manufacturing, transportation, and commerce are long past. Often ravaged by changes in the economy, many places adapted. Lowell did so by building on its history as the city of mills and immigrants. Since the 1980s, driven by the creation of Lowell National Historical Park, marking the American Industrial Revolution (and adding Lowell to the same list as the Grand Canyon in Arizona, the Everglades in Florida, Statue of Liberty in New York, and Gettysburg Civil War battlefield in Pennsylvania), Lowell has embraced culture (arts and heritage) as a means to attract visitors and enhance the community. The Boott Cotton Mills Museum and related Tsongas Industrial History Center attract thousands of visitors, students, and teachers. The Park itself, a downtown historic district and 5.6-mile power canal system, is a museum-without-walls, an outdoor classroom for place-based, lifelong experiential learning, an urban laboratory.

An outcome of the Vietnam War of the 1960s and '70s and later genocide in Cambodia was an influx of refugees from Southeast Asia (particularly Cambodia). They brought to Lowell new ideas, beliefs, food, music, and way of life. These are celebrated at the annual Southeast Asian Water Festival on the Merrimack River, which draws upwards of 40,000 people. The award-winning Angkor Dance Troupe entertains and teaches traditional Cambodian dance all year.

In recent times, immigrants from Brazil, Nigeria, Ghana, the Middle East, India, Puerto Rico, and Cape Verde, among other nations, along with American citizens from Puerto Rico added their stories to those of the Irish, Greeks, Portuguese, Polish, Syrians, Armenians, French Canadians, early English and Scottish, and others who have long made Lowell their home. Nearly every ethnic group has its annual festival, national flag-raising ceremony, or monument. Lowell's rich culture rolls down its streets every day.

Many industrial buildings have been transformed into loft-style residences and artists' studios. Lowell boasts one of the largest concentrations of visual artists on the Eastern seaboard. At the Brush Art Gallery and Studios downtown, artists work in public view. Western Avenue Studios has some three hundred artists. Or you can check out the Whistler House Museum of Art, birthplace of the great painter. Lots of innovative bands and singers play the pubs and clubs of Lowell. A new music mega-event, the Town and the City Festival, uses venues throughout the city. Bigger venues, like the Paul Tsongas Center of UMass Lowell, Lowell Memorial Auditorium, and Donahue Family Academic Arts Center at Middlesex Community College, showcase regional talent plus popular musical acts, national and global. The three-day Lowell Folk Festival, running since 1987, bills itself as the largest free open-air folk festival in the country, drawing tens of thousands of people. Readers and writers flock to the annual Lowell Celebrates Kerouac! activities, Parker Lectures, and author talks at the City's Pollard Memorial Library. The way of life includes a robust sports and recreation scene with professional baseball and top-level university athletics, both women's and men's teams, all the school- and community-based leagues, from high-school rowing to young soccer players, and active networks of runners and bike riders.

But what does this mean? The United Nations and UNESCO developed the term Learning City and the idea in its early years. The United Nations has long had a commitment to education and literacy developed within UNESCO, beginning with the creation of the UNESCO Institute for Education (IE) in 1950. Over the years, IE moved from supporting adult education programs in Europe and the developed world to emphasizing education's importance in developing countries. Later still, the focus shifted to the support of lifelong learning and non-formal education in all countries of the world. The original IE was transformed in 2006 to create UNESCO's Institute for Lifelong Learning (ILL), headquartered in Hamburg, Germany. The ILL created three signature programs, including Lifelong Learning, under which rubric it created the Learning Cities Program.

The Learning Cities Program is an international policy-oriented network providing inspiration, know-how, and best practices to current and prospective Learning Cities. The network supports the achievement of all seventeen UN Sustainable Development Goals (SDGs), in particular, SDG 4 ("Ensure inclusive and equitable quality education and promote lifelong learning opportunities for all") and SDG 11 ("Make cities and human settlements inclusive, safe, resilient and sustainable"). The Learning Cities program supports and improves the practice of lifelong learning in the world's cities by promoting policy dialogue and peer learning among members. It helps by forging links, fostering partnerships, providing capacity development, and developing instruments to encourage and recognize progress made in building learning cities.

Basing our work on this framework and opportunity presented by the Learning Cities Program, and with enormous and valuable support from our friends in Cork, the Lowell initiative has connected with the major educational institutions in the city and many of its community organizations to drive this initiative forward. The model that Cork has given us is inspiring. The result was the first Festival of Learning in 2019.

More importantly, the work led to connections and ideas for promoting learning activities and opportunities in Lowell and Cork. One significant part of these activities is the educational and cultural value of artistic activity in all its many forms. In the spirit of Learning Cities, we wish to raise the visibility of our writers and enrich the experiences of readers, stressing the flow of ideas and reflection between Cork and Lowell. Learning Cities helped create the forces that drove *Atlantic Currents*.

John Wooding
Coordinator, Lowell: City of Learning

Cork

How did Cork become a Learning City? That's a question often asked, particularly since international recognition by UNESCO in 2015. Wyndham, a suburb of Melbourne, and Burnaby in British Columbia, Canada, have followed in our footsteps, organising annual festivals devoted to learning—and now Lowell has joined them.

When I was appointed Coordinator of the pilot Cork Lifelong Learning Festival back in 2004, I knew very little about what was involved nor what could be achieved. What I was asked to do was organise a two-day event showcasing learning opportunities across the city, with the aim of working towards Cork becoming a Learning City.

The approach adopted was that everyone participating in the festival does so voluntarily, that all events are free, and that they are treated equally, i.e. a knitting class is as valuable as a PhD student discussing research. I believe that works as it truly celebrates learning of all kinds, regardless of the age of those taking part, their background, ability or interests, and removes any sense that learning in an academic setting is more worthwhile than, for example, in a craft group.

With just six weeks before the weekend chosen, I set to work contacting people. As I did, I learned about schemes and initiatives I hadn't known about—including Home School Community Liaison teachers, Community Education Networks, a training project for young cyclists, and many, many more. I realised then that lots of people wouldn't know about them either and that spreading information about what's available is a very important element of the festival.

So is taking part of course—as much as possible being more than a spectator—actually trying something new, whether it's a walking tour of the city you've lived in all your life, or trying pottery, experiencing a Third Level lecture, taking part in a choir rehearsal . . . .

What we've always tried to emphasise is that learning is fun— and that's particularly relevant to those who have not had pleasant experiences of education, or who dropped out of school or college without qualifications.

And so we adopted the motto "Investigate! Participate! Celebrate!" which captures the festival's aims: find out what opportunities for learning are available; take part in events; and have fun doing so.

What happened that first year was that the response was so enthusiastic that it spread over four days with more than sixty different events. It gradually grew since then—so that in recent years over six hundred events have been showcased during festival week.

From the beginning the festival has been inclusive—inviting marginalised groups including the disabled, the Traveller community, migrants—to not only attend events but also to share their learning opportunities.

Learning never stops—it happens everywhere, and Cork's festival events reflect that, taking place on sportsgrounds and in parks, in workplaces, libraries, theatres, on the streets, in family and community centres and gardens. Learning is not only about gaining knowledge or qualifications; it usually involves inter-acting with others—indeed, sometimes the social aspect may be more important to the individual than what is being learned.

Cork is not a large city—its boundaries were enlarged last year, but, during the years 2004 to 2017, when I stepped down, its population was roughly 120,000. That means people know each other or at least know who to contact if you are looking for particular information or a useful contact. I believe the city's scale helped establish the festival and ensure it succeeded in its aim of changing attitudes to learning, to seeing that it's not confined to classrooms or lecture halls or that it stops in our youth.

In Ireland, Cork is known as "festival city" with about thirty of them annually, among the oldest are those devoted to Film, Jazz, Folk, Choral Music. Different sectors in Cork often work together on various projects, and the Lifelong Learning Festival helped to increase and raise the visibility of that activity. In 2012 we adopted the EcCoWell initiative, which takes a holistic approach to city development, bringing together Ecology & Economy (Ec),

Community & Culture (Co), Wellbeing & Lifelong Learning (Well). EcCoWell was the brainchild of Peter Kearns, awarded the Medal of the Order of Australia for his contribution to education, who introduced it to us. It promotes the integration of strategies to maximise the positive impacts on the health and educational opportunities of all, as well as developing the environmental and economic sustainability of the city, resulting in greater equality, social inclusion, and ultimately a better quality of life.

One aspect of the festival of which I am particularly proud is our partnership with Féile and Phobail ("festival of the people") in West Belfast. The main reason we gradually built up that relationship is so people from different communities at either end of the island of Ireland can learn about each other. Over the years exchanges and projects have taken place—including mural painting, the building of traditional boats and learning to row them, writers reading their work. Relationships built up through these activities now continue year round and have extended to include participation by Cork in the Belfast City Marathon and vice versa. Festivals can help to break down barriers in places emerging from conflict, and, hopefully, others may learn how rewarding that can be.

The festival is central in Cork achieving recognition as a Learning City, and has inspired others to follow its lead, both in Ireland and overseas.

This collection of writing is aimed at building on links we have made with Lowell, and illustrates how we can learn from each other. Hopefully, it is only the first collaboration between our cities.

Tina Neylon
Former Coordinator, Cork Lifelong Learning Festival

ONE

Brendan Goggin

Cork: A Learning City

When Cork was designated in 2015 as one of only twelve cities worldwide to receive an inaugural UNESCO award for Learning Cities, the occasion was celebrated as a significant milestone for the city. That award was followed two years later by further United Nations Educational, Scientific, and Cultural Organization (UNESCO) recognition when Cork was selected to host the third biennial UNESCO conference for Learning Cities. The previous two conferences had been held in Beijing, China, and Mexico City. Cork with its population of 120,000 would not have come to mind as a natural successor to these cities, but its selection represented Cork being regarded as a remarkable exemplar of the concept of Learning Cities that UNESCO wishes to promote.

Tradition of Learning

How did Cork achieve these distinctions? The city, second biggest in the Republic of Ireland, has a long tradition of learning. Founded over 1500 years ago as a monastic settlement and continuously occupied since then, it has experienced all phases of Irish urban development. Educational historians point to the presence of a monastic school in its earliest settlement—the oldest extant document from a Cork source, dating back to 664 AD, makes reference to the school and to the care of its students. Historians also point to more recent times when educational developments in the city in the eighteenth and nineteenth centuries provided the firm foundation on which the primary, secondary and higher education institutions of the present day were built.

Ireland has always prided itself as being the "Island of Saints and Scholars." However, the reality was that up to the 1970s the vast majority of the population had completed their formal education by the age of fourteen. While the country had a well-developed system of primary education, second level and higher education was the preserve of a small minority.

Driven initially by new perceptions of the role of education in economic development, major changes in the educational system at all levels were initiated in the 1960s. Ground-breaking initiatives, such as the removal of the financial barriers encountered by families to secondary education and substantially increased investment by the state across all sectors, led to major changes. Participation rates at all levels increased dramatically and continued to do so in the following decades.

Learning and Economic Development in Cork

Cork's educational system became a key factor in its economic development. Traditional industries such as textiles, motor car assembly, shipbuilding, and tyre manufacturing, had provided a significant part of the employment base for much of the twentieth century. Under the influence of globalisation, Ireland's accession to the European Community in 1973, and a number of recessions, these had all but disappeared by the mid-1980s.

However, thanks to its education and training system, the city was well-positioned to adapt to the changing environment by attracting new high-technology companies. Many were set up through foreign direct investment, but many also resulted from evolving indigenous Irish companies. These industries required the supply of a highly qualified and highly skilled workforce, and this was to be found in Cork through the graduates of its higher education institutions, University College Cork (UCC) and Cork Institute of Technology (CIT), and from its other training and education facilities. In turn, these were dependent on the supply of students progressing to them from second-level schools, especially within the city.

Pre-eminent among the new electronics and information technology companies were Dell-EMC and Apple Computers, who established their European headquarters in Cork. Pfizer, established in 1969, was the forerunner of many pharma companies to set up in the Cork region, and now nine of the top ten pharma companies globally have a presence in Cork.

Planning the Learning City

The strategic plan for the development of Cork, approved by the city authorities in 2002, was entitled *Imagine Our Future*. It recognised the important role which education had played in the rejuvenation of economic life and adopted as one of its pillars of progress the development of Cork as a Learning City. The vision was, however, much wider than merely economic. The plan emphasised the importance of learning at all stages of life and its benefits in addressing issues of deprivation and social exclusion, in community and personal development, and in fostering a culture of creativity and innovation in the city.

The Learning City concept resulted in a number of initiatives across the city and within the education sector, with varying levels of success. The annual Cork Lifelong Learning Festival was the most enduring, high profile and successful of these, and has been running since 2004. With its motto of *Investigate! Participate! Celebrate!*, the festival seeks to promote and celebrate learning of all kinds, for all ages, for all interests and all abilities. From modest beginnings, it grew rapidly to a week-long festival with over 600 events in venues throughout the city and involves not only the expected education providers, but also community groups, libraries, voluntary organisations, and industries.

Learning City Renewal

The Lifelong Learning Festival also provided the platform for the relaunch and rejuvenation of the Learning City initiative following a period in which the initial enthusiasm had waned, and the statutory support structures on which it depended had themselves changed. An agreement between four major partners, Cork City Council, UCC, CIT, and the Cork Education and Training Board (Cork ETB), provided a new start for the Learning City initiative and a reformulation of the objectives which Cork set itself. As well as these four partners, the initiative also involved participation by other bodies in health, community services, business, environment, arts, and culture, all of which view learning as central to their successful functioning.

Cork's Learning City concept is about much more than educational establishments. It recognises that learning takes place not just in such settings, but also in families, in communities, in workplaces, in public spaces, and through digital technologies. Included in its goals are those of enhancing the quality in all spheres of learning and of contributing to economic progress, sustainable development, and social inclusion.

Fundamental to the approach adopted is recognition of the distinct and complementary roles of the various participants and the benefits of co-operation. As an instance of this, the higher education institutions CIT and UCC have remits and frames of reference that encompass the city but are not geographically limited to it. The Learning City structures assist them by providing a means of involvement with other sectors of education and with communities that would otherwise be more limited. In turn, that involvement assists them in addressing their aspirations of greater social inclusion and greater equity of access to higher education. This is formalised through the Learning Neighbourhoods Programme. Initiated by the Adult and Continuing Education Department of UCC, it is a working partnership of local communities, CIT, Cork ETB, the Health Services Executive, and Cork City Council. It operates at the local level in six different communities across the city and focusses on community engagement, promoting a culture of lifelong learning, social inclusion, and raising educational horizons where expectations may be low.

The size of Cork was important in determining its approach to developing the Learning City. Cork is large enough to have a well-regarded university and institute of technology in the higher education sector, three large further education colleges, and a leading training establishment under Cork ETB, a well-developed community education scheme, a diverse industrial and employment base, and a vibrant cultural life. At the same time Cork is small enough to facilitate individual contacts, networks, and partnerships across the entire learning environment.

Also critical to its success is that the Learning City is never an objective in itself and is focused not on institutions but on what can be achieved by the people in Cork collectively and individually. As such, Cork's Learning City will always be a work-in-progress—a journey and never a destination.

Matt W. Miller

Augumtoocooke

North side of the Merrimack is what the Pennacook called
    Augumtoocooke,
but as I drive east along Pawtucket Boulevard there's
    no seeing Augumtoocooke.

That road pours into Varnum Ave. then onto the VFW Highway
    so on my left I see
Heritage Park, the University, a Mickey D's, Dad's frat, but not
    Augumtoocooke.

The Pawtucket Falls lap lazy over the wooden flashings of a dam
    built to max out
the river's hydraulic head and where once fished first people
    of the Augumtoocooke.

Across the river, Fox Hall Towers, tallest building here to Boston,
    LeLacheur Park,
Tsongas Arena, ribbons of redbrick mills, all that looks down
    over Augumtoocooke.

Bang a larry at the lights on Bridge Street, roll past
    Little Caesars, Manning Liquor,
watch landscaping crews smoke morning butts by a Dunks,
    but no Augumtoocooke.

Down by McPherson Park, lithe Irish, Cambodian, Greek,
    and Dominican boys
sweat half-court hoops brilliant under the rim knowing shit
    about Augumtoocooke,

though it might get a mention at McAuliffe Elementary
    studying Indians a whole week
before Thanksgiving break, before Christmas snow blows in
    to bury Augumtoocooke.

Now I roll into what's left of Dracut, bought for four yards
    of duffel and a pound
of tobacco from the daughter of the sachem who hunted
    the marshes of Augumtoocooke.

There's no more game in the marshes. There're no more marshes.
    But at night, the reservoir
was a good teenage spot to drop boomers and think, *Wow, I am
    sooo about Augumtoocooke,*

*so deep in breezes of some better yesterday, and if only I could strip me
    down into that way
of life I'd be so pure, so alive diving into Beaver Brook under the moon
    of Augumtoocooke!*

Driving a busted-out Chevy, missing all I see to arrogate
    the used-to-be, dreaming absolution
from history, from my millboy misery, I seek a cradle
    in the crook of Augumtoocooke.

Such bullshit. Nothing but what I took, what I take and take,
    what I break to make my egg
bob in some unpoisoned pond where I can drop a line,
    some kind of Augumtoocooke

of my mind. But it's not mine. It's a land apart, outside time,
    and ever our infinite theft
milled from the sagging pines of this Augumtoocooke,
    Augumtoocooke, Augumtoocooke.

Robert Forrant

A Lowell Story

In *The Uprooted* (1951), Oscar Handlin writes: "Once I thought to write a history of the immigrants in America. Then, I discovered that the immigrants were American history." One could say the same for Lowell, Massachusetts, on the Merrimack River about thirty miles northwest of Boston. Immigration has transformed the city for nearly two centuries. An immigrant proverb goes like this: "I came to America because I heard the streets were paved with gold. When I got here, I found out three things. First, the streets were not paved with gold. Second, they weren't paved at all. And third, I was expected to pave them."

Irish immigrants dug the canals that produced waterpower and built the textile manufacturing mills. Newcomers from Armenia, Canada, Greece, Lithuania, Portugal, and other countries and regions of the world joined the cotton mill workforce or operated small businesses. This history is evident in neighborhoods that still contain, side-by-side, the trappings of the immigrant past, and the immigrant and refugee present.

Food stores, ethnic restaurants, social clubs, and religious institutions harkening back to the 1830s offer us ways to understand the past and present. In the last three decades, Buddhist and Hindu Swaminarayan temples, churches that serve diverse faith groups, mosques, and restaurants run by and catering to Southeast Asian, Latin American, African, and Indian customers opened throughout the city.

Early History

In the 1600s, Native Americans in two settlements, Pawtucket and Wamesit, lived within the boundary of what is today Lowell. Where the Merrimack and Concord rivers meet in downtown Lowell was the Wamesit cluster, while Pawtucket was found near the powerful falls of the same name on the Merrimack. The Algonkian-speaking Pennacook people lived in what is today New Hampshire, southern Maine, and northeastern

Massachusetts. They subsisted by farming, hunting, fishing, and gathering. Abundant with fish, Pawtucket Falls was a popular site in salmon spawning season. Inhabitants of Wamesit and Pawtucket also hunted waterfowl, turkeys, pigeons, deer, and moose. The frequent inter-tribal wars in the region and growing fear of attacks by English colonists caused local tribes to flee north. Eventually, their lands were sold to white settlers and the villages of Pawtucket and Wamesit replaced by new farms and trade shops like blacksmiths. Canals, mills, and dams on the river permanently disrupted the environment and ways that remaining Native peoples made a living.

By the mid-1820s, Lowell had a dozen large cotton textile mills, which had been built mainly by Irish immigrants. The laborers dug miles of canals to link the river with the factories and constructed a dam at Pawtucket Falls to generate the waterpower required to operate these mills. The impetus came in 1821, when several Boston businesspeople, many of whom had made their initial fortunes in the trade of human beings, purchased land and rights to an underused transportation canal that routed goods like timber around the falls and then seaward on the river to Newburyport and the Atlantic Ocean. Off the elementary canal grew a spiderweb of smaller ones feeding water to the mills. The first factory operatives included immigrants from the United Kingdom with some mill experience and young women from the countryside. More factories, worker housing, and an enlarged canal followed. For the next twenty-five years, much the same history dominated the economy. By 1848, Lowell, the largest industrial center in America, produced 50,000 miles of cotton cloth each year.

As factory cities like Lowell grew, the economy of the northern United States relied more and more on a labor force working for a wage, men and women selling their time to somebody else. Just twelve percent of the U.S. workforce in 1800 worked for pay; by 1860 this had reached forty percent. According to historian Thomas Dublin in *Women at Work,* in 1845 close to seventy percent of Lowell's mill hands were women, primarily from rural

New England, Yankee farm girls with limited work prospects outside their homes beyond teaching or childcare. Between 1825 and 1845, profits averaged twenty-four percent annually as workers strained twelve hours a day. Productivity rose through the application of ever newly designed machinery. Wages did not keep pace.

One female mill worker, just before leaving the city in 1840, described her days this way in the pages of the *Lowell Offering*, a magazine written and edited by women mill workers: "I am going home where I shall not be so obliged to rise so early in the morning, nor be dragged about by the factory bell, nor confined in a close noisy room from morning to night. I shall not stay here . . . . Up at the clang of a bell and out of the mill by clang of the bell—into the mill and at work in obedience to that ding-dong of a bell—just as though we were so many living machines."

A Portland, Maine, newspaper editorial cautioned Mainers not to let their daughters travel to Lowell. It read in part: "There are hundreds of young females shipped from this State every year to the factory prison-houses, like cattle, sheep, and pigs sent to slaughter." Their destiny was to labor in "the polluted and polluting manufacturing towns where they are prepared for a miserable life and a horrible death in the abodes of infamy."

Young women organized against their situation. The first significant walkout in Lowell occurred in February 1834. These words from their strike proclamation rang out across the region: "The oppressing hand of avarice would enslave us, and to gain their object, they gravely tell us of the pressure of the times, this we are sensible of, and deplore it . . . and as we are free, we would remain in possession of what kind providence has bestowed upon us, and remain daughters of freemen still."

By 1850, what had started out with a handful of mills had become a vast textile empire. Lowell mills produced 65,000 miles of cotton cloth annually, enough to circle the globe more than twice. The so-called "Boston Associates" controlled a fifth of the nation's spindles, a third of New England's railroad mileage, and two-fifths of Boston's banking capital. Steven Yaffa, in his book

Cotton: The Biography of a Revolutionary Fiber, summarizes this history: "Within a decade of Lowell's founding, New England's textile aristocracy had gained so much wealth and political power that they had become uncrowned royalty. Their money paid for schools, hospitals, museums, churches, and parks in and around Boston . . . . These Lords of the Loom lived with their clans in an exclusive Boston enclave . . . . When they traveled to Lowell . . . they soon departed. They were not about to make this mill community their home . . . ."

As the country careened forward to a violent Civil War, a significant element of Lowell's population remained in support of the institution of slavery. Historian Van Wyck Brooks, in *The Flowering of New England* (1936), described this relationship. "The wheels of the cotton factories revolved at a furious pace, and the Southern slave drivers plied their whips to feed the Yankee mills with Southern cotton. The more the prosperity of New England came to depend on cotton, the closer the propertied classes drew to the Southern planters, with whom they felt obliged to ally themselves, yielding to them in all political matters."

Nevertheless, female mill workers championed the anti-slavery cause. Thousands of them signed petitions to end the slave trade in the nation's capital. Aware and concerned that enslaved people produced the cotton they worked, they made donations to support the underground railroad and turned out in large numbers to hear anti-slavery orators like William Lloyd Garrison and Frederick Douglass. And, when the fighting began, a militia whose ranks were filled with Lowell mill workers answered the first call to battle. In fact, on April 19, 1861, members of Lowell's Sixth Regiment, Luther C. Ladd and Addison Whitney, became the first casualties of the war when attacked by a secessionist mob in Baltimore, Maryland. Though not born there, the young millhands enlisted in the Lowell Guards. The granite obelisk of the Ladd and Whitney Monument at City Hall stands in their memory.

Twentieth-Century Decline

As the years passed, thousands of European immigrants flocked to Lowell for mill jobs. The first significant immigrant arrivals were from Ireland, followed by waves of newcomers. Immigrants remained the primary source of labor until the 1920s when federal immigration restrictions blocked the incoming flow. They comprised close to seventy percent of the mill workforce by the end of the nineteenth century. Their wages supported family members they left behind in Ireland, Quebec, Greece, Portugal, Germany, Italy, and Eastern Europe. The money they earned boosted sales at city establishments. With an entrepreneurial spirit, they started numerous businesses catering to families in the ethnic neighborhoods.

However, by the early twentieth century, Lowell's competitive advantage dissipated with the advent of steam engines, coal-fired furnaces, and then electricity. Between 1909 and 1919, Merrimack Valley factories still employed 150,000 people, a labor force not equaled before or since. Rapid job loss starting in the 1920s resulted in a far less welcoming environment for newcomers venturing to Lowell. Moreover, the global economic depression in the 1930s added to the city's troubles. Reflecting the tough times and slowed immigration, the population fell from 113,000 in 1920 to 100,000 in 1930 and under 100,000 by 1940.

Factories got built in the U.S. South, where few unions and lower wages were the lures. Lowell's mills could not compete with Southern textile mills with their new machines, new technology, new production methods, cheap non-union labor, and a newly built infrastructure catering to the Southern mill owners' every need. In just twenty years, from 1919 to 1939, Massachusetts lost forty-five percent of its textile jobs. In 1936 only 8,000 people worked in Lowell's textile industry, roughly the same number who did so in 1836. The post-World War II years saw the final outsourcing of factory operations to the Global South, especially to countries in Central America and the Caribbean.

The Long Recovery

In the 1960s and 1970s, many Lowell immigrant neighborhoods and industrial buildings fell to the wrecking ball in the name of urban renewal. For a time, city leaders believed that the way forward for the once-thriving mill city was to cause a sharp break with its past. The concept caught on throughout the industrial Northeast. It represented the operationalizing of a belief that tearing down distressed and disinvested areas would attract new dollars. In Lowell's case, leaders searched for a new economic engine to replace cotton mills. Despite the aggressive knockdown of several neighborhoods, the hoped-for jumpstart never materialized.

Instead, city planners, education leaders, community activists, and members of the university community nurtured a different vision for the city's future, one predicated on historic preservation, enhanced public schools, and a dynamic cultural life. The federal government established a National Park in Lowell in 1978, and, instead of demolishing old buildings and paving over the city's history, the local story became central to Lowell's revitalization. Public and private investments in the repurposing of old mills for twenty-first-century business incubators, healthcare facilities, artist lofts and studios, spacious housing, and new retail shops soared. Today, more than ninety percent of the five million square feet of vintage mill space is occupied. Over the same period, what had been a small commuter college grew into an 18,000-student University of Massachusetts Lowell. A campus of Middlesex Community College has 5,000 students in the city.

Breathing further life into the city, following passage of the Immigration and Nationality Act of 1965, which abolished country-based immigration quotas, a renewed stream of global migrants entered the U.S. Many made their way to Lowell. Post-1965 immigration and refugee arrivals from several strife-torn countries in Africa and Southeast Asia transformed Lowell yet again. According to the U.S. Census Bureau, about twenty-five percent of Lowell's population in 2010 was foreign-born. The figure is likely to reach thirty percent when the 2020 census is completed. Like earlier generations, new Lowellians are shaping and enriching the city with their unique and diverse presence. They build and join religious institutions, start businesses, enhance the regional labor force, and contribute to the local economy. They are participants in and creators of cultural, social, and community organizations and institutions. The world has arrived here, changing the cityscape in dramatic ways just as it did in the late nineteenth and early twentieth centuries.

Alannah Hopkin

The History of Cork City

Cork is in Munster, one of Ireland's four provinces, and is the second largest city in the Republic. Corcaigh means "marshy" in Irish, and the city is built on low-lying land between two channels of the River Lee. As the city grew, other parts of the marsh were drained, and the river's channels diverted, so that today its commercial centre is on an island connected to its banks by a series of stone-built bridges.

Archaeological remains indicate that a pastoral community was thriving here by the sixth century. This is traditionally the date when St. Finbarr (the city's patron saint) established a monastic settlement in Cork. The Vikings arrived around 900, and lived in relative harmony with the original Celtic community, until the arrival of Anglo-Norman settlers in 1177. Prince John granted the city its first charter in 1185. The walled medieval city of those days had sea channels coming right up to its gates. The city's coat of arms shows two castles guarding a port, beneath the motto *Statio Bene Fide Carinis*—a safe harbour for ships.

The medieval population of Cork was decimated by bubonic plague in 1349. In 1491, during the Wars of the Roses, the Pretender Perkin Warbeck landed at Cork, and "Rebel Cork" supported him in a failed plot to overthrow Henry VII of England. The nickname has persisted down the years.

The Tudor conquest of Ireland ended in 1603. Cork City sided with the Crown in the ensuing conflicts, but Catholics were largely excluded from civic life until the process of Catholic Emancipation was completed in 1829. Economic prosperity came largely from exporting the products of Cork's rich agricultural hinterland— butter, beef, and wool—along with brewing, tanning, distilling, and the manufacture of fine silver and glass. Shipbuilding was also an important activity, as was provisioning the city's large garrisons of the British army and navy.

The prosperity and relative peace of the eighteenth century led to a building boom that created such classics as St. Anne's Church,

Shandon, Christchurch on North Main Street, and the red-brick Customs House (now the Crawford Gallery of Art), the Butter Market and the Greek-style rotunda next to it where the butter was weighed, the Firkin Crane. Shandon Steeple, belonging to St. Anne's Church, is a much-loved landmark, and Cork's most iconic building. The steeple has four clock-faces and is topped with a 3.3-meter-long salmon-shaped weathervane, thus giving the citizens both the time and the weather forecast. South Mall and Grand Parade were largely built by bankers and lawyers. South Mall was a waterway, lined by quays and substantial merchants' houses. The canals were later filled in, and further terraces of fine houses were built in North Mall and Washington Street.

The population expanded greatly in the early nineteenth century, reaching 80,000 by the 1840s. Many people took refuge in the city following failures in the potato crop from the early 1820s, culminating in the Great Famine of 1845. Cork's deep-water port, Cobh, grew in importance as the first and last port of call for transatlantic shipping from the mid-nineteenth to mid-twentieth century. By the mid-nineteenth century, Cork had gas lighting in homes and streets, and two newspapers. The railway arrived in 1849, the same year Queen's College, now University College Cork opened. The building boom of the late nineteenth century was responsible for most of the city's shops, pubs, theatres, and hospitals.

Because of the noise and pollution of the city's commercial centre, those who could afford it moved to elegant villas in more healthy locations on the hill north of the river or in the western and southern suburbs. The most prosperous people in Cork were merchants, who energetically developed the city, and were active in local government and philanthropy. These families became known as the "merchant princes," their names recurring in civic records—Beamish, Crawford, Murphy, Roche, Dwyer, and Skiddy, among others. From the late eighteenth century on, there was a growing Catholic merchant class, and several large Catholic churches were built in the late nineteenth century.

The city's best-loved landmark is a large statue on St. Patrick Street to a local hero, Father Theobald Mathew (1790-1856), a charismatic priest who persuaded thousands of Corkonians to "take the pledge" and stop drinking the alcohol that ruined so many lives. He was also active in the cholera epidemic and the Great Famine. The wide sweep of Patrick Street, as the main shopping street is called colloquially, remains a popular place to promenade on a Saturday afternoon, known as "doing Pana."

The importance of food in Cork's identity continues to this day, with the ever-growing popularity of the English Market. Housed in an elaborate Victorian brick-and-cast iron emporium in the city centre, over 140 stalls offer foodstuffs ranging from local specialties like spiced beef to the famous "fish alley" with its seafood displays, freshly baked bread, local cheeses, and fresh fruit and vegetables. A walkabout by Her Majesty Queen Elizabeth in 2011 gave the busy market and its amiable traders an international profile.

Queen's College, now University College Cork (UCC), was built on a naturally elevated site on the River Lee to the west of the city. Its motto, "Where Finbarr taught, let Munster learn," is most appropriate for a UNESCO City of Learning. Its Gothic quadrangle is based on Magdalen College, Oxford, and built in local limestone. These days the Gothic quad is complemented by an array of contemporary buildings, including the award-winning Glucksman Gallery (2004).

Across the river is the Mardyke, a riverside walk laid out in 1719 beside the city's cricket ground. The adjacent Fitzgerald Park was created in 1902 when Cork hosted an ambitious international exhibition attracting huge numbers of visitors. The park is named after the Lord Mayor at the time, Edward Fitzgerald. It is now the location of Cork Public Museum, which has a wealth of information on the city's history.

The War of Independence (1916-1921) was fought in the streets of Cork. "Rebel Cork" lived up to its traditional reputation, and one side of Patrick Street, the City Hall and the Carnegie Library were burnt to the ground.

Years of economic depression followed the war, but the city's commercial life picked up again in the mid-twentieth century with the establishment of factories by Ford Motors, Dunlop Tyres, and Sunbeam Wolsey. Cork City is widely reputed to be "sports-mad," and has some seventeen Gaelic Athletic Association clubs, a stadium, Páirc Uí Chaoimh, with a 45,000 capacity, as well as a popular soccer team.

Cork City has continued to expand its boundaries, most recently in 2019, a move that increased its population from 125,000 to 210,000. Cork is a popular choice with pharmaceutical and other multinationals since the opening of Cork Airport in 1961. A young well-educated workforce attracts many large employers to the city, including Apple's European Headquarters.

In 2005, Cork City hosted a successful year as European Capital of Culture. In 2015, Cork was designated A Learning City by UNESCO. The city's annual Lifelong Learning Festival, *An Féile Foghlama*, was first held in 2004, and continues to be a highlight of Cork's annual calendar.

David Daniel

2,860 Miles in Lowell

Roughly the distance from Boston to L.A. or back and forth to New York City seven times. That's how far we went. But this wasn't a lengthy road trip. These were unmapped city miles, walking miles, accrued at about ten per week, over fall and spring terms, across eleven years, as my students and I poked into the nooks and crannies, alleys and courtyards, rooftops and riverwalks of this fascinating old mill city.

As a teacher at the Lowell Middlesex Academy Charter School, part of my responsibility was to see that students got regular physical exercise. The class was called Mind & Motion and, in the absence of a gymnasium, the city was our gym, our library, our laboratory. We met last period of the day. I'd take attendance and off we'd go.

Some afternoons we'd ball up at one of the public courts or in the gym at the Hellenic School, or play soccer behind Tsongas Arena. For a time, I had a co-teacher, and she and I would alternate taking a sub-group of the class on runs. Most of the miles, though, were walking, autumn to winter to spring, open to the gifts of the season.

And, oh, the things we saw.

Everything afforded opportunities for learning. Markers, plaques, and gravestones taught history; campaign signs were civics lessons; ethnic neighborhoods spoke of sociology; sunlight and shadow on old brick walls gave us art; walks along the rivers and canals—where we saw beaver, turtles, great blue herons, carp—taught ecology. And there were the geometries of downtown buildings and intersecting alleys. Once we watched a large foam-fabric snowman floating down the Concord River on the spring flood, bound for the Merrimack, his carrot nose up-thrust like an orange mast. A meditation, perhaps, on impermanence.

Sometimes we'd buy a copy of the *Sun* and sit in Jack Kerouac Park. The game was: Suppose you know nothing about Lowell; what might you glean from reading a front-page story? An editorial? An obituary?

The city gave us entrée. Perhaps it was the school lanyards we wore, the bright, go-ahead green of traffic signals, or the alluring light at the end of Daisy Buchanan's dock in *The Great Gatsby*. We went where curiosity took us, over cobbles and asphalt, concrete and grass. If no sign expressly forbade it, we often entered, always respectful, quieter than a gaggle of high schoolers is expected to be.

The mighty Merrimack was both a destination and a journey. Some days we'd play touch football on its banks. One of our balls, and more than a few of our Frisbees, floated away. If I remarked that even on his best day Patriots quarterback Tom Brady couldn't toss a football across that expanse, invariably a student or two, taking the bait, would grab a stone. A *really* good throw—and those kids had arms!—might make it halfway across before falling with a soft splash. They'd shake their heads in good-natured chagrin. Another lesson learned.

Life lessons, for me, too. That the city is a web of life, of linkages, present to past and back again, time performing its magic act. A place where grunge co-exists with gloss and both keep company with beauty. A monument, not only to those who built it, and shed blood for it, whose names are everywhere, but to us who sustain it by living here now. Lessons that, like the river in its long journey, there are tumbles over rocks and spans of slack water, and, ultimately, a conjoining with the sea.

"Look at these buildings," I say as we conclude a September day's walk along Middle Street, just in time for afternoon dismissal. "Look up. See the dates? There isn't a person on earth now who was alive when these were built. And these'll be here long after we're gone—or after *I'm* gone, at least."

I want to add (but it's good to leave some things implied), "Make this place a choice, not a sentence. Live here because maybe you've been away for a while—off to college, perhaps, or national service, or a job, or for the grand adventure of love—and something in it called you back. Then, more than just a city, it's a home."

TWO

Joey Banh

My Father, He's a Soldier

A Vietnam War veteran, and he stands proud, back straight,
Left hand stiff at 0600, right hand right above the brow,
Saluting the South Vietnam Freedom flag as it dances
    next to my American one.
Draped in camouflage-green with a red beret tilted
    at the exact angle.
His shirt is 50 years memoried with gold stars, honorary badges,
    soldier stripes, and a purple heart.
Grown men in their 60s and 70s salute him as he walks on by.
    My father, he's a soldier.
That morning I see my father shine his old size-8 war boots,
    and ask if it is another rally.
He nods his head, and no words are ever exchanged
    when it's a rally.
As a child I remember waking up to the sound of
    my father screaming
Nam xuon nam xuon, Mien Mien
Duck down . . . Duck down, Grenade Grenade
Di Di Mao GI Di Di Mao
GO GO FAST GI GO GO FAST
I would stand at the crack of the door and watch my mother
    try to restrain his arms and legs and her own tears.
30 years past, my father tried to restrain his brother's arms,
    his comrade's leg and his nation's tears.
I would sit in the hall while my father pleaded to my mother,
toi co the cuu no
"I could've saved them, you know . . ."
Other nights I would catch my father at the base of the stairway
    gripping his stomach where four AK bullets entered long ago.
"*Ba ba* are you ok?"
Di ngu di
Go to bed . . . he would say.

The Vietnam War was a Civil War, yet many pointed at
   my father saying, "You killed my Uncle."
Many pointed at me saying, "Go home, Vietcong."
The Rallies are for Veterans rights . . .
Twenty Years of Rallies . . . still no rights . . . all wrongs . . .
My Father took bullets above a foxhole that housed
   South Vietnam and U.S. soldiers alike.
My father used to tell me, "We aimed at the same enemy
   and walked the same line,
Ate at the same table, took the same orders. The only difference,
   they didn't have to shoot at their own brothers."
My father fought in a war . . . ridden with guilt next to
   blue-eyed soldiers . . .
Took orders and gave them to soldiers with blond hair.
My father found me a home . . . ridden with guilt next to
   blue-eyed citizens,
Opened a business, took orders, and gave them to men
   with blond hair,
Took his vow to allied citizenship for a country where
   many find him enemy.

Ask hundreds of thousands, and they'll say, "Yeah, your father,
   he's a Veteran,"
But look in the American record books, and we're just
   a bunch of immigrants.
My father shakes hands with American soldiers every month.
Vets go to his house, salute him, and call him sergeant
   once a week.
He pulls out his old medals and that old soldier outfit
   six times a year.
He polishes his medals once a rally.
He shines his boots once a memory.
He tells a horrific story once a nightmare.

He goes to the doctor's once every bullet wound.
He has night tremors once every salute.
He has PTSD once a day with a glass of water.

He has rights once he stops being a soldier . . . but I told you,
my father, he's a soldier.

Just don't ask him about the war. Because we're still fighting it.

William Wall

The Mountain Road

James Casey drove off the top of Rally Pier. The tide here falls out through the islands and away west. It runs at a knot, sometimes a knot and a half at spring tide. Listen and you will hear it in the stones. This is the song of lonely places. The car moved a little sideways as it sank. And afterwards great gulps of air escaped, but it made no sound. I know these things, not because I saw them but because they must have happened. The sky is settling over Rally and the hills. It is the colour of limestone, a great cap on the country. Ten miles out the sky is blue. I heard it on local radio, suicide at Rally Pier. I knew who it was. His two daughters were on the back seat.

You cannot see the pier from my house. I got up and put my jeans and jumper on and climbed the hill behind the house, through heather and stone, to where I could look down. Bees sang in the air. Watery sunshine from a crack in the clouds. When I turned after ten minutes climbing, the whole bay lay before me, the islands in their pools of stillness, the headlands like crude fingers, boats pair-trawling a mile or more apart but connected forever by cables attached to the wings of the giant net. James was on the boats once. He it was who explained all that to me. I saw the police tape on the pier-head, a tiny yellowness that was not there before. If he left a note what did it say? Suddenly the song came into my head. "Dónal Óg." Even as the first words came, I knew what it meant for me. You took the east from me and you took the west from me and great is my fear that you took God from me. Are these lines from the song?

When the song was finished with me, I walked back down home. I was accustomed to think of it like that—not that I stopped singing but that the song was over. I made up the bed with fresh sheets and put the soiled ones in the washing machine. I washed out the floor of the bathroom. Why do we do these things when we are bereft? Then I had a shower and put on dark clothes. I got out the bicycle and pumped up the leaking tyre. My father had shown me how to mend punctures, but I could not remember now. I still have the same puncture repair kit, a tin box, but now I kept hash in it. Then I wheeled the bicycle down to the gate and onto the road and faced the hill to the house where the dead girls lay.

They closed the door against me when they saw me turn the bend. Cousins make these decisions, but I leaned my bicycle against the wall and knocked and then they had to let me in. Perhaps it was inevitable anyway. People around here do not shut their neighbours out. They showed me into the front room where the two girls lay in open coffins. Three older women sat by them. I did not recognize them. Aunts, most probably. They had their beads in their hands. I did not bless myself. I go to neither church nor chapel and they all knew it. I stood for a long time looking down on the faces. When old people go, death eases their pain and their faces relax into a shapeless wax model of someone very like them. People say they look happy, but mostly they look plastic. But when a child dies, it is the perpetuation of a certain model of perfect beauty. People would say the girls looked like angels. There was no trace of the sea on them, no sign of the panic and fear that bubbled through the ground-up sleeping tablets that their father had fed them for breakfast yesterday morning. According to local radio. His own prescription. He had not been sleeping for months.

When I stopped looking, I shook hands with each of the aunts. Nobody said anything. I went out of the room and found the cousins waiting in the corridor. I asked for Helen and was told she was lying down. The doctor was calling regularly all day. She was on tablets for her nerves. She was very low. I was about to ask them to pass on my sympathy when a door opened upstairs. It was Helen herself. She called to know who was there. It's your neighbour, one of the cousins said. She could not bring herself to name me.

Helen came unsteadily down the stairs.

Her hair was flat and moist. She was wearing the kind of clothes she might have gone to Mass in, a formal blouse and a straight grey skirt, but she had no tights on. Her bare feet looked vulnerable and childish. She stepped deliberately, stretching so that at each tread of the stairs she stood on the ball of her foot like a dancer. She came down like someone in a trance. I think we all wondered if she knew who she was coming down for. And if she did what was she going to say.

Cáit, she said, is it yourself? Thank you for coming.

Her eyes were flat, too. There was no light in them.

I'm sorry for your trouble, I said, taking her hand. I held the hand tightly as if the pressure could convey something in itself.

Helen shook her head. Why did he do it? she said. Even if he went himself. But the girls...

Helen will I make you a cup of tea?

One of the cousins said that. She was by Helen's side now, she would like to take her arm and lead her into the kitchen. They did not want her going into the front room and starting the wailing and the cursing all over again. Jesus, Mar, and Joseph, it would terrify you to hear the things she said. And here she was now talking to Cáit Deane like nothing happened at all. There was cake and several kinds of bread and honey and tea and coffee and a bottle of the hard stuff and stout and beer. The house was provided against a famine. They'd need it all by and by. This is the way things go at funerals.

He always spoke well of you, Helen said.

We were childhood sweethearts, I said.

He always said you should have trained professionally. He said you had a great voice.

I shrugged. I heard this kind of thing from time to time.

He said it was pity what happened to you.

I felt my shoulders straighten. I was fond of him, I said, everybody was.

He said you had terrible bitterness in you.

I moved towards the door but there was a cousin in the way. Excuse me, I said. The cousin did not move. She had her arms folded. She was smiling.

He said you were your own worst enemy.

I turned on her. Well, he was wrong there, I said. I have plenty of enemies.

Helen Casey closed her eyes. The only thing my husband was wrong about was that he took my two beautiful daughters with him. If he went on his own nobody would have a word to say against him. But now he cut himself off from everything. Even our prayers. If that man is burning in hell, it's all the same to me. I hope he is. He'll never see my girls again for they're not in hell. And the time will come when you'll join him, and no one will be sorry for that either.

One of the cousins crossed herself and muttered under her breath. Jesus, Mary, and Joseph. The doorkeeper unfolded her arms suddenly and stepped aside. I opened the door. I was taken by surprise to find the priest outside preparing to knock.

Oh, he said.

Excuse me, Father.

I pushed past him. I noticed that the tyre was sinking again; it would need pumping, but I could not do it here. I pulled it to face away. People say I'm cold. A cold-hearted bitch, some of them say. They say such things. The priest was watching me. He was smiling. Most likely he did not know who I was, the new man in the parish. They'd fill him in on the details in the front room with the two dead girls and the old women with their beads. The cousins would know everything. It was how crows always knew there was bread out. First came a single bird, a scout. There was always one. Then they gather. Before long they're fighting each other over crusts. You can knock fun out of watching them and their comical battles in the back yard. But the minute you put the bread out, one of them turns up to check it out and the others follow soon enough. If you dropped dead on your own lawn, they'd be down for your eyes.

I swung into my bicycle and launched myself down the tarmac drive and out onto the road. I turned for the hill down home but that was not where I was going.

I met the car at the place where the road was falling into the valley. There was no question of slipping past. I braked hard and dragged my foot along the road. By the time I stopped, I was by the driver's door and there was a drop of a hundred feet on my left-hand side. He rolled the window down. It was James's brother Johnny.

You'd think the Council would shore that up, he said.

The crows are gathering.

He nodded.

The priest was at the door.

He nodded again. He looked at me silently for a moment, then he said, He could have asked for help, Cáit. You'd have helped him, wouldn't you? I would any day. All he had to do was ask.

Johnny, I said, you know very well I was the last one he'd turn to. And the last one who could help him. And anyway, there is no help.

You could but you would not.

No, I said, I just could not. You know that very well.

Do you know what, Cáit Deane?

I probably do, Johnny.

He looked at me frustrated. You were always the same. You're too sharp for around here.

I shrugged.

My brother James, he said, you destroyed him.

He destroyed himself. I didn't drive him down to the pier.

Why did he do it if not for you? You took him. You took him and you wouldn't keep him and then you left him. Why else would he do it?

I got my foot on the pedal again and faced down the hill.

Spite, I said. He was always spiteful, like a spoiled child.

I launched myself forward and went clear of the car. In a moment, I was past the subsiding section. Fuchsia speckled the roadsides with their first bloody skirts. In the valley the last of the whitethorn blossom. The river at the very bottom gleaming like concrete in a field of bog iris. And ahead was the bay and its islands and the vast intolerant ocean.

I chained the bicycle to the stop sign outside the funeral home. The street was a long one that ran into a steep hill; the funeral home, the graveyard, and the church were all at the top of the hill so that the dead could look down on the town, and the townspeople when they looked up from the pavement saw death looming like a public monument to their future. People joked that it was the only town in Ireland where you had to climb up to your grave. To make matters worse, the funeral home was owned by the Hill family. There were several Hills in the parish, and naturally the funeral home was called The Hilton. They say that the only people making money out of the economic crash were accountants and funeral directors. Even the bankrupt had to be buried by somebody. At the door in a plastic frame was a poster with a picture of an anorexic bonsai plant and the words: Our promise to you, Phone ANYTIME, day or night. You will NEVER get an answering machine.

Funeral homes are always cold. There were pine benches in lines like a church. They had been varnished recently, and there was that heady smell. It reminded me of my father's boat, the wheelhouse brightwork newly touched up. It was the smell of childhood.

James Casey lay in a plain wooden box at the top of the room. I could see immediately that the brass handles were fake. Someone had examined a funeral menu and ticked cheap. I went to look down on him. I thought I had nothing to say but when I was standing there I had plenty.

You stupid bastard, I said, you stupid murdering fucking bastard.

There was more like that. I surprised myself at the flow of anger, the dam-burst of fury. After a time I stopped because I was afraid I was going to attack the corpse. And then I thought I might have been shouting. No one came, but perhaps funeral directors and their secretaries are used to angry mourners. I stepped back and found my calf touching a bench. I sat down.

They'll all blame me, I told him. They already blame me.

Then I cried.

James Casey looked tranquil and unperturbed. In real life he was never like that. After a time, I got up. I looked down at him. His eyes were stitched closed because when he was pulled from the sodden car of course they were open. They are not very expert in our part of the world; I could see the stitches here and there. The funeral director knows from experience that the eyes of dead people do not express emotion, but he knows that his clients would see fear in them. Nobody wants to look a dead man in the eye. It's bad for business.

Fuck you, I said.

I turned on my heel and walked out. A tiny sigh escaped when I closed the door like the seal opening on an air-tight jar. My bicycle lay on the ground in its chains. They knifed the tyres while I was with James. I was not going to give them the satisfaction of watching me wheel it down the street. I was going to leave it where I found it. Do not slouch, my mother used to say, stand up straight, put your shoulders back. But I slouched just the same. How many years since I first loved James Casey? I pulled my shoulders back, but I kept my eyes on the ground. The thought that I had done something unforgivable. It was always there in the dark. Things come back in the long run, the way lost things are revealed by the lowest tides, old shipwrecks, old pots, the ruined moorings that once held steadfastly to trawlers or pleasure boats. There are no secrets around here.

Masada Jones

This Is a Story of a Daughter

This is a story of a daughter
A girl
Learning to be strong
Her mother young
Unprepared for her daughter's fight
Girl birthed two months too early
Not fully cooked in the oven
Womb clinching to hold her in
Ma not ready
Sat legs crossed in hospital bed
She know that's no way to birth a baby
Sister and Doctors
Both say she coming
Girl gon' be born
First day of Fall
Head-first
Head full of hair
Head strong
Ma must have had heart burn all pregnancy
Took three slaps to make her cry
Ma had no name for her yet
Came too early
Already stubborn and nameless
Ma's sister said name her Masada
Said something of fortress and Hebrews fighting Romans
There the name settled
First time girl smiled
Felt important and necessary to be named
Was no easy task raising her
Her voice loud and clumsy
Said things kids shouldn't
Dreamt of being grown
Ma didn't know how to contain her daughter's wondrous spirit

Full of curiosity words and song
Ma did know how to calm her
Took her all up in her arms
Rocked her back in forth
Ease your mind
Words ain't going no where
Sometimes you just need to be
Sure to this day you can still see Masada rocking
Feeling her Ma's love and seeking solitude
Bang
One day Ma wakes at 4 a.m.
Sits straight up in the bed
Drinks water to settle herself
Then finds rest
Masada's been preparing to be strong
Her clumsy mouth now home to power and song
Little girl far from being hushed
Her brother left this world at 4 a.m. in search of better lands
Places where black and brown boys find work easy
A land where living is not just about survival
Dreaming is feasible
Seeing 25 possible
So many hope
He found that land
Finds comfort in the simplicity of everyday life
Masada's mom is broken now
She takes her ma up in her arms
Trying to rock her steady to calmness

Brian Simoneau

Sonnet for the Guy Who Told Me My Dad Was a Saint

Saints don't come from dumps like this. They come
from towns untransected by train tracks or tainted
rivers passing rows of molting tenements,
from cities where every block's a work of art

and spires scrape clouds, every window stained
in prayer. Sacred steps don't tread these streets:
even the blessed must feel the weight of brick,
history's consumptive grating in the chest.

But today—in the shade of a willow, water
gracing over the dam, walls of a mill rising up
to meet a ceiling of Sistine sky—a saint's

not an impossible thing, and the dust slipping
through sunlight's almost beatific, almost
beatific and almost beautiful.

Marie Sweeney

My *Anam Cara*

In 2015, the author was among the 2015 Anam Cara *honorees, an award recognizing local "soul friends" who have made significant contributions to the preservation of Irish culture and heritage in the Lowell area. Afterwards, she shared her story with readers of the* RichardHowe.com *blog in Lowell.*

Why am "I" in this place tonight? What is my story? Let me give you a little bit of the story. I'm proud to say that these are my people.

Patrick Meehan (1847-1913) and Margaret McDermott Meehan (1849-1916) arrived from County Sligo in 1864—when married they settled in the Acre neighborhood on Worthen Street. A bookkeeper and a grocer, Patrick was noted in his obituary as a "man of magnetic personality with a host of friends, a man ready to lend a helping hand to anyone in need and a prominent factor in the growth and success of several well-known societies of St. Patrick's Church." His passing was "a cause of genuine grief to all." Margaret or Maggie, as she was called, had nine children. They raised a family of the six surviving children. Patrick and Maggie died young, each at 60.

Patrick Kirwin (1844-1911) came from County Dublin, and by way of Blackstone, Massachusetts, came to Lowell early in the 1870s. He had a valuable skill as a wool sorter as well as management talent. Ellen Courtney (1854-1934), a bit younger than Patrick, also from Dublin by way of Blackstone, came to Lowell and married Patrick in 1876. They raised a family of eight children, first, in what we call the Flats for the flat-topped housing near the Concord River, but they soon moved up to 30 Agawam Street in what would be called the Sacred Heart Parish. Patrick was a pioneer of the Sacred Heart Parish as he was one of the committee members who often met in the Lyons Street School to organize this new Catholic parish. His son, William J. Kirwin, Oblate of Mary Immaculate, would later become its Pastor. With a large circle of friends, Patrick was known as a loyal friend and family man. With Ellen, who survived him by many years well into the mid-1930s, and their children, they formed a solid part of their community.

Six-foot-tall red-headed Thomas Deignan (b. 1864) came to Lowell from County Leitrim by way of Liverpool to the Acre. A laborer, he was into wood and coal and a teamster. The lively Elizabeth "Lizzie" Charles came to Lowell from Ireland with her sisters and married Thomas at the Immaculate Conception Church in 1885 (I'm wearing her wedding ring tonight). They had ten children and raised eight into adulthood. Lizzie lived until 1940 and was the center of the Deignan home on High Street, ensconced in her rocking chair in the family kitchen. Only three children married, and just two had children; the others lived at home well into adulthood and not surprisingly brought home their paychecks to Lizzie. (I suppose then it was a pay envelope!)

Joseph Burke (1871-1971) and Matilda Montgomery Burke (1877-1965) emigrated from Newtoncunningham, Londonderry, Ireland to the United States in November 1898, arriving on-board the *Nebraska* with two children in tow, Katherine and Bill. In 1900, they had their first child in America, in Lowell, my grandmother Matilda called "Tillie." They raised their eight children, first, in the Sacred Heart Parish on South Whipple and Gorham streets and then on Moore Street before settling by the late 1920s in the Highlands neighborhood on Stevens Street. Joe Burke was a physically strong man who could do the hard work of many. He walked long distances for most of his life usually with his dog Rigger (there were many Riggers), and Joe "Pa" Burke lived to be 100. Matilda sailed and traveled back to Ireland many times to visit her brothers. She enjoyed life. A fashion-plate in her time, she was a saleswoman in a department store for many years. Joe outlived her.

My grandparents were of these beginnings (the Meehan-Kirwin wedding was at St. Patrick's and the Deignan-Burke at the Sacred Heart). Grandmothers Agnes Meehan, a Notre Dame Academy and Lowell alum who trained for business and sales, and

Tillie Burke, a homemaker, great cook and founding member and President of the Ladies Ancient Order of Hibernians, Division #46, were strong of faith and family. Both grandfathers, Patrick "PJ" Kirwin and James "Jimmy" Deignan were charmers and worked in government. Papa Kirwin, born in 1884, worked more than 50 years at the Lowell Post office, and Papa Deignan, born in 1895 and a World War I Army veteran, worked at the Watertown Arsenal. Then for "PJ" there was the Meehan and Kirwin funeral business with his brother-in-law, the postmaster and former Mayor, and for Jimmy Deignan, with the beautiful tenor voice, Irish wit, and repartee, there was the B. F. Keith Vaudeville circuit. Appearing in local shows and gigs, he even produced a number of Keith Academy Shows and, in the late 1930s, served a few terms on the Lowell City Council!

These men and women, my great-grandparents who came to Lowell, left their marks and their legacy through their children, grandchildren, and great-grandchildren. Their influence brought men and women into all walks of life: education, military service, public service, service to the Church, medicine, healthcare and public health, government service. They became teachers, doctors, nurses, businessmen and businesswomen, laborers, librarians, maintenance workers, car salesmen, accountants and CPAs, a Mayor, a city councilor, a school committeeman, a postmaster, organists, pianists, music teachers, priests, sisters, funeral directors, social workers, religion teachers, computer and technology workers, writers, lawyers. They "got on the city," the telephone company and the electric, worked at the *Sun* newspaper, the bank, the hospitals, in public housing, ran nursing homes, were in private practice, became Tewksbury Hospital medical and nursing directors, got into food service, were civically and culturally active, and more.

For me, it's always been as I was taught, as was role-modeled for me: the legacy of faith, family, community, our Irish heritage and culture and service. And, well, a little Democratic politics thrown in.

I want to thank the committee on behalf of myself, my husband Bill, my partner of more than forty-seven years who I met in Sr. Rita's kindergarten at the Sacred Heart School, and my sons Bill and Ted, daughter-in-law Nicole and granddaughters Abby, Hannah, Eva and Mae, and for all those who came before me— for including me in tonight's honors. To be with this group of people is a great part of the honor. *Anam Cara*, an honor to be deemed a "Soul Friend" of Irish culture and heritage, along with Peg McAndrews, an old friend so committed to her Irish heritage, St. Patrick's Church, Catholic Charities, and to whom I had the pleasure of giving the Greater Lowell Area Democrats "1999 Distinguished Democrat" award; with Leo Mahoney, a good man, a humble and generous man, "the salt of the earth," as they say, with whose son and nephews and our sons and nephew share a friendship and a bit of history; with Mike Demoulas, another humble and generous man of the Acre whose friendship with my dad lasted for over fifty years of business and shared beginnings; and lastly, with the great leader Paul Sheehy, a colleague, a mentor and, actually, my boss for a while, but most of all my longtime friend, and as with the others, greatly missed.

Alex Hayes

FR8879

Warsaw to Shannon

We're leaving the sea of clouds behind now,
Suspended and frozen amidst the blue,
I looked for you in my chest and for all
those years saw nothing but mirrors and those familiar,
    youthful eyes staring back.

Soon I'll be home, and you still five years dead,
Slowly rotting, embalmed with unsaid words.

You were more alive in this last week than
in sixteen years past, shrouded in shadow,
Forever more mystery than mother.

The glass within is shattered now,
I finally feel the pain,
You've shown me the bleeding never stopped,
You did not die in vain.

David Daniel

As Lonely as Alice B. Toklas

After Gertrude Stein, her dear companion of decades, died in 1946, [Alice B.] Toklas stayed on alone in Paris for twenty years as the world tried to move beyond the great upheavals brought on by the lies of civilization.
—*F. Lowry Vincent*, 1945: France in War's Wake.

When he was a boy, Ross and his friends were jazzed over comic books, reading and swapping them, declaring which superheroes they'd most like to be. Superman, Captain America, and the Batman topped every list except Ross's. He wanted to be the Flash. The red bodysuit and the lightning bolt were part of it, and he thought being able to run really fast would be cool (he even went out for the track team in middle school, though it wasn't a success). What he really wanted was to find some way to get beyond the pull of earth's gravity. "Escape velocity," his science teacher called it. Twenty-five thousand mph. So mostly he contented himself with gazing up into space, wondering what might be out there.

His mom once remarked that what we think of as stars twinkling in the night sky are just light that is finally reaching us from unimaginable distances. Ross tried to conceive of an odometer that could log all those miles. In ninth grade science he learned that the light only *appears* to twinkle as it comes through the atmosphere, and that some of the light is from stars that burned out eons ago. Like incandescent bulbs, the teacher said. Sometimes Ross wondered if the light ever got lonely knowing its source was no more.

By high school his ideas about everything were evolving. He became intrigued by UFOs and the idea that we are not alone. The Flash, he perceived, was a distant cousin to the Ancient Greek god Hermes, and the Roman version Mercury, moving through the perpetual deep-space night, bearing messages. "One could argue," Ross said to his friends, "that superheroes are formed in response to our frailties or are just reactionary tics to the problems of society. Okay. But what if they are aliens, reaching out to us with a message?"

"What, you don't want to be the Flash anymore?" his friends asked uncertainly.

In college Ross came to admit that, for reasons of our own, we all lie; not always meaning to. Sometimes, something which leaves the lips as true or well-meaning can change to untruth en route. *I left my essay on the kitchen table.* Or *I'll call you soon.* Or *I'm sorry.* Or *I love you.* Then other people are left to sit in the glow of our intention, or in the pain of a true reckoning. Like the light of stars through imponderable vastnesses, our words only *appear* to twinkle. So, could the superpower of speed overcome the flaws inherent in language? Ease the pain of lies? Bring truth? Unite us all?

Since sound travels at 700 mph, Ross reasoned, could being fast like the Flash allow you to move to the ears of the listener so quickly as to be invisible, and clear up the message, soften the blow, tell the truth?

But the beery wonderings of early adulthood passed. Ross's boyhood friends were in their thirties now, none of them married. They, but not Ross, continued to read comic books and attend each new superhero movie as a group. Occasionally one would hit Ross up and suggest they hang. He'd say yeah, maybe, but neither would follow through. He sometimes missed the old friendships, but his mind was occupied with his job and his wife and children and his mother, who continued to share with him her understanding of the world.

Ross's mom was mostly right about things, in general terms, though in the particulars she was occasionally lacking. He didn't bother her with this, however; she was widowed and growing old. But, for instance, Ross now knew that light bends as it traverses space, so strictly speaking it's not the exact same light— or *lie*—that it once was. It's a space-time *continuum* lie. At night sometimes, his wife sleeping quietly beside him, he grappled with these and other matters, trying to imagine what superpower, if any, could overcome them. Or was *that* the superpower somehow? To imagine.

Kate Hanson Foster

Six for Gold

When my six-year-old asks me where
he came from—how he, you know,
got inside my belly, he is swinging a broken
tree branch around in the backyard.
Just swinging to feel the air molecules,
to hear the faint whistle of resistance.
The invisible turbulence satisfies something
for both of us—disturbing what you can't see.
You were a star I took for my own, I say.
But how does it work, he asks, you know,
getting the star into your belly? I rub
my hands together vigorously and then slowly
pull them apart like a wizard commanding
an invisible orb of commotion. I tell him to try—
keep rubbing your hands, as fast as you can,
and when you are ready, stop—wait
for the energy to arrive between your palms.
He doesn't know this is just a game, just
our nerves responding to friction. He gently
packs his hands around what he feels, a warm
snowball. I say imagine that energy gathering
into your belly. When you arrived, an old star
collapsed and exploded, and in a huge,
blast you landed inside me. He tosses his secret
ball into the sky—it's gone somewhere
we will never find. Like gold crashing into a rock,
or sinking into the bottom of a river, I say.
I can tell he is no longer listening, his eyes
are back to the branch. I smile and scoop
him up before he can grab it again, tickling
his side to make him giggle. He wiggles
in my arms, laughter bright and bursting,
this boy who came to me like gold.

Brian Simoneau

Poem for My Brother

We're not white trash, my brother said
to the kid who'd taken his hat.
He told my brother to shut up;
then he punched him in the stomach.
The early morning stung my eyes,
a church bell sounded in my head,
my lips quivered, let out a breath.
And I punched his ugly face once
then twice then over and over
until my knuckles burned and I
couldn't tell if the blood was his
or mine. He cried for me to stop.
My brother cried as well but
softly and without a word. Years
later, he tells me that he cried
because it seemed I never would.
My eyes were someplace else. Empty,
he says, or filled with something he'd
never seen until that morning.
He cried, he tells me, for brothers
unable to speak under cracked
open skies, morning light flooding
their mouths like blood, lips pressed against
prayer as they watch each other break.

Alex Hayes

Lacuna

The gentle arcing of her back
envelopes the cradle in shadow,
Tender gurgling, furtive laughter
which reverberates around the room
until it rips the roof away
and bathes the figures in cloudless sky.

Her wide smile buttressed by nine months
of terror and anticipation,
A patchwork cat of childhoods past
stitched together with crystalline twine
teeters smugly from the gable
mewling warnings as it is able.

She cannot hear them, nor can he
so absorbed are they by ritual,
He reaches for the thousandth time
for the polished marble of her face
abraded by a thousand nights
of visitation to this lost place.

The cat explodes in a shower
of leaves edged in golden filigree
that whirl above the silent pair
in a shimmering cyclone of air
composed of atoms unreal
and existing purely in darkness.

—

The man awoke to the rustling of leaves
falling gently from the eaves
of the house that he shared only with ghosts.

Gerry Murphy

Annual Anabasis

for the Murphys and the Buckleys

In the Woodford Bourne van,
Danny driving, my father up front.
My mother, brother, sister and me,
packed in the back
and swaying giddily from side
to side with the holiday gear.
On our way to Graball Bay
for two weeks in my aunt's
moth-haunted, ramshackle bungalow.
Excitement building since Douglas,
bubbling over at Carrigaline,
and as we rounded the bend at Drake's Pool,
holding on to each other for dear life,
we knew we would shortly
get our first teasing glimpse
of the yacht-bedecked sea at Crosshaven.
Upon which we would cry out in unison,
like the Ten Thousand on Mount Theches:
"Thálatta!" "Thálatta!" "Thálatta!"

Patrick Cook

Choristers

I recently came across an aged, yellowed, and tattered scrapbook filled with memories collected by my mom, Marie Cook, who passed away in 2011. Adhered to the book's fragile pages were dozens upon dozens of newspaper clippings documenting the exploits of a Lowell young women's singing group, the Christian Doctrine Choristers.

Growing up, I had always known my mom sang in her youth, and I would occasionally hear fragment recollections of some of the concerts in which she performed. My aunt Helen O'Neil, Mom's older sister, would often say my mom was a melodious harmonizer who had an unforgettable voice. My mom's grandchildren would hear those tones in her later years, albeit almost always as she was rocking them to sleep.

I've been trying to archive and get my arms around some of the historical artifacts my parents left behind, mostly black and white photos with no dates or IDs on them—a frustrating but thoroughly fascinating process.

But this book was different. It was distinctly focused on my mother's singing years, which began during World War II, and lasted into the mid-1950s. (My guess is those singing days ended when my brother Jimmy came along. I think everyone started singing a different tune when that happened.)

My mom's involvement with the group began when she was sixteen years old. It commenced as Marie Payette of Gorham Street received a letter from Father John L. O'Toole of the Oblate Fathers at the Immaculate Conception Rectory on February 22, 1944, welcoming her to a new radio program, the Cathedral Hour. She was told to report for her rehearsal at the League of Catholic Women Rooms, 53 Central St., 5th floor. Does that address even exist anymore?

Here's what I've been able to glean about the group and how it evolved beyond the Cathedral Hour, from yellowed *Lowell Sun* news clippings.

The Christian Doctrine Choristers performed under the direction of Rev. Harold W. Fraser, who was a graduate of the Catholic University School of Music. He was assigned to the Sacred Heart parish on Moore Street. When Fraser took over the weekly singing group, he changed the name of its radio program from the Cathedral Hour to the Christine Doctrine Hour, somewhere around 1944, right after my mom joined. It was broadcast locally on WLAW (680 on your AM radio dial) on Sundays at 5 p.m.

The group appeared in the first of a series of semi-annual shows in 1945 (my mother would have been 18) and continued performing throughout the area until the mid-1950s.

Their reviews in the *Lowell Sun* were stellar: "The Choristers, who have been presented four times on both National and Columbia Broadcasting networks, are consistent proof that the city abounds in talent which needs but correct training and the opportunity to succeed in the entertainment world."

The singing group attracted its share of star power.

I found one clip of Eddie Fisher (father of Princess Leia/Carrie Fisher) coming to town to perform with them on June 21, 1947, at the Lowell Memorial Auditorium on East Merrimack Street. Perry Como was supposed to have been the headliner for the event, but cancelled out, bringing in Fisher as his pinch-hitter.

At the time, Fisher was a private in the U.S. Army. My mother would have turned 20 one month prior to this concert. The *Lowell Sun*, previewing Fisher's Lowell performance, said, "recent appearances have led to near riots on the part of teen-agers to secure his autograph." A precursor to Beatlemania, no doubt. Don't believe me? A *Lowell Sun* photo shows Lowell Police Officers Frank Sexton, Sgt. Richard Cullen, Inspector George Handley, and Joseph Winn holding back the hordes. I believe, perhaps incorrectly, that this was the same Officer Joseph Winn who would be killed in the line of duty during an assault 22 years later in December of 1969.

In April 1951, Danny Thomas came to town, an event my mother frequently referenced over the next half-century. She was smitten by his jovial personality. He was always a favorite of hers, and because of him, she adopted his beloved St. Jude's Hospital as the charity to which she donated annually right up until her passing. Thomas returned for another gig with the group in 1953.

By the way, if you wanted to buy tickets to Thomas' gig, besides finding them at the LMA box office, you could get them at Gagnon's on Merrimack Street, Maloof's and the Epicure (where my Aunt Virginia worked) on Central Street, and at the Christian Doctrine studios in the Fairburn Building. Anyone under the age of sixty probably has no idea where any of the places I named once stood in Lowell.

The Choristers' setlists included standbys such as "Only a Rose," "Summertime," "Someday," "Moonlight Sonata," "Galway Bay," "The Way You Look Tonight," "Smoke Gets in Your Eyes," "Were You There," "Ave Maria," and dozens of others hits of the day.

Here are the names of the Choristers that I could cull from the various articles: Virginia McMullen, Margie Largay, Dolores Donnelly, Colette Grandchamp, Dorothy Allen, Florence Brown, Elizabeth Carolan, Patricia Cullinan, Pauline Gaumont, Rita Hennessy, Florence Kelley, Claire Kennedy, Helen Meagher, Elizabeth McGovern, Eileen Nestor, Dorothy Webster, Ann Smith, Phyllis Skaff, Ann Shugrue, and of course, my mom, Marie Payette. Admittedly, the names changed during the evolution of that decade, but that may be because some of the ladies married, and they dropped their maiden names.

My mom, along with Carolan (a dear friend of hers), Allen and Skaff, had a sub-group of the Choristers called the Chordears. Your guess is as good as mine as to the origin of that girls' harmony quartet's name, but I found multiple references to them frequently performing "Besame Mucho" (Kiss Me Generously) MOM!!!!!!!!!!!!

Sun scribe Alfred Burke wrote in one article that the Chordears again captured their share of the spotlight during one of their performances. "Their voices blend well together," he wrote. "Added to this is a natural gift for harmonic color."

Learning even more surprising facts about my mom, in a photo from April 27, 1951, just two months after she married my dad, Jim Cook, she's playing a ukulele during Thomas' gig at the auditorium. Until that point, I never realized my mother could play the ukulele! Go figure.

In March 1951, one month after getting married, my mom and the other Chordears were singing at the Policemen's Ball. Who knew we held Policemen's Balls in Lowell? Apparently, the city also hosted Firemen's Balls, too. And yeah, the Chordears sang at those, too. The group was frequently accompanied by Frank Simpson on the Hammond organ, Jack Payne, and Barbara Berke.

In a bit of familial irony, the Christian Doctrine Choristers, joined by Congresswoman Edith Nourse Rogers, performed at the Lowell Memorial Auditorium to honor 441 Lowell heroes of World War II. Among the 441 was one Gerald F. Cook, the older brother of my dad, Jim Cook, who would become Marie's husband just a few years later. She sang in memory of a man who would have been her brother-in-law had he survived the war.

Another weird piece of irony: one photo depicts members of the Christian Doctrine Choristers feting a fellow singer at her pre-nuptial shower at the home of Mrs. John McGoohan of 237 Nesmith Street—a few buildings away from Middlesex Community College's Nesmith House. The singer, Miss Payette, was scheduled to wed Jimmy Cook the following month on February 3 at 2 p.m. at St. Peter's Church. My mom's wedding shower made the *Lowell Sun*.

I could go on and on and on about the reviews, performances, and exploits of the chorus found in the scrapbook. Makes me wonder why they ever stopped performing.

Do you know any of the ladies I referenced (or perhaps some that I didn't, who joined at different points of that decade of performances)? If one of your loved ones—moms, grandmothers, sisters—has some history tied to this Lowell group, drop me a line at patrickecook@yahoo.com and I'd be happy to let you and your loved ones pore over a scrapbook full of Mill City memories.

So, this song's for you, Mom. You and all your fellow Choristers and Chordears.

Ave Maria, gratia plena,
Maria, gratia plena
Maria, gratia plena
Ave, Ave Dominus
Dominus tecum,
Benedicta tu in mulieribus,
Et benedictus
Et benedictus fructus ventris
Ventris tuae, Jesus
Ave Maria.

Kate Hanson Foster

Elegy of Color

Green shutters—white house.
Paper whites in the weak western light.
Brown mouse and its brown hush
across the stairs, four daughters
brushing long brown hair. Brown
beer in Black Label cans, black bible
on the nightstand. Baby Jesus
on the wall—incarnadine cheeks.
Shimmering red rosary beads. Red
garnet of my Claddagh ring. A leak
yellowing in the ceiling. The many
colors of my father singing. I was blessed
and I was blessed, like foreheads, like palm
wisps, like water my mother bought
from the church—colorless, colorless.

Elinor Lipman

A Tip of the Hat to the Old Block

I'll be careful on this St. Patrick's Day, mindful that sending a valentine to an entire clan of hyphenated Americans would reveal myself as sociologically backward. I won't generalize; instead, I'll narrow my focus to one subset of Irish-Americans, the residents of the Lowell neighborhood where I lived until I was twelve. What strikes me as remarkable from this distance is how my family and I were folded in, embraced, accepted as far back as the 1950s, despite our being the sole Jewish family for blocks around.

The 1950s were not a decade famous for open arms: No laws were on the books suggesting that religious animus was punishable by the courts. Pope John XXIII wouldn't until 1958 eliminate anti-Semitic pejoratives from prayers. New England hotels could advertise GENTILES ONLY or post signs that said NO DOGS OR JEWS.

My neighborhood was not the section of Lowell where mill owners, doctors, and lawyers lived. Ours was one of starter homes, clotheslines, one-car garages; no backyard was big enough for three bases and a home plate. Yet here was my childhood: my sister and I never heard an unkind or exclusionary word leak from the homes that surrounded us. From the day Marie McGowan moved in across the street, pregnant with her third, she was my mother's best friend, confidante, and cofounder of the daily kaffeeklatsch.

With five daughters between them, hand-me-down dresses hopscotched between our two households. Because my mother was the best cook in the neighborhood, with a range from gefilte fish to spaghetti sauce, her Irish bread inevitably won the title of most delicious and most authentic. At Christmas, she made wreaths of cinnamon buns for the neighbors from a recipe handed down by my kosher grandmother. I still don't know why Father Shanley regularly joined us for corned beef and cabbage, but it might have been a preference for deli-style over rectory-style boiled meat.

Marge Gibson was the neighborhood's best seamstress, with my mother, a tailor's daughter, a keen audience. Thus one fashion memory more vivid than any my own childhood offers up is that of Suzanne Gibson in white dotted swiss, brought by for inspection on her way to her First Communion, her mother's creation more beautiful than any off the rack, especially on Suzanne, the adored baby of the family, with her blue eyes and dark finger curls.

Every summer night, weather permitting, my father walked uphill to Eddie Reeney's veranda, where the neighborhood men smoked cigars in rocking chairs. My father marveled at Eddie's real-world skills; Eddie, in turn, treated my father, the English major and least mechanical man ever born ("Jets don't have propellers?!" he once proclaimed), with the studied patience of a shop teacher helping an armless student.

My father also revered the porch elder, white-haired Sam McElroy, a bachelor with a brogue, who lived with his two sisters from the old country. (I overheard my father tell my mother that it had not been easy for Sam growing up in Ireland: he was, my father confided, a Protestant.)

My sister, Debbie, and I dressed up for Easter, sans church, sans eggs, but kept our own council with respect to the Easter Bunny. Three years older than I, Debbie and her friends discussed religion just enough so that she came away accepting—not glumly, just a fact of life—that purgatory was the best she could hope for. St. Margaret's was our buddies' destination for church and catechism, but Temple Beth El, a closer walk, hosted the Brownies and Cub Scouts.

The McGowans, unannounced, came to my father's funeral—from some distance and thirty-nine years after we had left Cascade Avenue. And when my mother died, Marie, Pat (now Scanlon), and Carol (now Sullivan) were with us at a graveside service.

I should repeat: it's dangerous to characterize a whole group of people by their country of origin, or anything else. So today I'll keep it on a small scale, a salute to the McGowans, the Gibsons, the Daileys, the Shanleys, the Mullens, the Cullens, the Crimminses, the Timminses, the Lemeres (Irish mother), the Reeneys, the Hogans, the Gallaghers, and the McElroys, whose backyards ran into the Lipmans', and whose embrace hasn't released us yet.

THREE

John FitzGerald

Fota with Jerry

Egrets stilting streams, the broken walls of Belvelly Bridge
its toppled sandstone blocks bruising the dun shallows,
and so many years now since we circumambulated the island,
followed the railway line in search of Townsend's couch-grass
when we should have been in lecture hall or library.
But we weren't made for that. And this was all before
      the by-pass,
wildlife park, hotel, chalets, golf academy. Back then,
it was just the shuttered house and unkempt arboretum,
neglected farmland—somewhere entire set aside for
      our diversion,
the thick belt of holm oak and our own awkward bravura
useless holds against all that was to come undone.

Tom Sexton

Cummiskey Alley, Lowell, Mass.

It's Sunday morning with church bells ringing
as a family speaking Spanish rushes by me
in this narrow alley named for Hugh Cummiskey
the Irishman who led his crew of "white niggers"
thirty miles from Charlestown to dig the canals
that made Lowell's mills the envy of the world.
The old buildings on both sides of the alley sag.

When I reach the Market Street end, a man
sitting in a Caddy with its windows down
is listening to a talk show host with a Boston-Irish
accent loudly praising President Trump's wall.
"Send them all back, send them all to hell,"
he shouts, then smiling looks at me and says,
"The bastards never even try to learn the language."

Emily Ferrara

On the Morning of the Third Supermoon

I'm driving due North for the coast
past Kerouac's Lowell   the smokestacks of Lawrence
past Gloucester   its Man at the Wheel

powering past ramps and merges   *the clouds*
a skyless blue the driving question   this placebo
road   is not why   but how to persist

at the impasse of innocence toeing the fault line,
innocents seeking escape from near-death
  the clouds have fallen

asleep at the wheel sundogged swoon
the-too-much-with-us moon
I'm course correcting on cruise

past burning wrecks   promised auroras
the clouds an eyeless blue driving North to the sea
to the sea I love   the complicit and culpable sea.

Thomas McCarthy

REGent 7292

We haven't met since the last time it was beautiful
To fly. I was with Patsy O'Donnell at Idlewild,
Snug as an oily Irish bug in the engine shed.
Those damn radial pistons on the DC 7C
Kept us busy in a pool of oil: it was *Pan Am*, still,
And, boy, it was beautiful. You had gone ahead
And I had given you my number. What a party
We'd had, you and I, twelve hours in the air.
Your love was like all the cut flowers in Mayfair.
In them days youngsters in the air could be discreet,
But we are older now. I was checking an oil leak
On the pushrod housing when I saw, in *Newsweek*,
You'd married for the third time. We should speak:
I regret, Ma'am, giving you the wrong number. Sorry, my sweet—
Reach me here at the engine shed, not Regent Street.

Thomas McCarthy

The Horse Has Bolted

We look back along the fuchsia-covered road near Carroll's farm.
It is a pleasant day to be sure, a day no man should have to worry
About the least thing; least of all our current troubles.
A skylark has risen, blackguarding beneath ambitious clouds,
A cow is lowing in the dead stillness; a pheasant mutters
Its useless observations:
                              It was not your fault and it was not my fault.

But, Patrick, the horse has bolted—

It is an unpleasant business.

So, we thought the rules might be different in a Celtic *Arcadia*;
That a horse might be different.
                              Well, here is horseshit
And trouble brewing beneath braided leather.
                              The road behind us
    is full of dirt;
It was a road well swept when the times were good. Now,
    even the sky
Is stinking:
            A scarlet door swings from the injured afternoon.

David D. McKean

St. Patrick's Day in the Acre

St. Patrick's Day is one of my favorite holidays. Sure, there's the big three: Christmas, Thanksgiving, and Easter. Even Halloween and Valentine's Day have their good points. But March 17ᵗʰ is something special. Once, when landing at Logan coming from Dublin, a young Irish businesswoman, who was visiting Boston for the first time, turned to me and asked what it was about St. Patrick's Day and Americans. Some might say it's the search for identity. Others might say it's about the *craic*. Others might think of it as the Irish form of "Festivus for the rest of us" (a la *Seinfeld*). My family celebrates far differently than in my parents' time. My wife and I took a trip down memory lane and reminisced on how the day was celebrated when we were kids in the 1960s.

Growing up when and where I did in Lowell's Acre neighborhood almost made St. Patrick's Day a holy day of obligation. It was a religious and cultural day. Much like Advent prepares believers for Christmas or Lent for Easter, once the calendar turned to March the arrangements began. Certain foods had to be prepared, special songs rehearsed, and every item of green clothing readied. At St. Patrick School, the annual reunion show was planned weeks in advance. The show goes back to the late nineteenth century, if not earlier. Records show that the parish would present entertainments of by the different societies, grade-school children, and parishioners. In the Parish Archives are copies of programs going back almost one hundred years.

When I attended St. Patrick School, about half the class had Irish surnames. Most of the students were half Irish and half something else, like me. A few had no Irish in them, but still were required to sing "Galway Bay." A friend of mine of Lebanese extraction, with whom I am still friends, surprised me when I asked if he remembered the old songs. He confessed that he despised having to wear the green and to this day can't stand the sound of "Oh the Days of the Kerry Dancing." I still do not understand that. I thought everyone wanted to be Irish.

The show was the big event of the season. The Sisters would walk the entire student body, about four hundred kids, from the school to Market Street to Prescott to Merrimack and to Lowell Memorial Auditorium along the Concord River downtown. We walked two-by-two the full two-point-four miles. The show was always at 7 p.m. on March 16th. The entire Auditorium sold out year after year. I'm not sure if it is even there today, but behind the maroon curtain and stage was seating for the entire school chorus of more than three hundred students dressed in white shirts with green ribbons for girls and ties for boys. The Sisters, wearing a single green ribbon pinned to their habits, stood guard to ensure no shenanigans would besmirch the good name of St. Patrick School.

The show always began with the pipes and drums of Clan McPherson Band from Lawrence, another mill city downriver. The drum major in his tall bearskin hat led the pipers in with his silver baton flashing in the spotlight. The bass drummer wearing the leopard pelt twirled his drumsticks. We felt the vibrations of the drumbeats, not only physically, but in our very souls. Pipers lifted their pipes and marched into the hall playing "Scotland the Brave." For you purists, remember we're all Celts.

From the auld sod, singers sang "I'll Take You Home Again, Kathleen" or "It's a Great Day for the Irish." The audience frequently chimed in, after all these were the songs we were raised on. Little did most of us know that many of those Bing Crosby favorites were not from the auld sod and were not even written by Irish Americans. The genre at the turn of the century was an appeal for Irish-type vaudeville music and every musician, no matter the background, penned Irish sounding tunes. Those became the standards heard in every Irish-American home. But the music did its job, joining the crowd into one communal voice.

Part of the entertainment of the night was seeing the first and second graders do a little song and dance on the stage. What would really tear up Nana and the crowd was that the girls wore shamrock print skirts with aprons and dust caps. The boys wore green silk pantaloons with a cummerbund. We had to go on stage and act out Mick McGilligan's Ball. I remember this well, because I still have my pantaloons. I stole them. But my clearest recollection is how silk pantaloons, that were homemade using a loose elastic band to hold them up, can very easily slide down as you dance around a stage. And, how funny it is to see a six-year-old holding up his green silk pantaloons in front of hundreds and hundreds of people. Yes, I'm speaking from experience.

The high point of the evening was the Irish step dancers. Step dancing had been a tradition at St. Pat's School for decades. My mother-in-law attended St Pat's and took lessons in the 1920s. When my time came, it was common for boys and girls to go to the school hall each Saturday with their ghillies (soft shoes) and brogues (hard shoes) where Jim Madden put them through their routines. Jim was a taskmaster, but his mother (from Ireland) was more brutal. When my own kids took part in competitions, at their first *feis* (competition) who was there but Jim Madden, older but still with perfect posture. The crowd at the auditorium listened to see if the girls made their clicks with their hard shoes. Their green dresses with simple gold braiding were plain compared to today's outfits. (One of my daughter's dresses cost $1,500 and had to be imported from Ireland.) At that time, dancers could wear their medals won at *feisana* (competitions)—to see the medals lift and fall to the music beat was part of the thrill.

At the end of the evening the pastor would always walk out and declare the news every schoolchild had been waiting to hear: no school the next day. That did not mean you could sleep in the next morning. Mass was at 9 a.m., and it was not just any Mass, but a Solemn High Pontifical Mass. The celebrant wore the gold cope with the embroidered image of Patrick on the back. The opening song was "Hail Glorious Apostle Selected by God," and the closing would be "Hail Glorious St. Patrick, Dear Saint of Our Isle." Every seat in the church was filled. It was like Christmas when folks you hadn't seen all year would show up. They were coming home.

And then there was the feast, or so some say. I can't stand corned beef. I want to be very careful here when we talk about corned beef. Every Irish American talks about the sainted grandmother's recipe for corned beef and cabbage that she carried off the boat from Ireland. The debate about this can cause whole families to stop speaking to each other. Corned beef is not the most traditional of dishes in Ireland. In our ancestors' time, beef was pretty expensive. When they came to America beef was more accessible, and corned beef fit into their price range. So maybe Nana's recipe isn't so Irish. In my house, corned beef was served, but it was more likely to be a boiled ham shoulder with cabbage, turnips, and boiled potatoes. Hey, the Irish have great humor, literature, music, and poetry. No one ever said they had haute cuisine. Then there's the debate over soda bread. With caraway seeds or without? With raisins or currants? Let's not forget the green beer, too. To round off this Irish meal, my French mother would make cupcakes with green frosting, and then remind me that St. Joseph's Day was only two days away.

Maggie Dietz

Downtown

Hard not to notice the necklace
in the window, flashing in shadows
of passersby, draped on a stand
of flocked foam whose design
suggests clavicles, an attenuated
elegance even in the partial.
The pendant a threaded cymbal
or temple gong suspended from
strands of embroidery thread strung
at the base with carved, coral-painted
wooden beads then wound into twisted
ropes of glass—beads red and tiny as
tobiko—that meet in a loop and
coin clasp. Nothing I would wear:
nonetheless appealing, nonetheless
arresting in its almost-gaudy exoticism.
I'd like to meet who buys it. I'd like to
see in fifty years the granddaughter
with unusual taste inherit it, wear it with
jeans and a t-shirt and earrings she bought
for a song. I already miss her, that curious
girl from later, her bright eyeliner.
I've already gasped the day on the subway
the loop lost hold and the mercurial
beads went instantly everywhere, spraying
the seats like so many drops of blood.

Sean Thibodeau

Faux Chateaux

I pass a condo-plex of faux
chateaux backed up into pines,
pretty, really, under snow,
a ONE WAY DO NOT ENTER sign
saves the one-families up the hill
by the highway from undue traffic.
A woman I worked with in Boston
lived alone there on Robbins Road,
bought at the height of the bubble,
worst decision of her life, stuck
among the shit-box cars filling the
poorly plowed lots. Living in fake
luxury surrounded by all those *fixed
incomes* (her phrase). I read a story
in the paper, a Chinese man
attacked his family in one
of the units of the complex,
didn't say why. Façades
can be dangerous, but less
than our beating hearts.

Charles Gargiulo

from *Farewell, Little Canada*

It was a Saturday morning in March 1963, and as usual I got up to see Dad off to work. Our usual routine was he would wake me up around seven, kiss me on the head, and say he'd see me when he got back. Only he never came back.

Of course, I didn't know that when I watched him pull away in his 1960 black Pontiac Bonneville waving goodbye. I had no idea he wasn't coming back when I watched my Saturday morning cartoons, went out to play baseball all day, and got back for supper.

When I came home, I was surprised he hadn't got back yet, but didn't get worried until I noticed that my mom was acting weird. She got even weirder when I went to bed that night and he still hadn't come back. As the week went on, I stopped asking her when Dad was coming.

Before long it became clear that without Dad's income we were screwed. Three months later, Mom said we wouldn't be able to afford to live in Dracut anymore and that we would have to move to Lowell.

She found a place in the same building my Aunt Rose lived in on Austin Street in a neighborhood called "Little Canada." It's called that because a whole bunch of French Canadians left their homes in Quebec in the late 1800s and moved to Lowell to work in the textile mills. Back then there were a zillion factories along the Merrimack River, and the city was pretty famous for making all kinds of clothes. I heard even famous guys like Abe Lincoln and Davy Crockett used to visit Lowell. One cool thing about the place was they built lots of canals to use waterpower to help make electricity back then before they had electric companies. These canals crisscross the city, and we had a really big one that goes right through Little Canada called the Northern Canal.

The French Canadians moved down here and got to steal a bunch of jobs from the Irish, who were starting to get sick of the lousy mill owners screwing the crap out of them. The Irish started to band together and complain about the lousy pay and working conditions, so the mill owners just said, "Up yours," and recruited this big poor labor force up north in Quebec. The Canucks were desperate, and the owners said to the Irish, well screw you if you don't like it, we got these poor schmucks who will gladly take your place. That kind of quieted the complaining down for a while until the Canucks started to get just as sick of things as the Irish and decided to fight together against the mill owners. So, the owners hired the Greeks, who had just gotten to America and were desperate for work. When the Greeks got wise, the damn mill owners went and grabbed the even more newly arrived Portuguese. You get the picture.

My dad's family was Italian, but my mother was French Canadian, and her grandparents moved here in the 1880s from Three Rivers, a city in Quebec. Everybody who came from Quebec squeezed into an area in between the neighborhood where the Irish lived and the mills near the river. That area became Little Canada. It really became official when the French Canadians built their own church, a big giant stone one called *St.-Jean-Baptiste.*

About twenty years after Little Canada was formed, the Greeks moved in and scrunched a neighborhood in between the Irish and French Canadians. All three groups, the French Canadians, the Irish, and the Greeks had neighborhoods that were just like being in their old countries. They each created their own schools, the Canucks and Irish had Catholic schools, and the Greeks had a Greek Orthodox school. The Irish mainly spoke in English, but the French Canadians ran their school in French, and the Greeks ran theirs in Greek. All the adults still mainly talked to each other in French in Little Canada, or Greek in the Greek neighborhood, but outside of school, none of us kids did.

It didn't take long after arriving in Little Canada for me to figure out that none of the three groups got along. We stayed in Little Canada and God help anyone of us who went alone into the Irish or Greek neighborhoods, or if one of them came alone in ours. We hated each other. Each group of kids had its own main street.

We had Moody Street, the Greeks controlled Market Street, and the Irish had Broadway Street. The main street of Lowell itself was Merrimack Street, which was mostly made up of stores and led into downtown Lowell. I remember reading about the Korean War, and how after nobody really won between the north and the south, they just kept it divided and created this border line between them called the Demilitarized Zone or DMZ. It was meant to keep the peace by saying, we can kind of meet here without killing each other as long as we don't step into the other guy's land. Merrimack Street was sort of our DMZ. We could all walk down it without beating the crap out of each other so we could go to the movies, pool halls, bowling alleys, or to buy stuff in all the stores.

The apartment we moved into had four rooms and was on the second floor of a large, old three-story gray wooden tenement. There were nine apartments in the building. There was no bathtub or shower, and the toilet was in the hall. Kind of like an indoor outhouse. There was no heat when you had to take a crap in the winter, but at least there was plumbing so we could flush the damn thing. The kitchen sink acted as the shower/bathtub. Duck under the faucet to shampoo your hair and fill the sink with soapy water to take a sponge bath.

The stove was pretty cool. It heated the apartment and there was this little flame inside called the pilot light. When you wanted heat, you turned the dial on the stove and "WHOOOSH," a big row of fire would flame on inside. What was really neat was that in addition to heating the place, the top of the stove had burners on one side and on the other side there was a flat iron skillet-like top above the flames that got so freaking hot that you could spit on top of it and your spit would boil and sizzle the second it hit. Of course, the downside was it would melt your friggin' skin off if you ever accidentally touched it.

Mom and I had our own bedroom and we had another room where we stored stuff. The kitchen acted as our living room where people who came over hung out and talked sitting around the table. We had two doors in the kitchen. One led into the hallway, and the other led outside. Yes, that's right, a door that opened with no stairs right on the second floor. In fact, every apartment on the second and third floors of our building had a door that opened like a window. Don't worry, we didn't walk out and fall to our death because the really cool thing was that a wooden passageway with rails connected every apartment on the second floor to each other, same thing for the people on the third floor. In case of a fire, if we couldn't get out by our hallway stairs, we were supposed to run down the passageway to the end where there was a steel-rung ladder to use, one person at a time, to climb down to safety. Good luck with that.

Even though our address was Austin Street, there was no doorway facing the street. There were two different doorways to our tenement that were entered from a skinny alleyway between us and another large apartment building. The alleyway was so tightly tucked between our buildings that we could probably shake hands with the people across the alleyway if we opened our windows. So even though the sun never touched those windows, we had to keep the shades down unless we wanted to have our next-door neighbors peeking into our room all day.

Austin Street was a short one-way street that ran two blocks from Merrimack Street. It cut through Moody and ended at Ford, which ran parallel to Moody Street and alongside the Northern Canal. Austin Street was in between Cabot and Aiken Street and ran parallel to them. This four-block area, within the borders of Merrimack, Aiken, Ford and Cabot Streets, became my main territory. In it, there were literally just two tiny spots of open land the size of a torn-down apartment block. These open spots were both crappy hard dirt lots with small stones, no grass and about a hundred years of chipped pieces of broken bottles wedged in the dirt like rocks. One lot was used as a small parking lot for the brick Welfare Office building next to my place, and the other one was behind the tenements across the street from our house on Austin Street. That was our closest thing to open space. Our main playground was Austin Street itself, since it had very little traffic. Cars could only travel one way from Moody Street to Ford Street, and whenever somebody tried to drive the wrong way, we'd all yell at the driver "ONE-WAY! Hey dummy, it's a one-way street!" Then we'd chase and harass the driver if they kept going anyway.

I loved Austin Street. There was a stoop in front of the apartment across the street from my building that ended up being our main outdoor hang-out. My friends and I would gather there when we decided to go outside. What made it especially cool for me was that my Aunt Rose used to sit in a chair in her parlor next to a window that overlooked Austin Street. She used to love looking out her second-floor window and watch me play with my friends. I would toss her a wave when we played, and I think it became her favorite form of entertainment as she used to spend hours watching us. She also had a view of Ouellette's Diner and the Austin Provision meat market, across the street from each other on the corner where Austin Street met Moody Street. She could also see the giant *St.-Jean-Baptiste* granite church looming large behind the tenement buildings on Austin and Moody Streets.

If you crossed Moody Street and stayed on Austin Street it ended one block up on Merrimack Street, where on the right corner you had the rectory next to *St.-Jean-Baptiste*. Directly across Merrimack Street where Austin Street ended was a small food supermarket called Clermont's, where we bought our food. If you kept going right on Merrimack Street you passed the rectory and the front of the church and came to the corner where Aiken Street ended. On the other corner of Aiken, across the street from the church, was Louie's Drug Store. It was a tiny drugstore with the usual boring drugstore stuff, but it also had a tiny counter where you could get the only ice cream cones in Little Canada. Now if you headed back down Aiken you would come to an intersection with Moody Street, which had another even more boring drugstore which always seemed dark and foreboding inside. Then Aiken went another block until it intersected with Ford Street. There were large three- and four-story tenements lining both sides of Aiken. Then it would cross the canal and head all the way down to the Merrimack River where Little Canada ended near large red-brick mill buildings. Along the way was my favorite store, good old Harvey's Bookland. Across the street from Harvey's was another small food market called Dufresne's. Aiken Street crossed the Merrimack River into a section of the city called Centralville, which was a stupid name because it wasn't anywhere near the center of Lowell. The bridge that crossed the river was a big, cool, green, metal bridge that had strange metal grates, instead of tar, for the roadway. When cars passed over it, they would make a high-pitched humming sound. Everybody called it the "singing bridge."

Now going back to where Aiken Street intersected with Ford Street, if you took a right on Ford, instead of continuing down Aiken, you went between two- and three-story wooden tenements lining Ford Street as it continued one block past the end of Austin Street until it intersected the next block at Cabot Street. A left on Cabot took you over the canal and down to the factory buildings. But if you took a right on Cabot, the Welfare Building was on the right-hand corner and it was followed by about three different smaller apartment buildings until you got to Merrimack Street and Benny the Jips Variety store, a two-story building with a bookie joint upstairs. On the other side of Cabot, between Ford and Merrimack Streets, a long row of red-brick apartments led to the corner where the *Club Passé Temps* (Pastime Club) stood on Moody Street across from Benny the Jips. In this club, guys from Little Canada drank and played pool in their own private club instead of a regular bar.

Opposite the *Club Passé Temps* across Moody was the Holiday Diner, my favorite diner with a lunch counter and booths. They made the best hamburgers and fries in Little Canada and had a great juke box. There were a few smaller owner-occupied wooden homes between Benny the Jips and Ouellette's Diner on the right side of Austin. Across from Ouellette's there was a small shed that housed a tiny gas station with two pumps. If you continued down Moody past Austin, there was *St.-Jean-Baptiste* taking up the entire block until Aiken Street on the left side, and three gigantic four-story long tenement buildings on the other side. If you continued up Moody, you went past more tenements until you got to St. Joseph's School where the street continued until it reached the end of Little Canada, crossed Pawtucket Street, and went over an iron bridge far above the Merrimack under which were spread an amazing bunch of rocks that broke the water into rapids when the river ran high. When you crossed the river, you saw Lowell Tech college in a neighborhood called Pawtucketville, where the snobby French Canadians who looked down their noses at us lived.

If you went back to the corner of Moody and Cabot, where Benny the Jips, *Club Passé Temps*, and the Holiday Diner were, and turned right on Moody and straight up Cabot, you would be at the intersection of Merrimack Street. Marie's Oyster House was on the left corner, a big fried seafood restaurant. Inside were wooden booths, but the place's claim to fame was its Friday business. French-Canadian Catholics formed lines that left the building and curled a half-block along the sidewalk waiting to get a take-out dinner. We weren't allowed to eat meat on Friday. It was a church rule. It would be some kind of sin if we ate a hamburger. My mom bought fried scallops or clams and French fries packed in white waxed boxes that the staff loaded into brown paper bags. By the time you got home, the bags were wet with grease and the damned waxed boxes leaked. But the food tasted so good it was worth risking a heart attack. Across Merrimack Street from Marie's was the *Jeanne D'Arc* Credit Union where most of the people in the neighborhood did their banking. Cabot continued one more street until it ended at Market Street where there was the beginning of a large red-brick series of public housing units built in the 1930s. The Rainbow Bar, where my dad once decked a guy, was on the right side of Cabot Street between Merrimack and Market Streets. Behind the housing projects on Market and Adams Street was the North Common, a large park where there were baseball fields and outside tar basketball courts.

This area I have described was for me the heart of Little Canada.

The Little Canada neighborhood was razed in the early 1960s as part of federally funded "urban renewal" in Lowell, scattering thousands of residents and tearing the fabric of the Franco-American community. A decade later, determined to prevent a similar fate for the historic Acre neighborhood, Charles Gargiulo fought for social justice and helped preserve the Acre for its residents and the city.

CORK IN THE ROUND

Liam Ronayne

A Reading City

Cork City Libraries is at the heart of Cork: The Reading City. What this means in reality is our library branches hosting book launches, creative writing classes, the Cork World Book Fest each April, the annual "One City, One Book" initiative, and providing a range of supports and incentives to book clubs. Our catalogue and writing/reading blogs, and a range of reader development projects also help make a reading city a reality.

The Cork World Book Fest features readings by world-class writers in a variety of settings. When we put "World" in the title in 2005, it was an aspiration, but since then it has grown in range and breadth and, we hope, gets more interesting by the year. It combines readings by writers with a cultural street fair: book stalls, music, street entertainment, the spoken word, and more.

"One City, One Book" brings the city together through reading and discussion of a common book. As well as building a sense of community, the project aims to promote individual and social wellbeing through literature, local and international culture, discussion, and creative writing. Our book for 2019 was *Darkest Truth* by Catherine Kirwan.

Our Children's Book Festival is a month long celebration and promotion of children's books and stories, taking place across all our libraries during October. Events include author visits, workshops, performances, crafts—all free of charge.

Our library branches are at the centre of their local communities and offer a range of activities for adults and children, including exhibitions, book clubs, chess clubs, writers' groups, creative writing classes, art groups, gramophone recitals, conversational Irish sessions. They host classes in basic computer skills, literacy, and basic English in conjunction with various agencies. In partnership with the Centre for Continuing & Adult Education in UCC (CACE) we also make short courses accessible to local communities. Our libraries also regularly host events organised by local communities including many during the Cork Lifelong Learning Festival.

Cork City Council Library Service is a popular and well-loved resource, contributing to the social, cultural and economic life of the people of the city. It celebrated its 125th birthday in 2017/8.

- o Citizens borrow between 900,000 and one million items from the city's libraries each year;
- o Between 43,000 and 47,000 people are members in any given year; and
- o An estimated further 23,000 people use the libraries' services.

The library service continues to face major, perhaps unprecedented, change. Over recent years we have seen greatly increased demand for both borrowing and use of library spaces and facilities. Demand for study spaces, classes, and attendances at events are all on the rise. While heartening, and indicating the value of a library service, this presents obvious challenges to us. Furthermore, the digital revolution, now well underway, impacts on us in three main ways:

Firstly, the move beyond printed materials to eBooks, eJournals, apps, etc.; and changes in how people access digital materials: "renting" not "owning";

Secondly, major shifts in the media ecosystem, most of which are responses by the commercial world to digital developments; and

Thirdly, the demand and expectation on the part of the public that a modern public library should provide a range of digital services, such as more extensive Cork Past & Present web content, music downloads, web videos, etc.

Ireland has experienced widening socio-economic inequality over the years since the economic downturn, a decade ago. The library service had to re-focus its policies and programmes to respond more effectively to social, educational, and cultural exclusion.

Cork City Libraries face the future with confidence, based on the commitment and competences of library staff, and on the strength of the relationship between libraries and the people they serve. To respond to the challenges we face, we will need to reconfigure ourselves: in our staffing structure, in the adoption of appropriate technologies, and in the physical layout of libraries. The reconfiguration required forms a central part of this development programme.

Liam Ronayne is the Cork City Librarian. Cork City had a population of 125,657 in the 2016 census but, following a boundary extension in 2019, it increased to c. 210,000. It is the second largest city in the Republic of Ireland.

Alannah Hopkin

Literary Cork

Cork's poetry scene is thriving, and is very much part of the city's everyday fabric. For example, Cork's poets are celebrated in the Farmgate Restaurant in Cork City's English Market. Owner Kay Harte has assembled a wall of framed writings by mainly Cork poets, and Cork writers like to gather beside it for coffee and scones or a traditional lunch.

The cultural and economic capital of the south of Ireland, Cork has a unique identity as a university town and a cathedral city, and, until recently, a busy working port. It stands on a beautiful river where it divides into two main channels before opening out into Cork Harbour—Ireland's largest. The poet Edmund Spenser, who was appointed High Sheriff of Cork in 1598, described Cork's River Lee in *The Faerie Queene* as

> The Spreading Lee, that like an island fayre
> Encloseth Cork with his divided flood.

Cork's unique character is as strong today as it has ever been, revelling in a heritage that blends a strong Irish language (Gaelic) tradition from its surrounding countryside with influences from Norman, Elizabethan, and Huguenot settlers. This is in addition to the influence of the transient population of a busy port, and the many merchants and workers who have survived a succession of "boom and bust" years.

Cork may be officially the Republic's second city, but "Corkonians" are an independent, free-spirited people, who regard their city as the true capital of Ireland. Cork was the centre of resistance to British rule during the political upheavals of the early twentieth century, and the revolutionary zeal of that legacy lives on in its independence and open-mindedness. These days the streets of Cork are enlivened by posters and graffiti-inspired by the website, The People's Republic of Cork. This is a legacy of Cork's strong working-class tradition, which still glories in its songs and its ever-evolving slang. Take a look at its website [www. peoplesrepublicofcork.com] for a sample of Cork humour.

There has been a strong tradition of singing in Cork City down the ages, often in praise of the city itself. The best known is Cork City's sporting anthem, sung on every possible occasion, "On the Banks of My Own Lovely Lee." While it is the latest in a long tradition, the song itself dates only from 1933. Cork's song tradition reached its height in the mid-nineteenth century with John Fitzgerald (1825-1910), The Bard of the Lee, author of songs such as "Beautiful City," and "Cork is the Eden for You, Love and Me."

Cork also has a folk song tradition, which was revived in the late 20th century. Some of these songs—"Salonika," for example—had their origins in the army garrisons that were long a feature of the city. Others relate to the Cork's love of sport—"The Armoured Car" and "The Boys of Fair Hill," or drink—"Johnny Jump Up," and most are characterised by strong wit. Musician Jimmy Crowley worked hard to rescue words and music from oblivion, and they are still sung with gusto in the city's pubs. The Cork Singers, an informal a capella group, meet every Sunday night in the *Spailpín Fánach* pub on South Main Street.

Francis Sylvester Mahony (1804-1866), humourist and essayist, who wrote under the name Father Prout, is buried in the graveyard of St Anne's Church, Shandon. He is best remembered for his lines on the bells of that church, with its unforgettable rhyming scheme, so typical of the playful Cork humour.

> With deep affection,
> And recollection,
> I often think of
> Those Shandon bells.
>
> 'Tis the bells of Shandon,
> That sound so grand on
> The pleasant waters
> Of the River Lee.

There are many more stanzas following the same rhyme scheme.

While Dublin has James Joyce's novel *Ulysses* to immortalise its charms, Cork writers have excelled at the short story. Frank O'Connor (1903-1966), the greatest of them all, was born Michael O'Donovan in the city centre. He left school at fourteen, fought in the Civil War, and learnt Irish while a prisoner. He became a librarian in Cork City, but left when his books were banned by the new State that he had fought for, and advised all other Corkonians with literary ambitions to do the same. His story "Guests of the Nation" is a classic war tale, while others, including "First Confession," were inspired by his Catholic upbringing. O'Connor's influence is still strong internationally: the Chinese-born short story writer Yiyun Li claims to have learnt to write stories by reading Frank O'Connor, and has won numerous awards.

O'Connor became well known in London as an acerbic radio pundit, later moving to the U.S. where he taught at Ivy League colleges. He had a great love of the Irish language, and his translations of classic Irish poems into English, collected in *Kings, Lords and Commons* are among his finest work. He is one of many to have translated the famous poem "*Caoineadh Airt Uí Laoghaire*" ("Lament for Art O'Leary") written by Eileen O'Connell in 1773, one of the best-loved poems in the Irish language.

Another major figure on the Cork literary scene was Seán Ó Ríordáin (1916-1977) who wrote poetry in Irish, exploring the enigmas of death, human nature, the natural world and religion. Like Frank O'Connor and the Cork-born short story writer Sean O'Faolain (1900-1999), he learnt much from Daniel Corkery (1878-1964), a school teacher whose writing about Munster's Irish language heritage introduced many people to the province's great eighteenth-century literary tradition. Late in life, Corkery was appointed Professor of English at University College Cork (UCC) initiating a long connection between the university and the city's poets. Corkery taught Seán Ó Tuama (1926-2006), poet and head of the Irish Department, best known for the anthology *An Duanaire: Poems of the Dispossessed* (1981). When Seán Lucy, also a poet, became head of the English Department he appointed the poet John Montague as a lecturer, an inspired move intended to enliven the academic environment. An impressive number of UCC students from this era are poets, including in Irish Nuala Ní Dhomhnaill, Liam Ó Muirthile, Michael Davitt and Liam de Paor, and in English Greg Delanty, Theo Dorgan, Seán Dunne, Thomas McCarthy, and Gerry Murphy. Today, UCC offers a Creative Writing MA within the English Department and hosts regular readings.

Patrick Galvin (1927-2011) born into a poverty-stricken Cork home, travelled extensively before returning to Cork in the 1990s. His poetry is witty, anarchic and surreal, and he is equally well-known for his childrood memoir, *Song for a Raggy Boy*. With Mary Johnson he co-founded the Munster Literature Centre (MLC) and had a major influence on Cork's thriving poetry scene.

The current director of the MLC, poet Patrick Cotter, organises two major literary festivals every year, the Cork International Short Story Festival and the Cork International Poetry Festival, both of which present readings by major literary figures. Its journal *Southword* is published twice a year. Cork City Library on Grand Parade is a hub of poetic activity, and organises the annual World Book Festival in late April. A unique Cork institution, *Ó Bheal*, happens once a week at the Long Valley Bar in Cork's centre where poets meet to enjoy poetry competitions, a guest speaker and an open mic session. A fixture on the Cork literary scene since 2007, run by poet Paul Casey, the current generation of Cork poets, including Ailbhe Ní Ghearbhuigh, Doireann Ní Ghríofa, and Bernadette McCarthy, have honed their skills at this unique event.

Colette Sheridan
Theatrical Cork

While successful playwright Enda Walsh isn't from Cork, the second city likes to claim him because it was here that he launched his career with *Disco Pigs*, which premiered at the Triskel Arts Centre in 1996 and toured internationally. Walsh has gone on to a hugely successful career, including working with David Bowie on the rock star's musical *Lazarus* before his death.

Disco Pigs also launched the career of Cillian Murphy who played opposite Eileen Walsh. And the drama about two Cork teenagers with a close but unhealthy relationship also put Corcadorca Theatre Company on the map. Artistic director of Corcadorca Pat Kiernan has gone on to direct the company's myriad award-winning plays, most of which are site-specific, taking in locations including the city's courthouse, Spike Island (which used to house prisoners) and the former Sir Henry's Night Club (for a memorable production of *A Clockwork Orange*.)

For a small city, Cork punches above its weight when it comes to theatrical talent. There's the likes of London-based Fiona Shaw who began to make waves as an actor at the dramatic society at University College Cork, known as "Dramat." There, too, John Crowley, now a film director, started his career. Before turning to the silver screen, directing *Brooklyn* starring Saoirse Ronan and *The Goldfinch* starring Nicole Kidman, Crowley directed plays for Druid and the Abbey as well as on Broadway and in London's West End. Crowley's older brother, Bob, an acclaimed set designer who has won Tony and Olivier awards, attended the Crawford College of Art and Design in Cork before heading for the bright lights of London.

Less starry but nonetheless talented dramatists living and working in Cork city include Cónal Creedon whose *Second City Trilogy*, commissioned for Cork's tenure as European Capital of Culture in 2005, has been performed in New York following an extended run in Cork. Creedon, who is also a novelist and a documentary maker, lives and breathes the sights, sounds, and smells of Cork City. From his inner-city home, he casts an astute observant eye over his fellow Corkonians and is attuned to the local idiom, the sing-song delivery of speech, and the references, from sports to the Bible and drinking culture.

Former Arts Editor of the *Irish Examiner* Declan Hassett has been writing plays since his retirement, including *Sisters* originally for the late acclaimed actress Anna Manahan who performed it at the Everyman. There's also local journalist Liam Heylin, who moonlights as a playwright. And there's the former banker Geoff Gould, who tours the highways and by-ways of County Cork with his Fit-Up Festival, following in the tradition of the actor-manager Anew McMaster who brought plays to the provinces decades ago.

The city has two main theatre venues, the 1,000-seat Cork Opera House on Emmet Place and the smaller Everyman Theatre, a beautiful Victorian building on McCurtain Street, which used to be Dan Lowrey's Music Hall and later the Palace Cinema.

The Everyman Theatre, currently run by the dynamic artistic director Julie Kelleher, stages everything from Beckett, mostly by Gare St Lazare, the unparalleled champions of the absurdist writer, to the recent hit play about rape culture, *Asking for It*, by Louise O'Neill.

It was the Cork-born short story writer Frank O'Connor who always felt that no town or city was worth a damn if it didn't have some sort of drama going on. O'Connor was one of the founders of the Cork Drama League, but when he left the city for Dublin in 1928, it lost its impact. However, in the early 1930s, the Little Theatre Society was formed, encouraging members of local dramatic societies to put on plays, usually in Cork Opera House.

A major influence on Cork theatre was Fr. O'Flynn of the Loft whose main interest was the teaching of Shakespeare and the production of the Bard's plays. However, Fr. O'Flynn, who clashed with O'Connor, didn't like modern drama and had a somewhat narrow view of the world.

Cork theatre and the touring theatrical profession in Ireland was dealt a huge blow when the Opera House burnt down in

1955. It reopened in 1965. Theatre companies had to adapt to the loss of the city's main theatre for ten years. The Southern Theatre Group, for example, produced most of its work at the Fr. Mathew Hall.

Its most memorable production was that of John B. Keane's play *Sive* which opened at the hall on June 29, 1959. Word got out that *Sive* was "theatre dynamite." The play, about a match between a young girl and an old man, tapped into a dark vein of rural life that was about to disappear. The Abbey Theatre had turned it down, so it premiered in Cork, running for six weeks that summer, which became known by thespians as "the summer of Sive." Keane followed it with more ground-breaking rural plays which are still performed, sometimes at the Everyman Theatre, including *The Field* which became a successful film.

The Everyman Theatre Company took off in 1963, the year that American President John F. Kennedy came to Cork. It was formed by John O'Shea and Dan Donovan, both school teachers who have had lasting theatrical influences on their pupils as well as on their city. It was based in Fr. Mathew Hall, owned by the Capuchin Order, and used as a bingo hall, which meant that the premises wasn't available on Sunday nights when Corkonians played the numbers' game.

Cork Theatre Company was founded in 1980 by Gerry Barnes, Fred Williams, Emilie FitzGibbon, and Ger FitzGibbon, among others. The company first presented an annual summer season, including lunchtime shows. In 1982, the company leased the Ivernia Theatre on Grand Parade, where most of its productions were seen. During its existence the company presented new Irish plays, both full-length and one-act, classic texts, and new adaptations. Its theatre-in-education work has been continued by Graffiti Theatre Company, which evolved out of the group.

Meridian Theatre Company, with Johnny Hanrahan as artistic director, was established in the 1980s. The company produced new and experimental writing for over two decades, but is no longer in operation. In the '80s, there was talk of the Everyman moving out of the Fr. Mathew Hall and salvaging the Palace, which had been used as a cinema. The premises was sold to the Everyman for £120,000, a good price and an act of generosity to Cork from cinema owners Ward Anderson. What helped to purchase the theatre, whose auditorium is listed, was the sale of an asset, a house that had been left to the Everyman next to the Fr. Mathew Hall. The new Everyman theatre opened in 1990. It was a big change from the Fr. Mathew Hall and also the CYMS (Catholic Young Men's Society) premises on Castle Street which was a part of Cork's theatrical history. The purchase of the McCurtain Street theatre has proved to be a winner for the city's theatregoers.

Declan Hassett

A Sporting Revolution

When American President Donald Trump visited his golf resort at Doonbeg in County Clare in 2019, he could have been forgiven for thinking that the championship course on the mid-western edge of the island of Ireland was the only show in town. Not so, as County Clare is very much part of the sporting phenomena Gaelic games, which engross fans not only of Hurling and Gaelic Football but Ladies' Football and Camogie, the exciting female equivalent of Hurling. Hurling is the fastest team sport in the world, and that includes Canadian Ice Hockey.

The explosion of interest, particularly in Hurling, played with machine shaped sticks cut from logs of the ash tree, is now attracting interest all over the world and not just in traditional emigration centres of the Irish Diaspora.

In August 2019, over 82,000 fans gathered at the Gaelic Athletic Association (GAA) headquarters in Dublin, Croke Park, to watch teams from County Tipperary defeat Kilkenny in the All Ireland Final. Not quite the Super Bowl, but not bad for a little country.

A sense of history is key to understanding this remarkable success story.

Let us go back to the year 1884: Ireland is occupied as it has been for eight hundred years by our neighbours, Britain. Cricket is the sport of choice for many; an Irish village green would not be much different to one in Tunbridge Wells or Bath. After all, Cricket is played with bat and ball, Hurling with a stick and ball known as a sliotar. Hurling and Gaelic Football by then had evolved from inter-faction, village to village contests, to more controlled and organised, less bloody affairs. It was time to put things in order. A group of men gathered in Hayes Hotel, Thurles, Tipperary in that year of 1884 and established the Gaelic Athletic Association. Aptly, the hotel's address was Liberty Square. Those visionaries could not have known that the festering fight for identity and freedom would erupt just thirty-two years later in 1916. Ireland (twenty-six counties) would fly its own flag in 1922. There would be a terrible price to be paid: the dead of the centuries, 1916 martyrs, a vicious Civil War and Partition would foment further misery in the new century. After decades of murder and mayhem, mainly in the six counties which remain part of the U.K., including a period of internment, the remarkable Good Friday Peace Agreement was signed. Superstar Bono raised the arms of nationalist John Hume and unionist David Trimble in a dramatic display of unity before referenda on both sides of the border voted overwhelmingly for the agreement. Now it is threatened by the trapeze that is Brexit, an economic shambles, as the British and the EU search for an elusive safety net.

So much for the politics, from 1884 the competitive structure of the GAA continued to be based on the local parish. This meant that the club was the force and centre of attention and not the county. Thus, one of its most successful clubs was Blackrock in Cork (the Rockies). Change did come, and, from the 1930s, county teams were selected at the request of the County Boards.

The cult of the modern team manager, as in other sporting codes, was still light years away from the GAA. It must be remembered that at the meeting in Thurles in 1884, the GAA was set up as an amateur organisation. With a few modern tweaks it remains so today. The Gaelic Players Association ensures that its members are treated with the care and attention that they obviously deserve.

Interestingly, Hurling has a narrower base of appeal than Gaelic Football. The top counties in the main come from south and east plus pockets in the west and midlands. Vying each year for top honours are Kilkenny, Tipperary, Cork, Waterford, Limerick, Wexford, Clare, Galway, Offaly, Dublin and, in the north, Antrim. New competitions such as the Ring and McDonagh Cups have brought on such counties as Laois, Westmeath and Kerry.

The pursuit of excellence continues to put enormous pressures on players and managers. The contentious subject of pay for play comes up each year but, as far as the fans are concerned, their heroes play for the love of the game and their amateur status is seen as a badge of honour, rather than an obstacle.

Every sport in the world has its leaders and shining stars. I never saw them play but two of the greatest from the twenties and thirties were Lowry Meagher of Kilkenny and Eudie Coughlan of Cork. They figured in a sensational All Ireland series in 1931 when Cork emerged victorious. I was lucky in 1984 to interview Eudie and asked him about the offer from an American syndicate of an all--expenses trip to New York if he would agree to play a few matches in front of thousands of fans. The shy star of that time never went to New York. As a Cork Harbour officer and salmon fisherman, he decided he would miss his native village of Blackrock in Cork too much. All he ever wanted to do to play with the Rockies, walk the magnificent Marina by the River Lee and catch salmon in beautiful Loughmahon. Down the years, I watched the greatest hurler of them all Christy Ring, the boy from Cloyne in East Cork who came to the city and played with the famous Glen Rovers. Christy Ring was like no other player then or since. He won matches, scoring goals while on his knees.

Each decade reveals its stars: Limerick's Mick Mackey; Cork's Jack Lynch, a future leader of the country (Taoiseach); Jimmy Doyle and Tony Wall of Tipperary; the Rackard brothers Nicky, Billy and Bobby of Wexford; Philly Grimes of Waterford; Jimmy Langton of Kilkenny; Jimmy Smith of Clare. In modern times the crowd-pleasers have been Eddie Kehir, DJ Carey, and Henry Sheflin of Kilkenny. From Cork it has to be Jimmy Barry Murphy, Ray Cummins, Tom Cashman, Joe Deane, and Pat Horgan.

The game of Hurling has transformed itself. Lighter equipment and better stadia mean that it is much faster and more attractive with skill levels at an all-time high. Hard to believe in the space of just a century-and-a-half it has become the attractive force that the world of sport wants to know about. To think that the game of Hurling began simply as an expression of identity in an occupied land.

John Daly
Artistic Guerrillas Changing Cork

When Pablo Picasso declared that "Art washes away from the soul the dust of everyday life," it's unlikely he was referring directly to Cork. Yet that is exactly what is happening all across the "Rebel Capital" as a committed and enthusiastic cadre of guerrilla artists lend their creative instincts to brightening and enlivening previously overlooked corners of the urban landscape.

Everywhere you look these days, activity abounds with office blocks rising, new hotels opening, and the constant commercial melody of business traffic set to cruise control. And within this panoply of commercial and industrial progress, another less visible revolution is also underway on the city streets as a growing army of creative gardeners and radical artists commit their talents to transforming those forgotten corners this newfound prosperity has overlooked. A grassroots movement dedicated to urban renewal and sustained by a vibrant community spirit, it has taken root and grown from a simple idea into a powerful groundswell of colour and beauty across the entire city.

At the core of this improvement insurrection is Mad About Cork, a loose collection of artists and volunteers willing to give of their time and energy for the greater good of the city, and whose beautification footprint has so far been as admirable as it is arresting.

"It started out very small, a few friends getting together to pick up rubbish on the streets where we lived," explains artist Alan Hurley, one of the earliest members. "That led on to us painting blank hoardings, planting a few flower boxes and just generally trying to smarten up the city we all love."

Very quickly, whispers of this quiet regeneration made the news pages and social media, resulting in a trickle of like-minded souls that eventually became a torrent of assistance and goodwill. "It grew and kept on growing to the point where we're now out on the streets every week throughout the year. And as well as making the city a nicer place, Mad About Cork has become a really great way to meet people."

Holding regular weekly gatherings to plan street art, flower boxes and urban gardens, the results of this modern "*meitheal*"* for the city's forgotten spaces has gone far beyond its original objectives. Previously neglected and dilapidated areas such as Coleman's Lane, Kyle Street, Patrick's Quay and Douglas Street have been transformed, with the addition of floral window boxes made from up-cycled pallet wood, as well as numerous street art pieces celebrating all things Cork.

Using images of Cork legends above witty slogans, tourists and locals alike smile at mirthful takes on The Frank and Walters, Ashling Thompson, Cillian Murphy, Daniel Florence O'Leary, Mary Elmes and Tanora—Cork's favourite fizzy drink—all given their own tributes on electrical boxes across the city. My personal favourite is on the corner of Patrick's Bridge—an arresting image of Roy Keane over the legend: "It's always Cork first and Ireland second."

Local support from residents and businesses, allied to the willing ear of Cork City Council, has seen Mad About Cork continue to thrive as their projects get ever more ambitious and expansive. "People have been behind us all the way," says Alan. "They buy us paint, allow us use their taps for water and even buy us Lotto tickets for good luck. When we identify derelict sites we feel are ideal for artwork or gardening, we look for permission from Cork City Council, who have always been very supportive of whatever we do."

With over two hundred volunteers made up of locals and foreign nationals from over thirty countries who now call the city home, Mad About Cork resembles a mini-United Nations with urban beautification as its guiding ethos. Words of a typical volunteer, Kevin O'Mahony, sum up much of the movement's collective spirit: "It's amazing how quickly you take pride in the work and don't feel at all self-conscious about being in the middle of the street on a busy Saturday, acting like you own the place. I guess that's the whole point of this—we all do collectively 'own the place' and should take pride in its appearance. More than that we should act on that pride with our ideas, our voices, and our hands."

The original idea for this urban rejuvenation began back in 2012 when Eoghan Ryan and Alasdair Fitzpatrick, a pair of individuals driven with a passion for their city, founded Re-imagine Cork— the initiative which subsequently gave birth to the more recent Mad About Cork. "It was a simple idea to do something for the rundown laneways, urban green spaces and derelict buildings, and try to give them colour and character," Eoghan recalled. "We concentrated on the North Main Street area and its surrounding laneways which had suffered from problems of dereliction and anti-social behaviour. Our aim was to provide colourful murals that celebrated the area's history, heroes and humour. We hoped that the artwork would create talking points and breathe life back into the historic arteries of the city."

Fostering a sense of community and responsibility amongst traders, businesses and local residents, Re-imagine Cork found a willing population ready to lend time and talent to changing drab walls to eye-catching murals, and forgotten litter tips into havens of floral exuberance. "It was about working with traders, local voluntary groups and people with a love for Cork on ideas to enhance the streetscape and foster a greater sense of togetherness in the city."

*Meitheal *is the Irish word for a work team, gang, or party and denotes the co-operative labour system where groups of neighbours help each other in turn, for example with farming work, such as harvesting crops.*

FOUR

Cónal Creedon

from *Glory Be to the Father*,

a novel-in-progress

Chapter One

It's the things we has in common that makes us a family, that's what my Uncle Jojo used to say.

*

Me and my Mam had one thing in common; neither of us knew my dad. He fucked off before I was born. He didn't even stick around long enough to get to know her name or see my face. In fact, now that I think about it, me and my Mam had two things in common, 'cause neither of us knew her father either. Six months before she was born, her own father, my grandfather, walked. He just walked out the door and never said goodbye. Someone said he was spotted heading across St. Patrick's Bridge, but that was the last they ever heard of him.

It can't have been easy for my Mam when she found herself pregnant. She was only sixteen when it happened, for Christ's sake. It was her first dance, her first night at the Arcadia Ballroom, her first kiss, her first awkward, groping fumble in the back of a van with the drummer of the band; a charming, smooth-talking, drunken man.

He told her how beautiful she looked and all the things young girls like to hear. And after plundering her virginity he bought her a glass of milk and Chester Cake at the Red Spot Café, then dropped her off at the end of our street. And that was the first and last she ever heard of him. No, by Christ, it can't have been easy for my Mam when she found herself pregnant with me.

But all that was a long time ago, forty years ago or so. It was a time when people were buttoned up in the days before Velcro. It was a time when sex before marriage was one of those sins where confession just didn't make it right. It was too late for remorse, too late for repentance, the damage was done. And no matter how many *Hail Marys, Glory Bes* or *Our Fathers* she spouted; no matter how many Novenas, Benedictions, or Exposition of the Sacrament my Mam attended, once that seed was planted neither God nor man could stop it from sprouting.

In her innocence my Mam was branded a slut, and from that day forward she would live her life in the shadow of that vile and filthy, debased act. She may as well have been cast down into the burning fires of hell not only for eternity, but for the rest of her living days as well.

And if those who knew better had their way, they'd have stripped, whipped, and dragged her naked through the streets as an example to any other filthy scruff muff who as much as dared to contemplate sins of the flesh. But thank Christ, that sort of thing went out with witch burning. So all they could do was single her out and shut her out. That was the world I was born into, always on the outside looking in, living in the shadow of original sin.

To say that my Mam's life knew no joy would be no word of a lie, and sometimes I think that my birth must have marked the death of her childhood. Then again, my earliest memory is of my Mam telling me about the morning I was born.

She said, it was just past midnight, a few minutes into Christmas morn. An overnight sprinkling of snow had blanketed the town into a glistening winter wonderland. Uncle Jojo had a fire in the grate, belching out smoke and sending sparks up the chimney like a spray of shooting stars into the darkness, announcing my birth to the city and to the world.

My Mam swore that at that very moment she heard a choir of Angels. They were singing,—*Glory be to the New Born King ...*

> – You were wrapped in blue swaddling and I held you close to my breast, Christy boy. So perfect and so pure. I knew there and then, that you were the most special child in the whole wide world. You were my little Prince. A Prince of Princes.

> Your Uncle Jojo reached out to hold ya, and when he took you into his arms, he just cried. Cried like a baby, so he did,

and he kissed you all over from the crown of your head to the tip of your nose. Then he held you at arm's-length, studying your perfectly formed limbs, counting your fingers and toes ...

– *Look at the arms of him, Uncle Jojo whispered.—You mark my words, Sis girl. One of these years he'll make a fine hurler. I think we should call him Christy. Christy after Christy Ring.*
– *We're not calling my beautiful baby after no hurler.*
– *Not just any hurler, he said.—Christy Ring is God! Christy Ring walks on water ...*
– *It's Christmas morning, Jojo. A boy child born on Christmas morning. No way are we calling him after no hurler!*
– *For Christ's sake, Sis! You're not gonna call him something daft like Jesus, are ya?*

My Mam thought about it for a second or two.
– *Maybe we could call him Christy, she said.—Christy after Christ ...*
– *Fair enough, said Uncle Jojo.—You call him Christy after Christ and I'll call him Christy after Christy Ring*
And that's how they came to call me Christy. Christy Buckley, the boy with no dad.

All my life I had watched my Mam and Uncle Jojo fight like cat and dog. He'd say white. She'd say black. He'd say yes. She'd say no. They couldn't agree to agree. They couldn't agree to disagree. So it made me wonder how they managed to agree so easily to name me Christy. Then again, this town was never a winter wonderland, and our grate was always bare; no sparks like stars lit up the dark sky that Christmas morning announcing my birth to the city and to the world. God knows, the pieces of the jigsaw didn't quite fit, but the picture created in my mind was beautiful. I loved the story of my birth, and it was gospel in our house.

And if my Mam swore she heard the angels sing,—*Glory be to the New Born King*, well I've no reason to call her a liar. But it crossed my mind that maybe ...

Maybe the angels she heard that Christmas morning, were

the men of the St. Luke's Choir, staggering home from the Bell View Bar.

And maybe it was because my Mam lived such a joyless life that I loved the fairy-tale of my birth. For once she saw the sense in nonsense. For once she was willing to drop her guard, banish reality, and allow her imagination run wild.

God only knows what would have happened to me and my Mam, without my Uncle Jojo around to keep an eye out for us. The first four years of my life were spent being carted up and down four flights of stairs. Up and down, up and down, up and down.

> – *Like a bloody yo-yo*, my Mam used say.—First you Christy. Then all the way back down for the pram. Next the pram. Then all the way down for the shoppin'. Because whatever about me shoppin', I'd be lost without me pram. And ya couldn't leave a baby-sitting on the side of the street now, could ya? Well could ya!

And that's how it was, me and my Mam, living on our own, in our bedsit, up by the barracks.

> – We didn't need no help from no one, that's what she'd say.— But it was no place to rear a child. Quare hawks beneath us, students above us. Walkin' across our ceiling. Lookin' down on us. They were lookin' down on me, for Christ's sake. Couldn't swing a cat. Damp and draughty. Belchin' out smoke. Prayin' to God that the bedclothes would dry. Like a bloody yo-yo, up and down, up and down …

The following Christmas, me and my Mam went to visit Uncle Jojo for my first birthday. We stayed for a week, the next year we stayed for two. By the time my third birthday came around, me and my Mam going to Uncle Jojo's for the Christmas became a family tradition, and for a family with few traditions, Christmas with Uncle Jojo was one that we clung onto …

> – A good man, your Uncle Jojo, loyal and true, my Mam used to say.—He always kept an eye out for me, even before you came along, Christy. Always sayin' I should move in here, with him …

   – But sur' you and Christy is the only family I has, Sis, Uncle
     Jojo would say.

Eventually, Christmas became New Year, New Year became St.
Patrick's Day, St. Patrick's Day became Easter, on into summer,
and by summer's end, Christmas was only around the corner again.

   – I was thinkin', Sis, he said.—It's pointless you payin' rent
     on that little bedsit when you and Christy spends most of
     yer time down here . . .

And that's how we ended up moving in with my Uncle Jojo.

*

Christmas? A funny time of the year is Christmas. It's enough
to put the head spinning and the mind doing somersaults. It's a
time when bygones become bygones and those dead and gone are
remembered. It's a time when the pain of loneliness finds comfort
in candles and fairy lights, and the lonesome sound of Shane
McGowan singing of fairy-tale nights. It's a time when the mind
wanders to days of childhood, when everything was perfect in the
world. It's a time when memories become truths and the magic
of belief is restored. And I suppose that's it, Christmas is a time
of belief.

And maybe that's why every man and woman, boy and girl, cat
and dog from the four corners of Christendom will claw over each
other, just to get their legs under the table where they were reared.
It's a time when all the world stands still for one day to celebrate
the birth of Jesus.

And me and Jesus Christ have a lot in common. After all, that's
why my Mam called me Christy, in memory of another fatherless
boy, who just like me was born on Christmas day.

*

It's the stillness before the storm this Christmas Eve morn and
I'm standing on St. Patrick's Bridge. Not a soul scurrying through
the streets, no movement along the quays, nothing stirring. The
only signs of life are the sound of a squeaking wheel and the odd
flicker of light from the houses way up on the Northside. And
with only one more shopping day to Christmas, the city braces

itself. Because as sure as Christ was born two thousand, eighteen years and three hundred and sixty-four days ago this town will erupt when the shops open.

Not a light to my name; cigarettes, wallet and keys still on the floor by the couch where I left them the night before. But I'm free, and freedom is priceless, but priceless and penniless amount to the same thing when you're trying to buy a cup of tea, and it's pointless for me to be walking the streets without not as much as a brass cent in my pocket. And I'm asking myself, how in the name of Christ did I end up here.

From the day that I was born, I knew the pain of loneliness. I swore that if ever my time came to father a new generation, I would to do it right. I swore that the sins of my father and my grandfather would be flushed from our bloodline forever. So, from the moment Joan told me that she was pregnant I swore on my heart and soul, I swore on my mother's grave that I would be there for her. I would be there for her and our baby.

But as weeks became months something changed inside, and I knew it would only be a matter of time before I'd just have to walk away. Not because I couldn't handle the responsibility of rearing a child, no nothing like that, and it wasn't the call of the wild either. It was something more basic than that, something beyond my control.

And any plans I had of putting things right were just dead-end, side-track torments that led me exactly to where I'm standing right now, on St. Patrick's Bridge at the crack of dawn this Christmas eve morn.

And anyone who says that Joan is too good for me is probably right. And anyone who says she could have found someone better than me, I wouldn't call a liar. But anyone who says that I walked away because she was pregnant is talking through their hole. I was there for Joan every step of the way, the ups and the downs, the highs and the lows, the ins and the outs, for every grunt and every groan. And anyone who says I don't care? Anyone who says I don't care …

Well, I gave up everything for Joan, and everything's an awful lot when you've sweet fuckall.

I mean Jesus, it's like a family curse to be born Buckley without a dad. My Mam never really talked about my dad, and even if she did there wasn't a lot to say. What little I knew of him, I picked up from my Uncle Jojo. But usually he'd just shake his head and walk away.

Walk away, walk away, it's the story of my life. Because God knows, like my father and my grandfather before him, there comes a time when enough is enough, too much is too much and it's always too little too late, and sometimes you just got to walk away

*

What is it about Christmas? Woke up this morning thrown down on the couch, Joan standing over me with the big mad head on her, she's spitting fire and stamping her feet. There I was, on the flat of my back, head splitting, more asleep than awake, getting a feed of dog's abuse from herself, and for the life of me, I had no idea what I had done wrong. Fair enough, maybe I had a few pints, I admit that. But Jesus, it's been almost six months since I had a drink. I was bound to break out sometime, and she knew that.

It's Christmas time. Everybody has a drink at Christmas time. And you can be sure she wasn't standing over me every morning for the past six months telling me what a great man I was for not having drink. Oh no! But the one time I decide to go for a pint? Bingo, she's off. I mean, what the fuck is that about. I'll take as much crap as the next fella. I'll take a lot of crap. But I won't take that. So fuck her, it was time to go. I had to go, had to get out a' there. It was better for me, better for Joan and better for the child to be.

I mean, Christ almighty, there she was hissing, and spitting and throwing a fit. And I'm lying there with the eyes closed thinking to meself, how does it get to this point? How do two people fall totally head over heels in hate with each other? There I was, head splitting, trying to make sense of it all, trying to save what little we had.

105

- Jesus Joan, we loved each other! Where's the magic gone! What happened the fairy-tale?
- Fairy-tale? What fairy-tale!
- God almighty, Joan. You're Red Riding-hood, I'm the Wood Cutter. You're Cinderella, I'm Prince Charming . . .
- Prince Charming?
- You're Snow White, I'm . . .
- Yeah, well if I'm Snow White, you're Dopey.
- Enough is enough!
- Too much!
- For Christ's sake Joan, there must be something . . .
- Too little! Too late!
- Fair enough, says I. And I head for the hall door.
- You just keep on walking!
- I'll be back for my stuff!
- Stuff? she grunts.—What stuff! You had sweet shag all when I first met you!

I could have told her about stuff, stuff that I brought to this relationship, stuff you can't hang in a wardrobe or stack on a shelf. I could have told her about stuff. But, Jesus there comes a time . . .

– Fuck you! I shout and slam the front door behind me.

Fuck you? Now there's two words I've never said to Joan before. And I've said a lot to Joan. But,—*Fuck you,* always seemed so final. And right now, I can't think of two better words to say than,—*Fuck you!* Just two little words. It's like, after all these months of being a good boy, saying nothing, acting dumb, twiddling my thumbs, putting up with her and her carry-on, just to be able to turn around once and for all and tell her straight to her face to go fuck herself, it's like a weight off my shoulders. And just in case she didn't get the message first time around, I lift the letterbox lid and roar . . .

- Fuck you! Fuck yer mother! Fuck yer friends! And fuck your two-faced fuck of a brother!

The letterbox lid snaps shut, and that feels good.

That's when I notice the street sweeper. He's standing there beside me leaning on his brush. He raises his thumb and hisses the word ...

– Ressspect!

Respect from the street sweeper? Now that's something. Everyone knows that the street sweepers in this town are gods, and gods don't give respect lightly. And then I see the Chinese-one from number three across the street? She's standing there, key in the door, mouth open, staring into space, standing there like she's seen and heard nothing.

Funny, but I've always fancied the Chinese-one, ever since she moved in to number three across the street. It's probably got to do with the whole East meets West thing, a journey into the unknown, a taste of the exotic: sweet and sour, hot chilli, ginger and lemon grass. Something to get the blood rising ...

Not that I know the Chinese-one from number three across the street, no not at all. In fact, I don't know her at all, at all. I mean, I know her to see, see her up in the Golden Dragon every time I go in there for a takeaway. But she's the kind of girl who keeps herself to herself, and maybe that's what I find so attractive about her. She's a friendly sort of girl, quiet and mannerly, maybe a little bit shy, then again, you'd expect that from the Chinese. But sometimes at night-time when I'm lying there in bed next to Joan, and the light is low, and Joan is reading her book, and I'm looking at the ceiling, bored to death; I sometimes wonder what it might be like to go naked with the Chinese-one from number three across the street.

And maybe she has never noticed me before now, but at this moment as I stand here on my door step, barking loudest, telling Joan to go fuck herself, the Chinese-one from number three across the street can be in no doubt but that I am the man.

I am the man, and it feels good. It's like ever since I gave up the drink Joan has been chipping away at me, until eventually I was like a castrated dog licking my hole and wondering where my balls had gone, and I can take no more of it. I'm sick of central heating. I'm sick of weather glaze. I'm sick of the couch and sicker of sitting on it. I'm sick of curtains, cushions, tea and grocery shopping. And as sure as Christ, I'm sick to death of Joan. So, I turn my collar to the cold and walk away down McSwiney Street, into town …

That's when I realise my cigarettes are exactly where I left them the night before, next to the couch on the floor. My wallet and keys are there too. Two steps backwards, I whisper through the letterbox …

– Ehm? Joan? Joan? Open the door will ya?

I give a gentle tap to the letterbox.

– Pssst! Joan …

The street sweeper and the Chinese-one from number three across the street are standing behind me, looking on. I'm bent over whispering through the letterbox trying to attract Joan's attention without attracting attention to myself.

– Joan! Open the door will ya! Joan!

The street sweeper steps up.

– Are ya locked out?

I just look at him, like I'm saying,—*None of your fuckin' business.* He takes the hint and steps back.

I give another gentle tap to the letterbox lid and whisper,

– Joan? Open the door will you? Joan? Joan …

The upstairs window opens. Joan leans out.

– Ah, there you are, says I.

– Why? Where did you think I'd be? says she in her sarky sort of way.—Are you looking for something?

– Ehm? My cigarettes, wallet and keys. They're inside by the couch.

– Cigarettes and wallet? she says.

I notice she doesn't mention the keys.

– That's right, my cigarettes and my wallet, says I.

– And what's the special word?

– Special word, Joan?

– Yes, the special word, says she.

– Ehm? Thanks?

– Actually, she corrects herself.—There are two special words,

- Two special words? Ehm? Thanks, and, and, and sorry?
  Thanks, and sorry, Joan, says I trying to sound playful.
- No, she says in a sort of childish voice.—No. Not thanks
  and sorry . . .
- Ehm? How about, ehm? S-s-sorry and thanks?
- No, she smiles.—Not sorry and thanks either. . .

I'm squirming there, Joan up at the first-floor window towering over me, like a cat with a mouse, just playing with me. The evil bitch. And she knows, she knows damned well that she has me exactly where she wants me.

- Please Joan, just let me in to get my stuff . . .
- Ah, ha! she says.—So you're back for stuff?
- Joan, this isn't about stuff!
- Do you want to know what the two special words are?
  she asks.

I'm standing there totally exposed and vulnerable, so, I just nod my head,

- Well, says she.—The two special words are, fuck you!

And she slams the window shut.

I turn towards the street sweeper and give a sort of a half-laugh, trying to pass the whole thing off as a bit of a joke.

Again, the street sweeper raises his thumb,

- Ressspect!
- Yeah, right! Respect! I say . . .

In my heart and soul, I know this is not the best time for me to walk away, with a baby on the way. Then again it can never be the best time, only the right time and there comes a time when enough is enough, too much is too much and it's always too little too late. So, like my father and my grandfather before him, I turn my collar to the cold and just walk away.

Jennifer Myers

Martha Braun, Belle of Belvidere: A Sad Life

In the early morning hours of Sunday May 2, 1982, Martha Braun launched herself off the O'Donnell Bridge over the Merrimack River onto the jagged rocks below. She was fifty-four years old.

It was a sad ending to a life that started with a great deal of promise, but was tarnished by a short, controversial marriage.

Martha Braun, born in 1928, was the only daughter of Carl and Elizabeth Braun. The Brauns owned and operated the famed Commodore Ballroom in Lowell and were at one time part owners of Canobie Lake Park over the state line in New Hampshire; they also operated the ballroom at Lakeview Park in the Lowell suburb of Dracut.

On September 25, 1947, *Lowell Sun* columnist Barbara Brown wrote of the "exciting career of talented Martha Braun" a nineteen-year-old beauty who had "garnered acclaim galore since being spotted at a Yale University football game by a photographer from one of the glossy magazines."

A graduate of Rogers Hall in the city, the society girl attended finishing school at the Semple School, followed by the *Academie Moderne* and the Grace Downs Hollywood Modeling School in New York City.

Boasting "perfect" measurements (35" bust, 25" waist, and 36" hips), young Martha quickly became sought-after for modeling jobs in New York and was named "Miss Valentine 1948," beating out seventeen other girls.

"She's made several recordings, has sung at some of the plusher nightspots in Gotham and is being coached by two notables in the entertainment world, whose efforts have built some of the brighter lights in that field," wrote Brown. "This is why girls leave home, this kind of life with its overtones of champagne and caviar. But it isn't the way it reads. Martha takes her career seriously and, this being so, she gets a goodly amount of shut-eye nightly. No night-club beat for her, no cocktail chatter, either. It's a rough ground to the top and a girl has got to conserve her talents."

By 1949, word came back to Lowell that the hometown gal, who had won several small television and radio parts, had scored a screen test with 20ᵗʰ Century Fox; the *Sun* ran a photo of her auditioning for actor/producer Burgess Meredith (you may know him better as the Penguin from the 1960s *Batman* TV series, or as Rocky Balboa's trainer Mickey in the *Rocky* films)

"No Merman or Grable yet, but give the girl a chance," wrote the *Sun*. "Come a few years or less and the name of Braun may be as familiar to the nation as her dad's is to Lowell. At least that's the opinions of the experts in New York and how many times do they miss?"

Then . . . twenty-one-year-old Martha Braun met thirty-four-year-old Billy Daniels, a well-known crooner in 52ⁿᵈ Street jazz spots in New York City.

It was love.

The problem? It was 1949, and he was black, or as all of the news accounts pointed out she was a "wealthy white socialite" and he was a "negro jazz singer."

When her mother caught wind of the romance in late 1949, she went to New York to try to "cool" it.

Elizabeth Braun spent a few days with her daughter and her beau, even going to see him perform at a couple of hot spots.

"Martha was terribly in love with the man but, I told her she should gravely consider her future," Mrs. Braun later told the *Sun*.

Mrs. Braun convinced Martha to return with her to Lowell. She urged her to take a trip around the world to consider whether what she had with Daniels really was love and what she wanted to do.

After a month in Lowell, Martha left a note for her parents at the family home at 140 Clark Road, saying she did not want to be apart from Billy, and eloped to Weehawken, New Jersey. She called her mother at 2:00 a.m. the following morning to ask for forgiveness.

In a front-page story in the January 11, 1950, edition of the *Sun*, Mrs. Braun defended her daughter's decision to marry Daniels, noting:

"Daniels has a complexion lighter than most South Americans. Martha said he was part Indian, part French, and Spanish and might have a trace of some other nationality in him."

She described her new son-in-law as "suave" in appearance and "cosmopolitan" in makeup.

"While this wasn't what we had planned for our daughter it is her life," Mrs. Braun said. "If love is stronger than family influence we can't stand in her way"

By August 1953, the marriage was over. Martha Braun announced when Billy returned from Europe they would divorce.

"It's incompatibility; he's not for me," she said.

The divorce was finalized the following February, at which time Martha garnered attention by penning a piece for *Confidential* magazine titled "My Life with Billy Daniels," which emphatically stated the color of his skin had no bearing on the failure of their marriage.

"The feeling we had for each other was trampled to death by other women—white women," she wrote. "They chased him individually and in squads, coyly and with the brazen candor of nymphomaniacs."

Following the divorce, Martha returned to Lowell; her show business career dead.

In 1960, she married James McGrath, but that marriage too was short-lived. She dealt with bouts of severe depression. In 1970, forty-one-year-old Martha was arrested and charged with driving under the influence and drunkenness, for which she paid $110 in fines. In 1976, she and her then-boyfriend were accused of assaulting a woman in Lowell; those charges were later dropped. Over the years, Martha worked at Raytheon, the *Sun,* and as a clerk/typist in the city's CETA (Comprehensive Employment and Training Act) program.

On May 2, 1982, Martha left a note in the kitchen of her home at 140 Clark Road for her roommate, Carol Beauregard; in it she expressed her depression, but did not mention suicide. However, she left her mother's diamonds rings on top of the note.

Just before noon, her body was discovered washed up on the shore behind the Franco-American School by a kid throwing rocks into the river.

"I think she was trying to save herself after she jumped. It looked like she tried to swim to safety," Dr. John Karbowniczak, county medical examiner, commented after examining the scene. "But there's no mystery to this one; it's a suicide and she jumped from the bridge."

Beauregard told the *Sun* Martha had been suffering from terminal cancer, had undergone two mastectomies, and was left penniless.

A story in the *Sun* by Kevin Landrigan two days after her death, surmised Martha Braun's decent began on her wedding day in 1950.

"For Billy Daniels—the superstar black blues singer—it was a day in which he took the second in a string of lovely white women as his temporary bride," Landrigan wrote. "But for Martha Braun, that wedding day in New York brought a budding career to a grinding halt, turned close hometown friends and family against her, and aided in her eventual financial ruin."

By the time of their deaths in the early 1970s, her parents had forgiven Martha for the controversial nuptials, but many others in Lowell's social circles never did. She and her brother Carl only reconciled a few years before her death.

Beautiful, talented Martha Braun, once the toast of the town, was shunned when she returned to Lowell following the divorce and never regained her popularity or the acceptance of her hometown friends.

James Ostis

Mania in the Mill City

In what historic arena did The Rock win his first World Wrestling Federation singles title?

Madison Square Garden?

Joe Louis Arena?

The FleetCenter?

Try ... Lowell Memorial Auditorium.

On February 13, 1997, Rocky Maivia (prior to becoming Hollywood megastar The Rock) defeated Hunter Hearst Helmsley (prior to becoming Vince McMahon's son-in-law Triple H) right here in Lowell on a special Thursday night edition of WWF Raw (World Wrestling Federation) to capture the first intercontinental championship of his storied career.

Lowell's ring-based sporting history is, of course, famously tied to boxing, from which its produced major annual traditions like the Golden Gloves bouts, award-winning films like *The Fighter*, and politicians who didn't mind mixing it up (names withheld) either inside or outside the ring. Still others' thoughts about the terms "Lowell" and "wrestling" inevitably lend themselves to coach George Bossi and the dynastic success of the Lowell High School (amateur) wrestling team. But in addition to its status as a hub of the sweet science and competitive mat grappling, the Mill City has also been home to some classic moments in the bizzaro world of "sports-*entertainment*." With the biggest day of the wrestling calendar, Wrestlemania 34, set to occur this weekend, what better time is there to take a look back at Lowell's place in the professional wrestling history books?

The earliest recorded professional wrestling match in Lowell was held on December 9, 1904, when former welterweight champion of the world Harvey Parker defeated Eugene Trembley in a two-out-of-three falls match that took one hour and forty minutes. The wrestling of the early twentieth century was not the entertainment spectacle it would later become— although the matches were said to be no less predetermined even in its earliest days. While shows would occur among various local promotions through the years, the arrival of Worldwide Wrestling Federation in the 1960s ushered in a new era.

Many of the major moments in Lowell's pro-wrestling history occurred in the Lowell Memorial Auditorium—a staple of WWF live event tours for decades. A November 20, 1970, story in the *Sun* newspaper exclaimed: "The fastest growing sport in the area is professional wrestling!" The article hyped an upcoming "grudge match between the despicable 'Crusher' Verdu and the fans' favorite, Chief Jay Strongbow." Other wrestling greats of this era to appear at the Lowell Memorial Auditorium include Pedro Morales, Stan "the Man" Stasiak, King Kong Bundy, and Ivan Putski.

In most cases, these non-televised live events sought to entertain the crowd in attendance but were mostly inconsequential in the bigger picture. What really mattered was what happened when TV cameras were rolling. Lowell was the site of numerous television tapings in the 1990s with *Monday Night Raw*, *WWF Superstars*, and *WWF Wrestling Challenge* all airing nationally from the Mill City.

Lowell's most infamous wrestling moment took place at the same February 1997 Auditorium show as the Rock's title victory. WWF Champion Shawn Michaels forfeited his title belt not only because of a knee injury but also because he "lost his smile" due to the stress of the wrestling world. Michaels's decision to relinquish the title and temporarily "retire" (and thus skipping a rumored Wrestlemania 13 rematch with Bret "the Hitman" Hart) was a key incident on the road to the most controversial night in wrestling history nine months later in Montreal, Canada. Even Wrestlemania I was held at the Lowell Memorial Auditorium ... via the closed-circuit TV big screen.

Although the Auditorium is undoubtedly the most prominent venue for professional wrestling in the city, it's not the only local setting that has played host to pandemonium in the squared circle. *Sun* articles in the 1970s point to matches at the Janas Rink in Belvidere. The historic Rex Center played host to the matches of its day prior to burning down. The Paul E. Tsongas Arena began hosting WWF shows in 1998. Even LeLacheur baseball park got into the act in 2015 with "Wrestling Under the Stars," a first-ever outdoor wrestling extravaganza—although the ballpark concourse had seen its own share of some high-flying action before.

In an interview with the *Sun* in 2012, two-time WWE Heavyweight champion CM Punk noted, "There are a lot of places in the Northeast that have always been WWE towns. Lowell is one of them." Throughout the organization's rise from regional territory to worldwide powerhouse, the WWE has had a regular presence in Lowell, but other wrestling companies have promoted events in the city as well. World Championship Wrestling, rooted in the Southeast, had one show in town during its run, a 2000 Live Event at the Tsongas Arena. Total Nonstop Action hosted Lowell's first Wrestling Pay-Per-View with 2008's Lockdown. More recently, Ring of Honor chose the LMA as the spot to hold its 2017 Best in the World PPV, and that promotion will be co-hosting an event with New Japan Pro Wrestling at the Auditorium in May.

Smaller independent wrestling companies such as Northeast and Chaotic Wrestling also have had a footprint in the area. Four-time WWE Women's Champion Sasha Banks described her December 2016 Tsongas Arena live event show a homecoming, recalling her matches down at the P.A.V. (Polish American Veterans) club in the Centralville neighborhood before hitting the big time.

Another superstar who should have a soft spot for the Mill City is Nuufolau Joel Seanoa, or as he is better known, Samoa Joe. He won his first TNA World Heavyweight Championship by defeating Olympic gold medalist Kurt Angle in a "six sides of steel cage title vs. career match" at the Lockdown PPV on April 13, 2008. Eight years and eight days later, Joe shocked the wrestling world by defeating Finn Balor for the NXT Championship at an untelevised house show at the Lowell Memorial Auditorium. (An added piece of trivia: Samoa Joe is the only wrestler to compete at the Auditorium, Tsongas Arena, and LeLacheur Park, according to ProFightDB.)

But to the knowledge of this blog, at least, Stone Cold Steve Austin holds perhaps the most interesting unique local distinction. On September 1, 1998, he became the first professional wrestler to have a street in Lowell named after him—at least for one day. In advance of the first World Wrestling Federation event at the new Tsongas Arena, the roadway leading to the arena, John F. Cox Circle, was renamed "Stone Cold Way" in a ceremony featuring the then WWF champion wearing a New England Patriots 3:16 jersey alongside Lowell Mayor Eileen Donoghue, City Manager Brian Martin, City Councilor Armand Mercier, and a host of other local dignitaries.

Lowell may not be the world's most famous wrestling city, but it has seen its share of memorable moments. And that's the bottom line—because Stone Cold said so.

Alex Hayes

Mingled Red

I have hung my heart on your windowpane
and watched the curtains billow in the wind,
Neither of us knew what it would contain,
Yet when you learned, you never did rescind
that surety of grip that keeps my heart
balanced, level beside open window,
The maintenance of balance is an art,
While oblivion hungers from below,
And the weight of shrapnel lodged in my flesh
threatens to cast my heart into the dark,
And jagged metal tears your palms afresh,
And the mingled red of our wounds, so stark …

I marvel at you and I keep the faith,
You will not fail come fire, come storm, come wraith.

Stephan Anstey

As I Burn Away Leaving Me

the cigarette won't smoke itself under this almost-moon
so the man in the shadows stands
there holding the orange glow of burning
that reports the streetlight to the darkness.

the smoke reaches from the cigarette
toward the nearest star—the one
the man doesn't notice as he stands
in the shadows. If there is a question
between them, it remains unasked.

the man continues to smoke
the cigarette until it is done
the orange glow fades
until only the stars are burning
with questions for the moon.

Bob Hodge
Old Guitar

I got my first guitar when I was eleven, a Silvertone, lowest end model, good enough to learn on. My cousins taught me how to tune it, but it took a while to find my ear—some might say I'm still looking.

I'm not sure if I even suggested to my dad that I take lessons. I just bought a Learn Guitar book with my meager paperboy earnings and plunged right in. The book I bought taught me to read musical notes on the page and where to place my fingers to ring out the given notes, lead guitar. It also taught a bit about tempo, etc., to which I paid no attention.

I learned to play scales and could bang them out like nobody's business and then some very simple songs. I don't even remember which ones, but they were not cool, and I would have been embarrassed if any of my friends heard me playing them even though they might have been a little impressed that I could play anything at all.

I played all notes for months, not striking a single chord. One day a friend from school said, "Hey, Bobby, you got a guitar. Why don't I come by after school with mine and we can mess around?"

Dave came by, and I was sitting outside my three-decker in Lowell, Mass., on a little wall knockin' out some scales and "Greensleeves" or "Goodnight Irene." He said, "Whoa, that is cool. Do you know some chords?" He played Van Morrison's "Gloria," and then launched into "Louie Louie," and even sang— my jaw dropped. Twenty minutes and three chords learned, and I was playing "Gloria" non-stop until Dad knocked on my bedroom door and shouted, "Take a break, Elvis."

Dave took lessons, so he showed me some other stuff, and he and two of our classmates at St. Pat's, Jack and Mickey, played a folk Mass for our eighth-grade graduation. They were much better players than me, and I had to borrow a "real" instrument just so I wouldn't sound too terrible. That was my only gig ever, but I kept playing, and I got a bit better.

One Christmas I got a hollow-body electric jobber, a cheap one, and a small Kalamazoo amp. I did some damage with that baby. My friend George, who lived up Butterfield Street from me, the corner of Mt. Vernon, had a snare drum and also a vacant building, a former Greek church that we could play in when his dad allowed us. We had another friend with an electric guitar who could barely play—no matter, I taught him a few simple things, and we were off to the races. A band.

We had a songbook with chords that I borrowed from the library. Many of the songs were unfamiliar to me, so we just played it my way. Later, when I heard the song by the original artist—Lord have mercy, so that's how it's supposed to go!

We had fun, killed some time, even had a little battle of the bands with some guys down the street who had a full drum kit. When we played Donovan's "Hurdy Gurdy Man," one of our three audience members laughed, "What the hell was THAT!"

I worked the Bingo game at St. Pat's, setting up the small auditorium/lunchroom with tables and chairs. We even had overflow to the first-floor hallway where we set up—a fire hazard for sure. During the games we would cover the floor, running to check the cards of winners. I made some real money with which I bought a bookcase full of athletics books from *Track & Field News* and a Yamaha Guitar for which I had saved $180. That was 1971. I got the FG 180 red-label model made in Japan.

Well, five years ago I pulled it out of mothballs and brought it to a friend for a tune-up.

"Hey, Steve, I think I need a new guitar, a Martin or a Gibson, right, because I will sound better and everythang."

"Bobby, you got a real nice instrument here. I would definitely not give this up."

Turns out Yamaha just re-released this model they started making in 1969. Okay, maybe it's time to practice, take another crack at "Hurdy Gurdy Man."

Michael Casey

capitalism

a poem for Ruth Jensen

my landlady Ruth worked
for a computer startup company
in Buffalo
a secretary
she typed up the initial proposals
in an IBM Selectric MT/ST
an excellent typist
she could type faster
than the machine could keep up
one-twenty-five words per minute
her employee number was four
the first three were the owners
all brilliant engineers
from Lowell Tech
the principals
and the firm later
sold to Northrup Grumman
for a billion dollars
well seven-fifty mil'
and OK I am rounding up
and her pension
was forty dollars a month
yeah OK I am rounding up
but back to the one-twenty-five
words per minute
that's faster than I can think

Victoria Denoon

from *Keeping Éire's Secret*

This is an excerpt from Keeping Éire's Secret, *a novel-in-progress. It was inspired by a transatlantic archaeological excavation that took place in both Lowell and Ireland. The piece tells the story of a group of laborers who are fleeing a mysterious event in Ireland. Looking for a better life in Massachusetts, they discover what they thought they had left behind has followed them across the Atlantic.*

Chapter One

Hugh stared over the railing until the green fields of home were replaced by the icy waves of the Atlantic. Pulling the collar of his wool coat tight around his neck to keep the frigid wind off his wound, he sighed and headed below deck.

It had been a harrowing journey and, having finally made it this far, he was not about to take any chances. He lifted the makeshift mattress from his bunk and removed his rifle. With a damp cloth he rubbed hard along the barrel and forestock as if trying to erase the marks etched into the wood. After making sure that he had plenty of ammunition, he stowed the weapon under the loose floorboard that held the rest of his meager belongings and went to check on his traveling companions.

Walking down the narrow corridor, he placed one hand on the wall to steady himself as the ship lurched beneath his feet. Approaching his intended destination, he stopped and listened. He could hear strange, almost foreign, sounds coming from the cabin of his companion. Cursing to himself for not bringing along his dagger, he slowed his breathing, leaned against the door and listened. The noise had stopped. He knocked gently. There was a commotion on the other side. Fearing the worst and hoping he wasn't too late, he flung open the door.

Áine Ó Caoimh turned, the hood of her traveling cloak slipped from her head, revealing her long dark hair. There was a look of surprise and displeasure on her face.

"What do you mean barging into a woman's chamber unannounced," she scowled at Hugh.

"I beg your pardon mistress, I did knock, but then I heard a commotion and I was afraid that . . . . well . . . that we might have visitors, if you know what I mean?" Hugh stumbled.

"No, I don't know what you mean Master Cummiskey, and I would urge you to think twice about entering a woman's quarters uninvited," returned Áine without missing a beat.

Hugh begged forgiveness, closing the door and stepping back into the hallway. He began to walk away, then paused. "Funny," he thought, "I could have sworn I smelt candles," but there had been no candles in the cabin when he entered. Still, he could not shake that sense he had, or the sight of faint smoke rising from the table. Shaking his head, he walked on.

Back in his bunk Hugh tried to beckon sleep, but every time he closed his eyes his visions were full of tormented images. Determined not to witness the horrors of the past few months again, Hugh spent the night in the cramped quarters below deck half asleep, listening intently for any sounds that seemed out of place.

He awoke to the sight of Tomas, Cullen, and Ríordán tucking into bowls of rationed oatmeal. He rubbed his eyes, climbed out of the bunk and headed to the barrel of water that was supposed to serve as the washtub. Dampening a piece of cloth in the pungent water, he wiped his face and hands. From his pocket he pulled out the jar of balm that Áine had given him the week before and rubbed it into the gash along the side of his neck wincing as he did so. Miraculously, the wound was healing despite the less than sanitary conditions on board. While he didn't usually trust druid healers, he couldn't argue with the results he had seen thanks to Áine. But no matter how well the wound healed, it would be a long time before Hugh was able to close his eyes and not see what happened in the bog that fateful night.

For now, he turned his attention to what waited for him on the shores of the new world.

Chapter Two

Hugh felt the ship slowing. The nausea that he had been feeling over the course of the journey began to subside. Boston Harbour came into view through the early morning mist. He leaned over the side of the ship, holding the rigging, as if by doing so he could hasten it to port. He made out figures scurrying like ants on the bustling wharf—harbormasters waiting to tariff incoming vessels, dockers calling out as they unloaded cargo, merchants flogging their wares, and those greeting family and friends or just hoping to hear familiar voices and news from home. With an ocean between him and every relation he had on earth, there would be no one waiting for him, Hugh knew that, and he was glad.

He gathered the others from below decks. He wasn't really sure how he came to be in charge of this group or why they trusted and depended on him so much, but he was determined not to let them down. As his eyes adjusted to the dimness below, he saw Cullen and Tomas packing their few belongings into sacks. There was no sign of Ríordán, and neither Cullen nor Tomas had noticed he was missing. With his belongings, Hugh headed to Áine's cabin to let her know they were close to shore.

As he rounded the corner, Áine's cabin door opened and Ríordán entered the passageway. He watched as Ríordán turned to say something to Áine. Motioning for him to be quiet, she took his hand and placed something in his palm. The crepuscular lighting in the narrow corridor meant Hugh couldn't see the object was, nor did he know what Ríordán was doing in Áine's cabin. He decided it was best to not let them see him. Placing his back to the wall of the passageway, he counted to ten before resuming his journey. Reaching Áine's cabin, he knocked on the door and waited. There was no answer. He tested the door, it was unlocked. Despite Áine's previous rebuke for entering her cabin uninvited, Hugh pushed the door open.

The cabin was empty apart from a bowl resting on the small table by the door. The bottom was blackened and there was a smell of spice mingled with sweetness in the air. The aromas stirred up unanswered questions in Hugh's mind. Who was this Áine Ó

125

Caoimh? What did he really know about her? She was certainly a woman of mystery. She had been there that terrible day, and from then on she had been with them. But where had she come from, and what did she carry with her in that satchel that always hung from her shoulder? He couldn't deny that she had been helpful to them, but was that all there was to her? Hugh wasn't sure. Pocketing the bowl with a promise to investigate it later, he headed back to meet Tomas and Cullen. Everyone on deck was packed and ready to go ashore. Now at the height of the journey, Hugh felt as if the adventure was beginning.

Chapter Three

Stepping onto the dock, the travelers' senses were assaulted by the sights and smells of Boston Harbour. The group pushed through the throng of people near the dock. Walking by carriages and carts, they headed for the nearest alleyway. Ducking in from the street they gathered to discuss their next move. They needed to find work and lodgings, and after surviving on meal rations, salt pork and bread, their stomachs were also a priority. Asking around on the wharf, they headed to the Bell in Hand, a local tavern, where they were told they could get a meal, hear the latest news, and rent rooms.

Walking to the tavern Hugh noticed Áine glancing back every few paces. Looking past her, he could see a black dog baring its teeth and following them. At the tavern he waited for the group to enter and took a cursory look for the dog that had been following him. It was not hard to spot. Where one dog had been a few minutes before, there were three. He pulled his jacket collar tight round his neck, shivering from more than the cold, and hurried through the door.

The taproom was crowded. Tomas, Cullen, and Áine pushed their way to an open table while Hugh and Ríordán asked about finding work. Securing rooms for the night, and with a lead on possible jobs at the Charlestown docks, they settled down for their evening meal.

There was a strange mix of accents in the tavern. Over the din of the room, familiar words rang out. A man sang in a lachrymose tone:

> *All the dames of France are fond and free*
> *And Flemish lips are really willing*
> *Very soft the maids of Italy*
> *And Spanish eyes are so thrilling*
> *Still, although I bask beneath their smile,*
> *Their charms will fail to bind me*
> *And my heart falls back to Erin's isle*
> *To the girl I left behind me.*

The group ate and listened in silence. They didn't feel pangs of homesickness; the tune just made them remember what they had come here to escape, and as one they got up and headed upstairs.

Chapter Four

Weary from a day working on the docks in Charlestown but unable to sleep, Hugh left the crowded boarding-house lodgings for the solace of the empty streets.

Lost in thought, he walked the neighbourhood that just weeks ago had been foreign to him. It was becoming home. Early morning mist clung to the streets and alleys, blurring his vision.

One street turned into another and another. Hugh sidestepped to avoid colliding with stevedores hurrying to unload the latest arrivals in the harbour and street vendors, setting up their carts and preparing to hawk their wares to passers-by who would soon be filling the streets. The city was eerie yet so alive at this hour. Hugh loved the level of activity happening around him and was grateful for the isolation. Everyone about their own business, hurrying to get somewhere, heads down, lost in their own company.

Suddenly, Hugh realised that he was lost in more than his own company. He no longer recognized the streets in which he now stood. The mist had turned to a heavy fog. The light from the few streetlamps that were still lit in the early morning were subsumed by its oppressive nature, casting shadows on the street. Hugh was forced to run his hand along the cold, moist brick of the buildings in order to find his way.

A feeling of fear started to overtake him, one that he had not known for some time. He fought to quell the panic that was rising inside him when he heard the sound of water being displaced. Something had rippled the puddle he had stepped over only moments ago. He could hear breathing and a familiar smell reached his nostrils. The hair on the back of his neck stood on end. Turning his head, he knew exactly what he would encounter. A black dog stood behind him. As Hugh faced the animal it began to show its teeth, snarling. It seemed to be staring at something behind him, but Hugh was reluctant to turn his back to see what the animal might be growling at. Unwilling to show signs of fear that he knew the animal could smell, Hugh stood his ground. After a few moments, the dog turned and retreated back into the fog from where it had emerged.

Hugh instinctively raised his free hand to the side of his neck feeling for the wound that was once there, he felt only the scar that had taken its place and he was strangely comforted. Taking a moment to collect himself, he turned back into the fog and looked for any signs that would help him get his bearings.

Turning the corner as the fog parted, he caught a glimpse of her. It couldn't be, and yet, there before him stood the most beautiful woman he had ever seen. But she was not a stranger. That long dark hair, slender body, and piercing brown eyes were as familiar to him as his own name. He stood for a moment, unable to move, staring into those eyes he knew so well. He saw her smile widen in recognition. He had thought about that smile the whole way across the Atlantic.

He felt a moistness on his cheeks as he began walking towards her. Suddenly he was running. Something was wrong; despite his exertion, he was no closer to her. Just then, her smile started to fade as the fog swirled about her. For a moment Hugh lost sight of her, of that smile, those dark locks. He fought to propel himself towards her. In a second, she was gone in the fog.

Hugh whirled around looking for any sign of her. She was nowhere to be seen. Just then a face appeared, not the smiling loving face he was searching for, but the face he had been trying to forget. The mouth opened in mocking laughter, a laughter that echoed in Hugh's ears bringing him to his knees. He knew what came next, but this time he was alone and helpless. As the apparition came closer, Hugh prepared himself for the inevitable. He wasn't afraid to die. He closed his eyes and waited for death.

He heard the apparition calling to him as it reached out and touched him. The touch was oddly familiar as it shook him where he knelt calling out his name as if inviting him to get up. Louder and louder the sound of his own name rang in his ears, until he opened his eyes and saw Ríordán bending over him, a look of genuine concern on his face.

Drenched in sweat, Hugh sat up and looked around at the familiar boarding-house walls.

Stephen O'Connor

Fallen Among Greeks

I've never been to Greece. I almost arrived once, but that ill-fated pilgrimage is a story that only serves to assure me that the gods do operate in the affairs of men, as Homer promised. For just as Odysseus saw the hills of his native Ithaka before Aeolus roused the teeming winds that flung his ship to unknown shores, so it was my destiny to board a ferry in Brindisi that broke down in the Adriatic Sea, to be towed back to port, and to have my wallet stolen at the Carpe Diem Hotel while I was in the shower. And the will of Zeus was done. I always thought I would go back, but I'm beginning to doubt if I'll ever raise Greek land on that unbelievably blue horizon.

Still, if I've lived and worked among Greeks, if I've danced in a circle to the bouzouki and clapped my hands and waved a handkerchief and gotten cocked on my ass on ouzo, while the guys on the little stage at The Zorba Room played "The Road to the Peloponnesus;" if I know *The Iliad* and the *Odyssey* better than my own Bible, and I've read Kazantzakis, and eaten *spanakopita* and roast lamb and *octopodi* and *kalimari* and egg-lemon soup, and washed it down with a Retsina—then who among you would say, "You've never been to Greece." The transcendent truth of the matter is that in some way I have been to Greece.

And yes, I have dreamed about it, too. I've seen the bicycle warming against the whitewashed cottage, the narrow, crooked island streets, the blue dome of faith above an equally blue sea, the empty tables in the Aegean sun outside the café; all the patrons crowded at the tables under the awning, and the frantic marketplace of Athens with its fog of pollution chewing the marble of the Golden Age. Above it all, the Acropolis standing there—inconceivable—as if it had slipped through the fingers of heaven and all that lives in our collective unconscious and landed on that height to remind us that the pageant, though faded, was once substantial enough.

How did I, Sean Spellissy, fall among the Greeks? I was raised in the Acre, a neighborhood of small single dwellings, tenements, and vacant mills, dominated by the Gothic spire of St. Patrick's on one side of the Western Canal, and the Byzantine dome of The Holy Trinity Greek Orthodox Church on the other.

I first became aware of a separate people called the Greeks when Moe Murry, who worked for my father painting houses, told me sincerely, "There are two kinds of people in the Acre—the Irish, and the Greeks—and one of us gotta go." I wondered why one of us had to go, and where we, or they, would go. My father was not one to encourage such nonsense. "Don't fill the boy's head with that old malarkey," he said. In any case, by the time that I explored the Acre's alleys years later, the brawling Hiberno-Hellenic wars on the North Common had passed into remembered but unrecorded history.

Whether it was the priests on both sides who prevailed on their flocks, intermarriage, or that we just grew accustomed to each other—I don't know, but as a boy I was permitted to play with Titus Paleologis, the young Greek who moved in with his family across the hall. We all lived in a triple-decker on Fletcher Street that overlooked the O'Malley Funeral Home. Those Irish who could afford it waked their people there, but most of us waked our dead in our homes, while Padraig Leahy from Youghal Harbor scraped a fiddle for free whiskey in the kitchen.

Titus was bright, and a good athlete. He pitched for the Holy Trinity Little League. He was tall for his twelve years, like me, only he had dark hair, and I was what they called a "tow ead."

The Greek—what a strange and captivating race! I peeked through the windows of the coffee houses where men with sweeping moustaches read newspapers in words that weren't even made from our alphabet. I heard their language, spoken in strange aspirations; their lips and tongues seemed to fire off fierce fusillades of p's and k's and t's, while they sat drinking tiny doll cups of coffee. A rare tribe.

An Irish poet wrote, "Like dolmens round my childhood, the old people." The old Greek women, in widow's black, were the dolmens in the Acre's landscape—from another time, mysterious, inexplicable. The women leaned on canes, chatting outside the Pappas Funeral Home. I heard one say something like *Zow-ees esas* when another departed, and I said it over and over to myself on the way home, trying to remember and so break into their secret. Titus pronounced it correctly for me, and said it meant, "Life with you." That arcane and suggestive phrase only augmented my confused reverence for the mystery of their being.

One Saturday, I walked over to the Pollard Memorial Library and ambled through the young adult section. Perusing the rows of colored bindings, I stumbled upon a book called *Gods and Heroes of Ancient Greece*. On the cover, a warrior mounted on a white, winged, stallion brandished a sword as he charged upward through the air. It was the most beautiful thing I had ever seen. I brought it to the librarian, a balding, bespectacled man with tufted wings of hair above his ears, and was annoyed when he looked at it and laughed, "I'd hate to be on the ground when that horse lets loose." I gazed over my shoulder and pretended I hadn't heard.

I went to the St. Patrick's Day show at the Lowell Auditorium with my seventh-grade class. My father, famous in the Acre for his rich tenor voice, sang:

> *I kiss the dear fingers so toil worn for me*
> *Oh God bless you and keep you, mother mo chree*

Mo chree was Irish, my father had told me, for "my heart." We had had a language, like the Greeks, once. But we'd pretty much lost it. How do you lose a language? The crowd cheered and called for another song.

> *O the strangers came and tried to teach us their ways*
> *They scorned us just for bein' what we are*
> *But they might as well go chasing after moonbeams*
> *Or light a penny candle from a star.*

The strangers were English. "John Bull" my grandfather called them. "Do you want to know the story of the Irish?" he asked me,

"It was all *John Bull!*" Not long after St. Patrick's Day came Greek Independence Day. Instead of green, the Greeks wore blue. And Titus was in a play at the Hellenic American School. A moustache was pasted above his lip and he carried a wooden scimitar. The play was all in Greek. I didn't understand it, but I could see that the Turks were the strangers who came and tried to teach the Greeks their ways. The Turks were the Greeks' John Bull.

I envied Titus the language he had not lost. The Irish language was gone, for us, except in little phrases and songs and words that survived. My grandmother blessed herself in Irish. *In anim ahair agus avic agus a spear a niwher*, or so it sounded to me. She sang, "*Guday ma shanta voney gramma crema criushkeen, lawn, lawn, lawn.* And *Come back to Erin, mavourneen, mavourneen.* She said that "mavourneen" meant "darling." I only ever heard the two Miss Mahoneys really talking in our old language. They sat on their front porch, talking the old language and eating dulce. Was that all that was left of our language? Two old ladies eating seaweed?

And the more time I spent with Titus and his family, the more I began to feel that we Irish had lost our soul. One day, when the sun was shining in the window on the table where Titus and I were playing checkers, I heard his mother say something in Greek with the word *helios*, as she pulled the shade. Helios, the sun! *Lord Helios* in his fiery chariot. Their language, their everyday words, held their identity, their mythology, their gods.

In my library books, I read of the wrath of Achilles, the fall of Troy, the wanderings of Odysseus, and his terrible vengeance on the suitors. Grey-eyed Athena! There was a goddess companion a young boy might wish for. Not the pale, long-suffering Mary, her face ever upturned to a greater power, pleading, but Athena, who bore the Medusan shield and the long ashen spear; the visor of her war helmet raised, she smiled on her mortal champion. *Though a hundred swords sing for your blood, with me by your side you will come away unscathed, and steal their cattle.*

Like a young Don Quixote, my imagination filled with all I had read. Hermes, a gold star, falling through air, lame Hephaistos, and the bloody war god Aries, sea nymphs, Ino and Thetis, and the shape-shifting Proteus. I wanted to know more. I read the tragedians Aeschelus, Euripedes and Sophocles, the comedian Aristophanes, Hesiod's *Theogeny*, the birth of the gods, Ovid's *Metamorphoses*, and even the philosophers, Plato and Aristotle, though I understood much of it but dimly.

I told my parents that I wanted to transfer from St. Patrick's to the Hellenic American School and learn Greek. My father explained that though it would be wonderful to learn Greek, and he had the greatest respect for the Greek people, it would not be possible to attend the Hellenic school because the Greeks did not believe in the Pope. There was no more to be said. The Pope stood between me and a classical education. *Anagnorisis*, a recognition of something one hadn't known before. It was religion, even more than culture or language that was the wall between the two groups struggling to rise out of the Acre.

That summer, Titus and I enlisted some of the neighboring children. While others played cowboys and Indians, we played Spartans and Persians. We armed ourselves with sticks drawn from the dilapidated lattice work of the back porch and ran about proclaiming brave words in what we thought was the diction of heroes: "We shall return victorious, or upon our shields!" One humid afternoon, sweating from our warlike exertions, we walked down to the canal that flowed under Broadway from the Francis Gate House and past the Gas Company, and clad in our underwear and sneakers, we threw ourselves into the dark water, where we imagined other noble adventures, until we saw a rat scurrying into a crevice in the stone wall.

Not long after, I became quite ill. I couldn't eat. I was nauseated. Doctor Bleckman came and prescribed rest and a bottle of thick green, foul-tasting medicine that made me shiver in disgust. I only grew worse. I was frightened by my own weight loss, and felt my strength failing. I had been sleeping for some time, when I woke and heard my mother crying to my father, who was home for lunch, "Oh, he'll never make it, James." My father comforted her in a low voice and left again for work. There was a knock on the door soon after. It was Titus and his old grandmother. I heard my mother thanking her for some lentil soup.

"I want he be strong again. He's good boy," the old woman said.

"Yes, he is," my mother said, and her voice was choked in her throat.

"My ya-ya has something for Sean." Titus said. "It's good luck. Can we see him?"

"Yes, if he's awake," she said.

I smiled weakly as my mother opened the door. "You have some visitors," she said and turned toward the kitchen, adding to the old woman, "I'll put on the kettle for a cup of tea." I didn't think Greeks drank tea, but they accepted. The slim handsome youth and the aged woman entered. She made the sign of the cross over me and said something rapidly in Greek to Titus.

"Sean," he said, "Ya-ya says that someone put the *matia* on you."

"*Matia?*"

"The evil eye."

"She put the oil in the water, and she could tell," he said.

The old woman picked up my forearms and held them. Her hands were cold. She mumbled something in Greek, and then she turned and spat on the floor. "Sorry," Titus said, smiling apologetically.

She dropped my arms and put her cool, withered hand on my forehead. She pulled a dark shawl over her head and began to incant in Greek for a minute or so. She held out a hand to Titus, who handed her a small vial of something oily that she rubbed on my face. "*Livani*," she said, and Titus struck a match and lit some incense. A thin stream of smoke rose from her hand, which she circled above my body. I coughed weakly as she blew it toward my face. Then, from somewhere in the voluminous folds of her dress, she drew out a tiny object on a black string. She lifted my head and lowered it around my neck. Then she picked up the object and held it in front of my face. "*Mati*," she said, "strong good." I saw a small blue eye with a tiny black dot in its center. The kettle was whistling in the kitchen. I heard the women's voices, and I slept again.

My dreams were strange and vivid. I saw ya-ya standing on the canal wall. She described a circle with her cane above the water, and it began to churn and boil, and rats emerged from the water and clambered up the walls, fleeing for their lives. And I saw that it was not ya-ya, but Athena; the cane was the ashen spear. She was beside my bed, and leaned over my face and whispered, *Though a hundred swords sing for your blood, I am with you, and you shall come away unscathed.* I awoke from that sleep holding in my fist the tiny blue eye. And I felt I would be better.

I called my mother. She came immediately, wiping her hands on her apron, harried with worry. "How are you Sean, darling?"

"She brought lentil soup?"

"Yes. Yes, she did."

"Can I have some?"

"Oh, Mother of God!" She kissed my forehead and ran to the stove, and when my father came home, I was sitting at the kitchen table drinking a cup of tea with my mother, who was smiling for the first time in days.

"He had two bowls of lentil soup, and toast," she said, as if it were the greatest accomplishment of my life. My father threw a newspaper on the table and patted my back. He peered into my eyes for a few seconds and said, "You had us worried, boy."

My mother recounted the old woman's visit, and he examined the curious gift she had hung around my neck. "Well, the Greeks may not believe in the Pope," my mother told him, "but they have the power." He laughed as he sat down and spread the paper out with his paint-stained arms. "Well, they're an ancient race, and they must have their secrets. Though why they prefer coffee to lager is a mystery to me." He rattled the paper as he found the obituaries, and said, "All right then, Sally, let's see who's dead."

The obituaries—the Irish funny pages they called them. But it wasn't funny a few years later when the small picture of Titus Paleologis appeared there. The war was almost over when he was lost in the hedge rows of Normandy. I was stationed in the Philippines. My mother sent me the clipping, along with a devotional card, and a prayer to the Sacred Heart. I walked into the jungle and carved his name in a Balau tree, and while I recited the prayer that my mother had sent for poor Titus, a monkey cackled and gibbered at me from a branch above, and I wondered if my prayers sounded like that to God.

I sat there until the shadows were eaten by the dusk, holding a black rosary in my idle hands. I didn't imagine Titus in peace among the saints. I saw him charging skyward mounted on a winged stallion, leaving the stunned Persian archers and the toil of all our battles far below.

David Perry

Women, Not Unusual

There has long been a myth, even among some of the most long-suffering men, that women think us fools. That they do not like the things we do. So, they do not join us. They leave us to our silliness.

And we go into the record store.

We browse, we loudly boast insipid things like, "I had all o' these at one point."

We point out to our children, in a volume meant for the clerk's ears, "So, this is how we used to listen to music." Just to make sure, we wink at the clerk.

Women still know better than to engage in such charades.

I know. I am the clerk.

Three days a week, I sit behind the counter. The counter is a witness stand from an old courthouse. So, I am not the first to judge from its confines.

I actually own the place. In 2013, my son and I opened Vinyl Destination in a magnificent, refurbished mill in a corner of downtown Lowell, Mass., whose only purpose was once to act as a drop house for the Mill City's heroin and hookers.

Things have changed.

The new point-of-sale at Vinyl Destination, or POS as those of us *in the business world* like to call it, lends us a certain lofty air.

We judge.

The beautiful old wooden piece we sit in is from a courthouse, that is for certain. Which one, we don't know.

We envision it as a witness stand where thugs, cronies, and co-conspirators have broken sweats and betrayed blood oaths. We tell people that. It's a better story. The truth is, we don't know for certain.

But we now see everything with clarity.

And what I saw today I would not have seen until the last couple of years. Women. Women in a record store, shopping with intent. There always have been exceptions, of course. Most often they would drop men at the door, frown, roll their eyes then head off somewhere else.

Men carried the weight of their obsessive need to look at records with a shrug and then did what they do—form clubs of common misery. *Oh, the wife/girlfriend won't let me bring in any more records, ha-ha. Woe is me.*

But yesterday, a day when lots of people came in, women shoppers outnumbered the men. It used to be a man's sickness, record collecting. Not anymore. The annual year-end stories noting whopping percentage increases in vinyl sales are fun and certainly telling of numbers. But this is something else.

Women are right up there at record shows, elbowing their way to first shots at boxes of new arrivals with the best.

I wish I knew what it meant. I wish I knew where and when this all turned. I don't.

But I do know the coolest customers I had yesterday were female. And they had *Taste.* The guitar player from Boston who clutched the obscure Wayne Shorter alum, snagged Lee Konitz and then asked, "Do you have any Prefab Sprout?"

The perky twins with the new turntable who sprouted goosebumps upon finding *Cosmo's Factory.*

The former babysitter, now a mom, bringing her own fifteen-year-old daughter to buy a copy of *Rarities* by The Beatles.

The older woman who bought a new turntable and was slowly replacing the collection she dumped years ago.

"Now," she said in a hushed but determined voice at the checkout, reminding me of my own mom, "how am I going to know if these are okay?"

Reassured, she bought the used Otis Redding and Robert Cray records. I felt an urge to clean my room.

There was the young woman who messaged the night before to ask if we had any punk/hardcore/metal. She grabbed a Death record, Air's *Virgin Suicides* soundtrack and Godspeed You! Black Emperor.

The woman right behind her was beyond thrilled to find a copy of *Ella in Berlin* to fit in the bag right next to the Stones' *Black and Blue.*

But my favorite was a woman, thirties, who wandered in followed in short order by her two children. The pink-cheeked boy was in his teens, the girl a bundle of unbridled energy in a Batman costume, her tongue red from a bottle of sugary juice she sucked. You could see the tongue every time she screeched. I saw the tongue a lot.

The boy stood in front of the Soundtracks, pulling each record up as he went. The row began to look like a cresting wave.

"Mom, look" he said at one point, "they have *Star Wars*."

Mom wasn't there.

She stood directly behind him, her back to his, in the rock section, staring longingly at a copy of the Steve Miller Band's *Greatest Hits*. She smiled faintly, then fidgeted with the tight kinks of her red hair.

She looked at that cover for the longest time, as if it were a mirror and she were Kim Kardashian.

Batgirl broke the spell, screeching her restlessness. "Let's go *somewhere!*"

It pierced the perfect pop of the Chills song on the store stereo.

A man appeared in the doorway, looked at the scene, nodded at the woman and left. Did they know one another? Was this a husband?

The woman picked up the record and took it with her to the New Arrivals section. The kids vanished into the hallway. She shopped longer, holding the time like a life jacket. She dropped Steve Miller back into his slot and picked up the *Hunger Games* soundtrack.

I had read too much into this. Was it silly to think a record jacket would bring back so much?

Maybe this new perspective was too tempting. Stop judging. Stop reading things into this. Shut up, play records, swipe cards.

The lone customer left in the store, she approached the bench. She plunked down a greatest hits collection from the dollar bin. Then, that *Hunger Games* record.

One more. Cyndi Lauper. *She's So Unusual.* The one with "Girls Just Wanna Have Fun."

D-Tension

Roaches

The old neighborhood ain't what it used to be.
I went back and nobody knows who I used to be
Soon to be coming to a theater near you
The Hollywood blockbuster Gentrification, Part Two

You know the story, it writes itself
Take the land over, put the natives on the shelf
Ain't even stealth, they paved the trail
Of tears, you can't live here, pass the craft beer

Over here, this is where I went to school
Forty kids in a class, thirty desks, ten stools
It wasn't cool, we had to share books
Now all the new kids got iPads and Nooks

Look, here comes the marching band
We had plastic flutes, they got saxophones and
Drums and trumpets, fuck it, good for them
It ain't their fault that it used to be a prison

I witnessed, pimps and hoes at age five
Crack dealers on the corner, near the five-and-dime
But every time the cops did a sting or a sweep
Two hours later, they was back on the street

Missing no beat, the developers arrived
Much to my surprise, the crime subsides
I wonder why? What was different this time?
Then we all got evicted just like I predicted

It sickens me, cops never came around
Even if you was shot, down, bleeding on the ground
Now they're found, chilling with the hipsters
"Howdy, officer Bob. Why hello there, mister!"

I miss the bodega, where we got all our goods
Groceries, hardware, check cashing in the hood
Then the rent went up and we couldn't stop it
Now the old bodega's artisanal chocolate

Stop it? We can't, it's a losing battle
On to browner pastures, not so free-range cattle
I straddled broken glass and needles in the park
We played ball all night, now it's closed after dark

And if you wanna take part in a friendly game of soccer
You got a get a permit, rent a key for a locker
When it got hotter, we pumped the fire hydrant
Now they got a water park with swing and slides &

They took us for a ride, now they don't even hide it
This place got paid a visit by the great King Midas
As I write this, I realize that it's over
The battle is lost like I already told ya

But before I go, I have just one question
For the fence whitewashers, please teach me a lesson
I'm not pretending, I really wanna know
Where the fuck did the cockroaches go?

We were infested for 30 years
I lived my entire life in fear
Of water bugs the size of sunflowers
Flying in the tub when I'm trying to take a shower

I'd hide for hours while they multiplied
Then the white people came and what they all died?
How? why? I really need to know
We had exterminators once a month, was that for show?

Cuz god knows the roaches didn't care about them
They'd squirt some poison in the kitchen and then

142

The bugs got bigger and bolder and smart
They knew to wait until after dark

And when the light went on, they scattered like rats
While we're on the subject what happened to that?
The rats the size of cats, they spoke English and Spanish
Then you moved in and they all vanished

Goddammit, it's one thing to take my house
But please tell me how you kept the cucarachas out
Don't hold out, what's the secret, you owe this to us
You must tell us how to get rid of roaches

What's the hocus pocus, are there magical potions?
Tell me how the fuck you got rid of the roaches
This is my focus, there's a way and you know this
Tell me how the fuck to get rid of these roaches!

Do d-CON no Raid, we'll pay you to show us
Just tell me how the fuck to get rid of these roaches!
Please tell me how the fuck to get rid of these roaches!
Man, tell me how the fuck to get rid of these roaches!

FIVE

Chath pierSath

America, My America

Indebted to you, America,
My eyes aren't enough, for I have seen freedom.
My heart you can take
For I have felt hatred and war.
My gratitude in every limb born to you and for you,
Perhaps is all I have to give.
Take my ears for I have heard the Liberty Bell from
    Mount Rushmore.
Mark me a donor. Take my spleen, kidneys, and lungs.
My privileged American life can take my eyes, after all.
My arms and legs, I am willing to sacrifice.
Let me die for freedom and democracy,
For peace and prosperity, justice and liberty for all.
I salute you, America, for helping my dream take flight,
Letting me be, see and become, to work and play,
Eat and sleep to life's breathlessly beautiful hills,
Mountains, valleys, above and below.
"This land is your land . . . this land is my land,"
Field to field, "from California to the New York Island,"
Wheat and rye, Iowan corn, grassland,
Native sacred paradise,
On earth and beyond the sky,
Galaxy, and beyond every universe man must explore,
Stars and planets near and far.
To every free spirit, may American-born freedom roar,
Echoing far and wide until all
Tyranny be gone, like doubts and fears,
Gone from the ears I have given America.
From the eyes that witnessed human cruelty,
From the heart that felt freedom, the highway
Paved for kings and queens, the magician
Who appears and disappears by his own magic,
I give all of me, the entirety.
Claim me, America,
A sacrifice worth more than the life I knew before.   147

Matt W. Miller

Invocation at the Merrimack

And now I take a tongue into your mud,
into your syringe and soda bottle banks,

to beg your braided silk, your Pennacook
ikwe, your sliding tar of snake, your mouth
of stones, your clavicle

                      of roil and moan,
your lover ghosts thrown from Pawtucket Falls,
your whitewater of bread and roses,

                           your creak
of locks and lifts, your leap from burning windows,

your fished-out crib of salmon and shiv, of shell
casings and shad, alewife and boosted tires,
your cradle

             of flywheel, of factory, your mill
girl offering, your doffers, your biddies, your boom

and your busted. Penitent palmed I stand
in this, your sun tussling dawn, to call a song.

My river, roll your blueblack big hips under
the oxidized iron of cantilever and cable,

deluge and slip bridge ribs and sing between
the redbrick and brackish heft of textile mills
turned art galleries with crack alleys.

                    You,
bender of flashboard pins, come

                              sing to me,
sluice me, double back and seduce me to

your flood, tenor me down to your Irish blood
canals, your Greek restaurant ghettos,
fluorescent Cambodian groceries, chunk heeled
Brazilian bakeries,

                    your cobblestones
exposed to sell some rheumy history.

Bones old and broken of flesh, in sack and ash,
I call a song.

            You ferried me home, now drink
and spit me out where city hall has crouched
inside downtown's diverticula,

down to the fountain at JFK plaza where
my brother was suckered by a kid I wouldn't
hit back.

            And there, just one of ten police stations,
Pollard library, and across Arcand Ave,
Lowell High, its field house named after
our grandfather,

                the columned Masonic temple,
the bring your own wine Viet Thai, and bars
and bars and bars, one for every St. Anne's,
Immaculate, and St. Patrick's.

                        In your
hydraulic drop prayers are tossed like toasts
to tilted pints. There, here, my palms unfold.

Give willow to me against
my flooded nights, against my broken rites.

So you flow down and roll stones old river,
and moor me here for what I am and not.

Wake my song and pluck me to your pulse.
I'll stay down in your valley,

                                drink your ink
of water and dream myself

                                back into you.

Make me small again, roll me in your lap,
your mud, your moon lit blood.

                        Supplicated,
by the greasy vents of a train car diner, I beg
your lip of water to whisper.

Trish Edelstein

Returning for Good

After ten years of living in a dusty, brown and barren landscape in Amman, Jordan, it was time for me to return home for good. Home is Cork, the second-largest city in Ireland that settles on the banks of the River Lee. I arrived with one bag on my back at Dublin Airport, as the rest of my worldly belongings were following me somewhere across the oceans on a container ship. Outside the airport, I hopped onto a bus that goes directly to Cork. The journey passed by counting and enjoying the various shades of green, looking at fields, trees, plants, hedges, bog land. I lost count at seventy-three colours. No wonder Ireland is called the Emerald Isle in promotion videos. The contrast between the Middle East landscape and Ireland could not be more different.

The bus trundled down Cork's quays and we passed the container ships being unloaded by the cranes. I thought about the men who struggled daily for employment and who contributed to the economic development of the city, a way of life that is fast disappearing. As a young girl I always imagined what these ships coming through the double-decked bridges might be carrying; cedar wood, spices from India, and clockwork toys from China were on my list.

We pass the limestone Bonded Warehouse, which juts out on the port, it's a landmark for the city and today it is a listed building. It was built in 1820 by prisoners. The curved roofs are fragmenting in places and their supporting struts are drooping gently. The turrets hold spiral stairs leading to alleys vaulted like a cathedral undercroft, with white-painted brick interlocked in rows of arches.

If someone were to ask me where I like most in Cork it would have to be a swimming place on the Lee called the Hell Hole or its other name Poul an Ifrinn. For generations, Corkonians have come to this place to swim. It is situated on a sharp bend in the River Lee where one is able to jump in and immediately find yourself in deep blue water, with shoals of small fish passing by.

I became a two-season swimmer many years ago, where I swam every day there. A group of hardy men swim all year round and have done so for years. Some of the men are in their eighties, and swear that it has kept them in good health.

To get there one has to pass along the green pastures of the Lee Fields, pass Carrigrohane House recognised by its stone wall covered in wild flowers in the summer, pass Carrigrohane Castle which looks as if it is about to topple down from the cliff (If I am cycling past I make sure to go quickly). Finally, one goes over the bridge and there, opposite the Anglers Rest pub, is the final destination.

The Hell Hole has a very ominous name and certainly strange stories have been circulated over the years I have been going there. One is about seven monks who all drowned, each one trying to rescue another. John Windele writes way back in his 1846 *Guide to the South of Ireland* "at a sudden bend of the river is a deep pool bearing the fearful name of Poul an Ifrinn or Hell Hole." He goes on to say, "One of those fanciful eels of the supernatural class is said to inhabit this part of the river; he is of monstrous dimensions, has a mane of hair like a horse and two short feet. He is the guardian of enchanted abodes beneath, containing vast treasures. Heretofore, he can often be seen in the morning on the neighboring grounds, but of late years, his visits have been rare as those of Angels."

My children spent hours trying to find the bottom of the hole and there was one area that they held with suspicion as they were convinced there were whirlpools which could suck them down.

Despite all these stories, I saw the place as my paradise with its sandy bank and the poplar and ash trees bowing over on the other side, framing the swimming area.

All sorts of people came here, but the days that the male Travellers came with their horses was always a spectacle that was not to be missed. Suddenly over the bank they would appear, ten riders and sometimes more, they would ride bareback with great finesse and walk their horses steadily into the river. There was always a reluctance at first from the horses to wet their pelts, but with the encouragement of deep tenor sounds of "huup" coming from the men they would glide smoothly into the deep river. There would be a great scurry of swimmers leaving the waters as the horses entered the water. The horses would swim up and down and the riders would kneel on their back to avoid getting too wet. All too soon they would come back out and shake their manes and the rest of their bodies, spraying water into the air. As quickly as they arrived, they would leave and within minutes everything at the Hell Hole would return to its tranquil self.

The bus stopped close to Patrick's bridge and I waited my turn to step down onto the pavement. I smiled immediately for there was a very surprising familiar sight. I saw the same two men from ten years ago looking a little more worn, hanging over Patrick's Bridge with their fishing rods and wearing dark sunglasses, fishing for mullet. They swore the sunglasses helped them spot the fish coming downstream. The sight rekindled the love I have for the city and the River Lee.

Peuo Tuy

2000 Riels to Rouge Rage

I summon the tuk-tuk driver outside of Phsa Orrisei,
Choeung Ek Genocidal Center. How much?

2000 riels, he replies.

As we drive through two kilometers of unpaved roads,
I find myself inhaling dirt particles, clearing my throat with saliva.
Finally, we see a gigantic entrance sign to the center—500 meters.

The night before I made an international call to Ma.
Told her I was determined to find out
what all these nostalgic nightmares were all about.
It's been thirty-two years, Ma, I want to know.

We come upon a few ditches, I am scared witless, terror struck.

>   In re-education and concentration camps
>   they starved us to death,
>   overworked us, 12+ hours.
>
>   We ate worms, dogs, cats,
>   crickets, wild mushrooms, raw rice,
>   mice, muddy live shrimp, leaves, toads,
>   tadpoles, centipedes, scorpions.
>
>   Some of us lived.
>   Over 1 million corpses unburied spiritually.
>
>   They made us have edema.
>   We died from malaria. Gave us brittle bones.
>   Our shiny long hair shortened,

bodies thin like black bobby pins and
walking dreary shadows.

Our families separated—
Killed fathers, raped mothers and daughters,
shot children, manipulated kids,
buried us alive, made orphans.

Some of us lived.
Over 1 million died unblessed.

They slaughtered the educated: doctors, lawyers,
professors, artists, English and French speakers.
Patrolled our every breath.
Massacred the light skinned.
Burned clocks, watches, temples,
hospitals schools, shops.
Killed monks and destroyed Buddhism.

Some of us lived.
Over 1 million people died without a wake.

Their ultra-left rage
separated my family for 10+ years.

Meng, Meng, my cousin nudges me,
I don't want to be here.

We call our tuk-tuk driver.
None of us said a word to each other on our ride back.
I felt the spirits follow us back to Phnom Penh.

Resi Ibañez

Port Authority

// there's something about that bus terminal. //

I wonder about those people there,
at Port Authority.

You know the people I'm talking about –
the ones who are always there.

They have their tickets,
they're ready to go.
       no, going.

they're not waiting – their feet
are already out the door –

      but they are always there.

I wonder.
I wonder where they are going –
      if they're going home.

I wonder where home is,
      since they never leave this bus station.

I wonder
if those people are really

all white.
      Or if that is a mere accident?
      Unintentional coincidence
      of the sculptor's material?

You know those people I'm talking about -
The Commuters.

always stationed
in the ticket lobby
for the buses bound for Jersey.

Maybe they're like me -
white plastered exterior,
but cast in bronze //
      true colors
      underneath.

I also wonder
how they are always moving,
en route
to someplace else -
      and yet,
      standing still,

      here.

Permanently
passing through
      through this door

And how many doors have I passed through here? //
      there's something about
      that bus terminal //

      always on my own ways
      to get home . . .

even though
home is a moving target

home is
having each foot
on opposite sides
of a fault line

home is
always passing through

revolving doors, through

this bus terminal //

> *there's something about*
> *that bus terminal*

because I'm always here too //
> *something always brings me back*

here,
always on my way
        to someplace else —

home is being
in transit

sitting uneasily on a fault line,
on borders between continents
on boundaries between binaries

wanting so badly to not be locked in closets
        fighting my way out everyday
        my foot out the door,

the threshold, the border, the dividing line:
        crossed

crossing
pushing back against, out of this
hard white plaster, covering
bronze casting.
     sculptor's mistake.

home is
always always crossing that threshold,
being the first person in line …

I was born to run, you know.
     and not just through train stations at rush hour, either.

these commuters are bound for New Jersey
and I was bound to leave. //
     you ever think about how much time is spent
        running after
        your way out
           of someplace?

I was born under Sagittarius //
     (the sign of commuters and movers)

so it was written in the stars,
this Bruce Springsteen prophecy:
blood doesn't run in my veins
but my veins are the map of my body, my history
     how my mother immigrated from the Philippines
     and I left New Jersey to continue that legacy

because lines and borders are something I feel
very viscerally:
     moving and
     border-crossing -
        all coded in me,
        genetically:

to be

always
in
transition

in // between // places //
destinations // *The Commuters,*

always
in
movement —
		they are the company I keep.

They're not going anywhere,
		but they go everywhere with me //

*there's something about
		this bus terminal.*

Anthony Lawrence

Tracklist

In 1979, I left Australia on a one-way flight to Israel. I'm not Jewish, and Israel would have been low on the list of travel destinations had it not been for a chance encounter with an old friend from school who had just returned from working on a kibbutz in the Negev Desert. "Go and sign your name under mine on the back of the door in the Volunteers' hut," my friend suggested. I was working as a tree-lopper's offsider at the time and had saved some money. That night, over beers and games of snooker, I decided to find that hut and sign my name under his.

When I think of the Negev Desert, I think of long waits by the side of the road, hitch-hiking down from the oasis that was kibbutz Revivim into extreme heat and dusty limestone. While waiting I listened to a lot of music on my Walkman. In the years before leaving Australia it would have been rock music (Lou Reed, Rolling Stones, Led Zeppelin, Uriah Heep—the usual suspects) but another chance encounter, shortly before flying out, led me head-and-heart-first into folk music. Hitchhiking in Sydney, I was picked up by a young man whose car was filled with wonderful acoustic guitar and one of the best voices I'd ever heard. I saw the cassette cover: *Welcome Here Kind Stranger* by Paul Brady. There were others. Planxty, De Dannan, Stockton's Wing, The Bothy Band. I wrote the names down, and before I got out, he gave me a tape he'd made of some of his favourite bands. I listened to that tape while waiting for rides in the desert.

Cutting a quick swathe through a curious and adventure-packed itinerary that covered Israel, Greece (and a near-fatal night ride on the Magic Bus), Italy, Spain and England, I find myself on the ferry between Holyhead in Wales and Dún Laoghaire, Dublin. It's a rough crossing, and a ragged group of Punks are eating pork pies and swilling Guinness. I hear a guitar and find my way to the source. A young woman is playing and singing. She's very good. I ask her the name of the song. "Now Westlin Winds," she says, and suggests I listen to the Dick

161

Gaughan version on his album *Handful of Earth*. Sometime in the morning I step out into Ireland and the beginning of one of the most important years of my life.

Time and memory have conspired to shift the shapes of much of what happened in the next couple of months. Somehow, I found work at a fun-fair outside Youghal. I remember the blue ceiling sparks of the dodgem cars, clowns, and tough young men smoking on the margins. And as befitting the musical direction I'd been taking since that day in Sydney, I heard a great version of John Martyn's "May You Never" around the campfire one night. My folk music education was a curious mix of mostly live encounters and a backpack filled with cassettes I'd picked up along the way.

I fell in love with Cork the day I arrived—bus, train, hitch-hiking, walking—who knows, but I did know this was a place I wanted to spend time in. So many things about the city appealed to me: the steep hills and sweeping views of the city, St Anne's church in Shandon with its bells and golden fish, the pubs of course, but mostly it was the generous welcome of the locals and the accent, which I'd first encountered on the kibbutz when I befriended a Corkman. I was amazed by its musical complexity. I had arrived with Irish, Scottish, and English folk and folk-rock music set indelibly into my conscious and subliminal thinking. There was poetry, too. It had always been there. Poetry and music. Inseparable. Interchangeable. I was about to discover just how influential this city was to be on my life as a poet and my wide reading of poetry.

I first met Tina Neylon at what was the humble beginnings of the Triskel Arts Centre, founded by Robbie McDonald. I consider this meeting to be the most important in my life as a poet. Tina suggested I submit some poems to *The Cork Review*, which she was editing. My first published poems appeared in that journal. This was a huge moment. It came at a time when I was very much in need of the company of people for whom poetry, music, and culture in general was a priority. I'd felt cut adrift in Australia, at odds with my environment and people. Ireland, and Cork specifically, made me feel welcome and gave meconfidence to pursue a life in writing.

I was soon introduced to the poets the late Sean Dunne and Thomas McCarthy. These men were already widely published, in book form and in many journals in Ireland and internationally. They were kind and took interest in a young bloke from Australia. I also met Frank O'Donovan, another writer with a great sense of humour. Through my friendship with Tina I became involved with the Granary Theatre, and acted in two productions, directed by Gerry Barnes: *Biko* by Donald Woods, and Boucicault's *The Shaughraun*.

Life in Cork was rich, eventful and diverse. I played cricket for Munster, opening the bowling, and travelled to many extraordinary places. I have maintained contact with friends there, and recently returned to read as a guest at the Ó Bhéal poetry series at the Long Valley pub, where I used to write, have a sandwich and pint, and listen to the proprietor Humphrey Moynihan's classical music records.

Frank O'Donovan

The Stranger's Story

He first came into the pub at the start of that summer, walking slowly in the dog day heat up the hill past the Guardia di Finanza headquarters. He sat at the bar counter, and at first he was dour, didn't seem to want to talk to anyone. As the weeks wore on, he'd exchange a word or two with some of the regulars who happened to occupy the stools on either side of him. Mostly he drank alone, always beer. Rome was the best of cities, but the way Sammy kept to himself and focused his attention on his beer, he might as well have been in the middle of the desert. He'd sit at the end of the bar, swirling the foam in his beer and occasionally glancing out the window at the street life passing by. The heat that summer was particularly difficult to take. Bedroom windows had to be kept wide open all night, even though all that drifted in from the night outside was the suffocating heat and the mosquitoes that buzzed in your ear until you woke up, the heat heavy on your chest, making it difficult to breathe. Yes, if it wasn't the mosquitoes keeping you awake, it was the noise of traffic, trucks, loud voices merry with Peroni and Sambuca or your troubled past.

The Fiddlers' Bow is the kind of pub that seems to attract all types. The story went that Sammy arrived at nearby Termini Railway Station late one night, got off the train and walked straight over here, past the looming magnificence of the Santa Maria basilica, like he'd been here before. I've been working here for ten years now and the clientele are mostly tourists, a lot of Irish who are here on holiday. I've often seen people like Sammy wander in and out for a week or two. Drifters, the local English and Irish expats who are the regulars here call them. But Sammy hung on for longer than usual and began to drift in each evening during that long hot summer. Inevitably, the local expats got the rumour mill grinding: he had served time in prison, he had murdered his wife, he was an armed robber and was on the run from the law.

Sometimes when I see people sitting over their beer with their heads down, I wonder about where they came from and often imagine them as small children, speculating about what happened in their lives to transform them into what they are now. I imagined Sammy as a small grimy kid with scuff marks on his shoes and crooked teeth. Now he's about five-six, a shock of hair that had once been black but now streaked with grey and, from time to time, some green highlights. Snub nose on a round face and a small scar across his chin. The words LOST SOUL were tattooed in Gothic lettering on his brawny right arm. I imagined that his deep brown eyes had twinkled with devilment when he was a kid, but they had long since lost that sparkle. His expression was passive, always inscrutable. He wore shapeless nondescript tee shirts and jeans with sandals that had seen better days. The kind of guy you'd pass by on the street without a second glance.

After a week or two, I knew by the accent that Sammy was Irish, but for a while his reticence hid from me the fact that, like me, he was born and raised in the Red City. The Red City is on the southern coast of Ireland. It rises high above the oily dirty brown river that winds its way through the city. There are 100,000 souls crammed in there and in winter smoke rises from rooftops that are stepped and close together. The cross of the highest church in the city stands out against the dark sky, lighting up red to guide the faithful to its door. Sammy was from the north side of the city and, because I lived on the west side, we'd never met. But the night he mentioned his surname, it rang a bell and stirred my memory and my curiosity.

That particular night, when the punters were thin on the ground, I offered to buy Sammy a drink and we got talking. His surname was Holland. I've no idea why but that night he opened up to me and told me his story. As he spoke into the early hours of the morning, I knew that he had never told this story to anyone before and I could only wonder why he told me then. He spoke in a slow methodical way, as if he had laid out the various landmarks of the tale deliberately so that he wouldn't forget any of the details, measuring his rhythmic narrative with careful swigs of beer and the lighting of a fresh cigarette from the end of the previous one.

By his twenty-fifth birthday, he'd shot at least a dozen people in hits paid for by the drug lords of the Red City. Most of them drug dealers on the north side of the river. The way he saw it, he was just moving them faster along a road that they'd probably reach the end of sooner or later. No way back, no side turns. It was like they were hitching a lift and he came along in a hearse, smiling as he opened the back door for them. It was simple maths. When you grow up in the north side estates you learn the one great lesson of the life of crime. Sell drugs you end up one of two things. Dead or banged up. In the case of these cold and ugly streets, mostly dead. Two and two was four.

He took another swig of beer and lit a cigarette, blowing the smoke in rings toward the ceiling that was faded from years of smoke. He looked out the window at the young people hurrying by on foot and on scooters, furrowing his brow as he recalled the details of one cold evening in mid-December.

It all started out like so many other nights before: Sammy and his friends sitting around the bonfire in the field at the rear of the housing estate where they lived at the edge of the Red City, the backdoors of the terraced houses behind them neatly lined up like coffin lids. You could see the orange glow of the flames even when you closed your eyes and the acrid burning smoke got up your nose and fiercely burned your eyes, making them water and sting like you wanted to cry for a long time. There was Sammy and Baz, Hosty, Sting, and Angel. Sammy watched Sting chugging a bottle of beer, his boat like feet almost touching the fire, turning his drowned man face to Sammy as he passed the bottle. A feeling of disgust rose up in Sammy's craw but then Baz leaned in from the other side, asking him if he could get a gun for his mother's boyfriend. Sammy laughed straight in his face.

"Why does he want it?"

"Never mind, I just said I'd ask."

"Go back and find out what he wants it for. You can't hand a gun over to just anyone."

Baz said nothing, bit the end of his lip until it bled before slugging the dregs from the bottle. He shifted from side to side on the stone he'd perched on like it was molten. He got up and paced up and down until he pissed everybody off with his dark grey, then black mood. He was the last one left in the early hours of the morning, staring into the smouldering bonfire of tyres and blackened branches of wood, like he was looking for an answer to his problem.

But Baz couldn't let it go, spent the next few days acting like someone facing a life sentence trying to find a way out of a prison cell. The following week he was back on again at Sammy for the loan of a gun for his mother's boyfriend.

"I don't sell or loan guns. Why are you on my case about it?"

"I dunno why he wants it. Maybe he needs to do a job and doesn't want the piece traced."

"Can't help you with that boy, don't want to get into nothing illegal." That got a good laugh around the fire.

"Yeah, Sammy is up for hitman of the year, so he don't want to blot his copy book," Sting said.

Baz looked like someone kicked him in the head, so he dragged himself off to the far side of the bonfire and whipped out his phone, muttering into the mouthpiece like a madman.

He loomed back into view, his eyes staring out of his head like hot coals.

"He wants to know how much it would be to shoot someone."

Now that was more like it. Sammy could handle a shooting, like he was born to do it. Sammy gave him a flick of the eyes and a brief nod and Baz grinned like a maniac. Whoever his mother's boyfriend was, he'd sure got under Baz's skin.

"I'll be happy to do the honours," Sammy said with a bow. "Looks like your mother's friend isn't the shooting type."

So, the following night Baz drove Sammy in his vandalised old Honda Civic that belched black smoke to a garage on the east side of the city. The dangerous part of the dodgy Red City. They parked at the side of the garage and Baz lit a cigarette and fiddled with the radio. After a few minutes a middle-aged, balding man with a pot belly and a narrow moustache opened the rear door and creaked into the back seat. Sammy could hear him patting the side of his leather jacket, like he was checking for his wallet. It was the boyfriend. Sammy knew him only by the name of Judd.

167

Sammy tried to sneak a look at Judd, who was staring hard at the back of the seat, breathing heavily through his nose. He could barely see him in the darkness. "Eyes front," Judd commanded. Sammy shifted around in the passenger seat but kept his gaze straight ahead.

Judd's target was his wife. He was leaving her for Baz's mother, but he didn't think she could manage without him.

"We have no kids," he said like he was reading out bingo numbers. "I can't think of her in the house night after night on her own with dirty dishes piling up and the fridge full of rotting food." He paused like he was just about to say something else. Sammy snuck a look in the rear mirror but still couldn't see his face. Judd's breathing got heavier, his breath, filling the small car, smelled of cigar smoke.

"Think it over, make your mind up over the Christmas." He was gone as quick as he came.

Through the thick cigarette smoke Baz and Sammy peered out over the twinkling lights of the Red City that spread before them like stars, the semi-circles of the Seven Arch Bridge looking like they were suspended in dense fog in the distance. Baz said nothing, flicked his half-smoked cigarette out the window. His hand shook as he reached in for another smoke. Sammy couldn't hold it in. "Who the fuck says something like that? *I can't think of her with the dirty dishes and the rotting food.* Tell me she's torched his beamer or that she's poisoned his mother for the insurance. A prick like that don't deserve to live."

Back in the old days, before all the shooting madness started, before the gang started spending the evenings sitting around smoky, eye-burning bonfires summer and winter, hatching plans that never went nowhere, Sammy and his gang used to go swimming in the freezing water under the Seven Arch Bridge that spanned the river on the edge of the Red City. They fished there with twine and rusty hooks when they were kids. It was out of the way of things, a place you could be yourself with no one bothering you. A place to hide away, to scribble *Baz loves Dave* on the red sandstone of the bridge and not get in trouble for it.

Down through the years, dozens of people topped themselves by jumping off the Seven Arch Bridge. The stories were told and re-told by generations of city people. Sammy would relate these stories to the gang around the bonfire on winter nights, freaking out the younger ones. The jumpers were from all walks of life, dealing with their own crap in their own way. Only a handful survived. The survivors were asked what they thought about on their way down the long drop to the surface and they all had exactly the same thought. I wish I hadn't jumped. I had so much to live for.

Two days after Christmas Sammy met Judd for the second time. This time he was alone, waiting in his green Escort at the side of the same garage where he and Baz met him a few weeks before. Sammy had a pistol in a holster behind his back and a mind that was firmly made up. He planned to do a job all right, but not the job Judd was going to pay him ten grand for. He was going to shoot Judd, two hot pops in the back of his head as soon as he turned around. Prick didn't deserve to live after what he wanted to do on his wife who, as far as Sammy could see, had never done anything to him.

Sammy tightened his grip on the piece as Judd walked up to the car from behind, in his blind spot, and sat in the rear seat. And then it hit Sammy, like a train thundering from a tunnel. He should have spotted it the first time. *Fuck, I should have spotted it.* The way he crept up and got in without a word, the fluid movement of arrogance. Sammy's instinct kicked in, but too late. Cop. Judd was a fucking cop. He held the piece for one mad moment longer, that contained in its palm all the potential screwups of his short life. But he knew it was useless.

Sammy was shitting a brick now. Without turning his head, Judd said he would bring his wife to the train station the following evening because she was heading off to stay with her sister overnight. He said he would ring Sammy around eight and pretend to order a pizza. He'd park near the front of the station and go into the pizzeria, leaving her in the passenger side of the car.

"When I go in, you go over and shoot her. Make it quick and make it clean." He handed him gloves and plastic sleeves to keep the gunpowder off his arms, ordering him to throw them away afterwards.

"Get rid of the gun," he droned. He got out of the back seat as arrogantly as he had got in and was about to disappear into the night. Then a disembodied voice. "Don't even think of snitching. You'll be dead before the first word leaves your mouth."

Judd knew who he was, where he was, what he was. He had him where he wanted him and Sammy knew he had to go ahead with the hit. He was trapped. When he'd gone Sammy was drenched with sweat and his heart pounded like an out of control piston. He thought: I could do with a drink, a long, long drink. As soon as this job is out of the way, I'm going on a bender from hell. And then take Baz out.

It was 8:45 p.m. the following night and Sammy waited in his car outside the red-brick station. A few minutes later Judd drove up with his wife, jumped out and crossed over to the pizzeria, looking furtively at Sammy for an instant as he walked past.

Sammy had to act and act fast, even though this was risky, went against all his instincts. Self-preservation and not getting caught were always foremost in his mind. When carrying out a hit he would plan meticulously, prowl the scene of the crime like a panther for days beforehand, considering every detail, second-guessing every danger, watching exits, entrances, anything that could get in the way of the cleanly-executed hit. He'd shadow his victims, observing their habits and preferences, didn't act until they were in the middle of a group, to make sure there were people around. Then determined, swift, silent he'd drift into the group, two quick pops from the silenced pistol and he'd blend, then fade into the crowd, the darkness. That's how he was so successful, how he never got caught. But here he was dealing with Judd, an amateur in the world Sammy knew so well. Amateurs could get you caught or killed.

He moved fast, strode over to the car and broke the passenger window with a wrench. To make it look like a robbery, he demanded the frightened woman's handbag. She screamed and reached for something—her seat belt, her bag, he couldn't say in the sudden confusion.

But then there was a feeling he'd never experienced before, and even before he pulled the trigger, he knew this was going to be different than all those other times he had popped bullets. Time slowed down, all his movements slowed right down to almost stop. His chest tightened so he found it hard to breathe and the thought of what he was about to do felt like a juddering bolt from a gun that he held against his own temple. He was fighting with an inner voice about whether he should fire or not. He tried to say something to the panicking woman, but the words were like fire, choking him in his throat. He was rooted to the spot like a statue, his fingers made of stone as he tried to pump the trigger, but nothing happened.

The woman stared at him like a face deep under water, as if she were suddenly calm, then her mouth seemed to open and close like a large fish's and she shouted something at Sammy who didn't understand what she'd said and he don't wait to find out as he shot her three times and she slumped over the gearbox. He was back to his car in a flash and there were screeching tyre marks and smoke on the roadway.

Sammy got back in time for the TV news and learned that Judd's real name was Sgt. Terry Cole, a cop based in the western suburbs of the Red City. His wife's name was Dora. Sammy rushed out the back door of the flat and threw up before burying the pistol in a hastily dug hole in the flower bed. He couldn't remember much of the rest of that night. The TV droning in the background, moving pictures and flashing blue lights, disembodied voices, dabbing his sweating face with a tea towel. Dora's picture was flashed repeatedly on the TV screen. A young dark-haired smiling woman with high cheekbones and serious blue eyes. Sammy couldn't get the image out of his mind and even when he closed his eyes it was still there, like the afterimage of the orange flames of the bonfires.

I looked at Sammy who had been silent for a time, seeming to drift off into the reverie he'd been telling me about for the previous hour, ignoring his beer bottle and cigarette that was propped against the counter, its white smoke weaving a narrow white path up to the ceiling. With a sudden shock, he was present in the bar again and looked at me with wide eyes, as if he had just woken from a nightmare. "Christ, I killed an innocent person," he said, as if it had just happened. "I said I'd never go down that road and when I did it, I knew nothing would ever be the same again." He looked at me for a long moment, and his eyes seemed to dance in his head, and then he looked past me, out into the street where the light was fading, and his expression relaxed. He buried his face in his hands and remained silent for a long time before continuing the story.

From that night on the heat was intense, cops were crawling all over the Red City and anyone who was even remotely involved in crime was being turned over. A cop's wife had been hit and every seedy stone in every low life's nest was being forensically examined. Suddenly, armed cops were poking their noses into the well-oiled enterprises of low life criminals all over the city. Sammy left his flat through the back door and wandered around the city over the following days, sleeping on floors and broken sofas. He was frightened all the time. Not, like you might think, about being caught or about anyone coming after him to get revenge for what he had done. He couldn't have cared less about that. He was frightened all the time about what he had done to that woman, about what he'd turned into. And bit by bit he became weary of being frightened all the time.

A week after the shooting he made his way to the silent bridge in the weak dawn light and stood on the parapet, holding to his left temple the gun he'd used on Dora. He held his breath and closed his eyes but, before he could pull the trigger and send himself hurtling headlong into the cold waters of the river that would be turned red in the morning light, he felt Dora's presence near him. He sensed her as she put her hands to the side of his head, stopping the bleeding before it had even started. He had a feeling of inexplicable well-being and opened his eyes to see her looking softly at him, her eyes sad, her brow furrowed.

Sammy stepped back from the edge that morning. The next day he heard that Sgt. Cole's body had been found in a local park overnight. He's shot himself with his cop pistol. The following morning he left the Red City, cloaked and hidden by backstreets and sideroads. He hitched a lift to Dublin, got a lift to Paris from a haulier and eventually made his way to Rome, where he got a job as a cleaner.

I didn't see Sammy for a week after he told me the story. One morning as I was moving back the shutters to open the bar for the day's trade, he was standing in front of me with a grey backpack by his side. He looked closely at me with those dark inscrutable eyes and held out his hand, which was moist and hard when I shook it. He said nothing but I knew that he was heading back to the Red City to hand himself in. He turned on his heel and walked back down the sun-drenched street towards Termini, past the finance cops who investigated fraud and smuggling and who stood at the doorway of their headquarters, leering at women walking past in high heels, until he blended like a shadow into the crowds of tourists.

LZ Nunn

Argentina

I.

A road stretches along the pampas
like a run-on sentence.
All those rusty station
wagons and Peugeots so old
your grandfather could be grinning
from the driver's seat like a scene
from Fellini—wearing a Santa hat
and green boxers, his eyes blazing
with weird joy.

II.

Between the rolling stones, an ocean
stained by iron ore
all the way upriver
in God-knows-where
South America, where the land
of silver began, where bees swirl
in drowsy backwards circles,
the piranhas tangle beneath the murky
surface, and high above
in the slick dark leaves
the jaguar waits, poised
over earthbound prey
in suspended animation.

SIX

Michael Casey

a poem for Emily Blunt

at the reunion
I had a nice talk
with a girl
I never spoke to
in high school
I enjoyed talking with her
and thought she enjoyed it too
also as well
and then she said
I should like to talk
with you longer
but I don't want to

David Moloney

Too Late for Beginnings

When John gets lazy, I try to pry him off his sofa, the one he sprawls across, hugs the throw pillow under his chin, and we play darts. "It helps with coordination," I tell him. He groans like an indifferent teenager on summer break. "Hit one bull's-eye and you can lay there till I leave."

He pushes himself up into the downward dog, his hairy arms shaking. He laughs madly at himself. When he gets to his feet, I hand him three green darts. I can see in his face determination. He wants the couch. He wants Judge Judy. He wants Dr. Phil.

He positions his socked feet at the toe-line, a piece of electrical tape on the carpet. John closes his left eye and throws his first dart. It travels half the distance of the board and dives into the carpet. It sticks and wiggles. John laughs again, a gruff, guttural laugh. It takes much effort, but it is his favorite thing to do, laughing.

"I thought you were a muscleman," I say. "You throw like my Aunt Beth."

John punches my arm but not with a clenched fist. His knuckles hit straight bone. It stings and he rocks back and forth as if we are about to fight.

"Take a joke, big man."

He lines up another throw, practices by bending his elbow a few times, then fires a dart and scores a five. He doesn't blink. He's a half-a-foot taller than me, about 6' 4". He wears a *Star Wars* T-shirt with Han Solo wielding a blaster pistol, jean shorts high above his knee, and bright white tube socks pulled tight up his calf. John never left the decade where he lost part of his brain.

He mouths mockingly, "*Take a joke, big man*," a minute after I said it. He lines up another throw, cocks his large hand behind his ear, and fires his third dart into the bull.

An hour later John snores on the loveseat and I'm stuck watching Judge Judy. If I change the channel, his eyes will pop open and he'll snap his fingers at me until I change it back. I rifle down a sleeve of Oreos. The screen door in the kitchen screeches open then smacks shut. John wakes up and licks his chapped lips.

Grocery bags crash on the linoleum kitchen floor. "Don't help or nothing!"

I follow Tammy out to her van and hoist bags of food out of the back of it. "What's he like today?"

"Same as always," I tell her. I wonder if I have black cookie stuck in my teeth.

"Explain to him I'm in a rush," she says, but she says it like she isn't sure he'll buy it, and unconcerned if he doesn't.

I ask, "How's Kerryn?"

"Happy." My face must have changed. "Don't pity yourself so much. It isn't attractive." She drapes the last of the bags on my outstretched forearm. "Get him moving. A few days of lying around takes weeks to get back. Go for a walk on the boulevard. He likes to pet the dogs."

He's afraid of dogs.

While I'm unpacking the groceries, John shuffles into the kitchen. He makes his way to the sink and peers out the window. His groceries are much like mine: white bread, pound of American cheese, boxes of mac 'n' cheese, taco kits, ground beef, mini-marshmallow spiked cereals, chalky nutritional shakes, corn chips. Things food stamps cover. As I put the last of the cereal away in the pantry, John backs away from the window.

He asks, "How she look?"

"Same as always," I say. "She was in a super rush." I search his face for a sense of longing. I'm not sure if I want him to feel loss, or undoing, or if it's better for him that he can't conjure those sentiments.

He cups his chest and smiles. "Her boobs?"

"Covered up, John. I didn't get a look." He always asks. I entertained him once and he got a visible hard-on behind his wind pants. He wasn't shy about pointing it out.

He plops belly first on the couch. "It's the deal," he says when I disapprove. I feel like I'm not doing my job. I don't get paid much but I like John. I used to come over and visit with Kerryn. I guess Uncle John liked me enough to get me on Aunt Tammy's budgeted payroll. I never let him beat me at chess.

John sleeps heavily, his deep snores loud enough to knock the Bruce Lee photos off the wall. I'm bored. We are mostly confined to the kitchen, living room and bathroom when I hang out with John. The bathroom is the trickiest room to navigate, with John's big frame and all. Plus me. I sometimes wonder if that's why Kerryn brought me around, kept me around. To help John lower his pull-on jeans, get in position, and half-the-time make it in the bowl, and then wipe up where he missed.

His bedroom door is shut, and when I open it get a strong whiff of meat sauce, remnants trapped inside from last night's dinner. The room is small, his twin bed covered in tossed sheets and a throw blanket. The walls are bare, unlike the living room. It isn't much. A picture on the dresser shows a normal John in a white button-down, Tammy with a permed mullet, and a toddler in the same outfit as John. Most likely Cody. The room depresses me.

John's house is small. It's one of those modular homes built remotely, trailered in and set on a foundation. There's a good amount of them in this neighborhood, close proximity to the ever-flooding Merrimack River. A kid I grew up with lived in one. He told me it was similar to the military housing he lived in in Alabama. I always thought it'd be cool to live in one of those, as if a military home was equipped with experimental gadgets, laser beams that cooked whole chickens, alarm clocks with hands that reached out and tickled you awake. Until I was in one. It was nothing more than a tiny apartment with ordinary coffee makers, where you still had to mow the lawn and shovel the driveway and take care of the roof.

"You're a lazy ass," I say to John when I notice he blinked himself awake.

He snaps at me. "You. You want to see lazy?" He snaps again while he sits up. He has drool on his chin and sleep marks on his cheek. The late afternoon sun comes in hard through the picture window and beats on his face. His sideburns are wet with sleep sweat.

I say, "Tammy is going to fire me if she sees you sleeping all day."

He points to a stack of VHS tapes on top of the VCR.

"What about them?"

"Find one says MJ con . . . MJ contest."

It's the one on top and I put it in. I ask him if the VCR is hooked up and he nods sarcastically with his eyes wide. When he opens his eyes wide, he looks normal, like he hadn't had a piece of his headgear break off and lodge into his brain during a kickboxing match. Like he hadn't gone from man to child in the blink of a swift roundhouse.

The tape starts fuzzy, the borders static, then the picture settles in. The view is from a stationary camcorder at the top of a basketball hoop. It's a high school gymnasium. The rolled-out bleachers are full of people. The noise is loud with "Kiais" and wood snapping and fists tumbling stacks of stone. Men in Karate uniforms of different colors pace the gym floor and watch as other men compete. After a few minutes, John snaps again and points to the top right of the screen. I recognize him, but he's limber, standing tall in a snowy white uniform, his black hair wavy, his shoulders wide. He towers over the man stacking stone. TV John settles up, raises his hand and practices a few times, slowly, like he had before throwing the dart, and he smashes through the stack, his hand following through to the floor. People cheer but he keeps his head down and walks off to the bleachers and sits alone.

John claps a single clap. "Fuck yeah."

"Jesus," I say. "How many stones was that?"

"I dunno."

"Did it hurt?"

"You think?"

We watch some more. There's an intermission, and the floor is cleared. A group of men roll out a wooden frame, which looks like a bed, and leave it in the center of the gym. On top of the frame looks metallic. I ask what it is with a little too much excitement in my voice, and John tells me it's a bed of nails.

"Nails?"

"Yes," he says, and laughs in a deep, hee-haw stutter.

The bleachers fill again and the PA kicks on. The announcer

explains this is a contest only for the wicked, the toughest badasses on the planet, only the ones who can walk the walk, talk the talk. The crowd loves it, wants more. The contest calls for contestants to lie on the bed without a shirt. There are four men with paddles around the contestant. Whoever can withstand the most blows without quitting, wins tickets to see Michael Jackson in concert. John tells me to fast forward. I do and stop when he snaps.

"Watch."

TV John walks up to the bed of nails to cheers and hisses. He pulls off his shirt. He looks like a gladiator. He plays the crowd, looks up to a spectating emperor somewhere off camera. He rolls onto the bed and stretches his arms horizontally above his head. The announcer yells, "Begin!" The paddlers whack, and the crowd keeps count. John is the final contestant. The top score is thirteen. When the crowd yells "Fourteen!" John doesn't move. The paddlers stop for a moment, but John lowers a hand and snaps like he does to me. They hit him until they reach twenty, then the announcer says, "Enough is enough. Okay, okay. We get it!" John stands. His stomach is roasted.

Back in the living room, John snaps. He makes a jerk-off motion with his hand. "Tammy. In the parking lot. Parking lot after the concert."

***

Kerryn used to say I was annoyingly cute. She said it was endearing, though when I pressed her on *how* I was, she couldn't place it. "Maybe because you're always so fucking quiet. Or you're full of shit. Either way, it's cute." I can remember it because she'd said it the same way twice, and I had thought maybe she said it to others, it was a thing she did in the early push and pull of romance, but that was giving her too much credit. I'd been cute, then I became dull, then annoying, and she didn't have a nicer way of putting it.

The Ferris wheel brightly lit and dazzling in the night sky, stops to let passengers off. We sway at the apex and I look out over the boathouse, the Merrimack, to a line of cars idling on the Rourke Bridge, and hope maybe the occupants are jealous of people young enough to be dazed by the greasy seduction or old enough to be attracted by the carnival's oddball charisma. The bridge was supposed to be temporary, ten years max, but just surpassed its thirtieth year. A Bailey truss design, constructed of rectangles ganged together, the bridge is pleasing to drive across at night, passing the metal sides creates an illusion that you are driving faster than possible on a bridge that may never end. I shouldn't know of its design, but a bridge that shouldn't still be a bridge is much discussed—to fortify or to tear down—but never a consensus for a decision to be made, and from this view it wouldn't be a bad time to see it snap at its ends and splash into the black river, car lights poking through the wreckage like flashlights in a collapsed mine.

From afar, at least.

The operator of the ride has a freakishly long beard and a half-smoked cigarette tucked behind his ear. He gives a smile to the ground, which is more a suppressed laugh, one that I see far too often when I have John in public. I think *retard*. I don't think John is retarded. I fear others see that word right behind their eyes, in big, block letters, but try to shake it away, contain themselves, like a fart in church. *Retard*. Even in a place people regard as a refuge for castaways, misfits, a carnie can't help but accommodate his inner immaturity at someone different. *Look at this retard.*

To a child, the carnival can seem like the center of a universe. Games with promised winners, fast, clinking rides eliciting roars and screams, fried dough and French fries stuffed inside cups summoning a bubbling drool, the dings and blinks from the laser-guided shooting gallery, mechanized horse race standings, it all becomes *something*, a thing in itself, the dark world outside invisible behind the brilliant lights, a Nebula which sucks all existence around it, a great celestial event.

John loves the carnival. I'm ready to leave.

I eat fried pickles soaked in ranch dressing. I get him a cotton candy. We wade through the crowd, him bumping passersby, focused only on the blue swirl in his grasp. I'm fixated by his body presence, by the looks he gets as he trips on smooth grass, chin pointed at the sky, a glob of cotton candy escaping his furious chewing. I wonder if he's begun moving slower or if it's the end of the day tiredness or if he's too concerned about one task at a time.

"One more ride, big guy. Your choice."

We stop and he looks around. He chooses the Haunted House. There's no line. It seems more for huggy teenagers, but we mosey over as we finish the last of our snacks.

The operator looks very much like the Ferris wheel one, except this guy has a loop nose ring. Maybe it's a joke. Maybe he's followed us through some secret carnie tunnel, lazily messed with a disguise, only to get another look at John. A deeper look to better describe the *retard* over beers and smokes later sitting on milk crates, eating excess fries and rubbery foot-longs.

He asks to see our bracelets by wagging his wrist at us. We sit in a too-small cart, John tight up against me, and after two tries at buckling him in, the attendant gives up and flips a switch. We motor slowly through the corny ride. A Frankenstein monster rocks and shakes across our path, though there is no danger of collision. John says "Boo!" to rouse me. A mummy drops from the ceiling and he grabs my knee. It smells like a fog machine's belt is out. The spooky music is far louder than it needs to be. I watch John giddy and boyish, see him crashing through the stone. Him mounting Tammy in the backseat of a car. Him teaching Cody to kick above his head. I want to rush off the ride and tell that bearded carnie-fuck that John isn't a retard. He's a black belt. He's a lover. He has a son. But John lives in the past and present. John can't be a retard because he *isn't* anything.

A killer clown with long, yellow teeth pops out on John's side, and John jerks back then chops its head clean off.

**

When I first agreed to watch John, Kerryn had taken a job at a Residential Home for pregnant teenagers. She has a way with the downtrodden. I thought it noble at the time, heroic, and delivering chicken wings to college dorms and frat houses made me feel a bit inadequate. But now I think she did it to propel herself from my sunken orbit. Neither of us went to college or ever plan to now, being twenty-five and townies for life, but there are tiers in the workforce and non-profit certainly trumps food service. And I know it isn't that simple, her ghosting me, but it could be, right? My plan was to find something to do that was endearing, maybe even hopeful. Climb a tier. But I think John is too close to Kerryn, being her uncle, and she can't quite see the sad case he is or the decency in the leap I've taken. Jesus, I can barely care for myself.

Today, Tammy has asked me to take John to the gym. "He belongs to one, you know, so maybe we should be taking him there? Thanks." She speaks like she has phlegm in her throat. I keep imagining her with a perm, a *Ride the Lightning* T-shirt, her face soft and young and not a wrinkled mask of bloodless coloration that comes with heavy smoking. And also without the poorly painted-on eyebrows and sagging double chin. Her condescension is fleeting because her only pedestal of superiority is that she'd married John and borne his son and collected the settlement. But John took the heavy blow.

I didn't know about the gym. Getting John into my KIA Optima wasn't impossible, but it felt like it was. We maneuvered it like we were moving a couch into an apartment. He tried one leg first but couldn't lower his head far enough to squeeze in, so we backed out. Then we tried his ass first. He backed in and fell, whacking his head on the car. He laughed at the clusterfuck we'd entered. I asked him how Kerryn or Tammy got him out of the house, and he said, "Van, dummy." Our final attempt had John kneel on the driveway and lay his chest across the seat. I leaned over him and guided his hands to the steering wheel across the center console. He grabbed tightly. It was a humid day, as late July tends to be, and I could smell his sweat, earthy like soil. I hoisted his heavy legs like a wheel barrel and slowly drove him deeper into the car, him giggling, pulling his weight on the steering wheel. Once his entire body was inside, I lowered his feet to the passenger side floor mat and his body fell into place. We both exhaled deeply, and I wiped my hands on my shorts.

We listen to classic rock with the windows down and John plays stunted drums on the dashboard. This becomes an everyday thing, at least the days I work. John enjoys the gym and I don't mind spotting him. While his hands are a bit gnarled, he can still grip the bar tightly and push decent weight for high reps. Leg work is the hard part, but I don't push him to do squats. He does leg extensions, which are enough. Sometimes, especially if the gym is busy and we catch other gymgoers staring, John plays up his spotty speech. He mumbles and drags his feet then lies down under a bar and pounds out twenty reps of 135. The scrawny high schoolers sometimes tap each other on the arm, and some take out their phones to get digital proof.

The summer goes by slowly. Some afternoons, after he'd lifted and showered, John would pass out on the couch, leaving me to cable TV and my own thoughts. Whenever I heard a car pull up to the house, I ran to the window to see if it were Kerryn. It never was, and I had that sallow heart condition of lost love. It was pitiful and childish but instead of getting over her I waited for her. Sometimes I am glad to see her move on. I am waiting for—what? There has been no search for my future and no involvement from my mother. She is the kind of mother who goes to the Billerica Library on Wednesday nights to meet local authors and pretends to care about their books. She does yoga on Friday nights with other divorcees on the Play-Doh-covered rug in the library's Children's Room. She watches *The Bachelor* with passionate concern for the contestants. Each night, she makes a hamburger for her Toy Poodle, Sebastian. I imagine she was the curly-haired, freckle-faced chubby girl who had good grades, sat alone in the cafeteria, but knew all about the cool kids' relationships, down to the intimate, fly-on-the-wall details. Or, she'd make them up and fantasize about them. She's the kind of wife a husband cheats on.

But my mother has never asked about *my* relationships. After my father left for the west coast when I was eleven, I was allowed to roam the city on my Dino BMX bike, find places I could wipeout safely enough to leave a superficial mark but not break anything. I always asked for Band-Aids, which she started to keep well-stocked. She made pasta-heavy meals. I tried to compliment her. I'd say, "Nice earrings, mom." Or, "That shirt looks good on you." The compliments landed somewhere between her commanding me to wash my hands or telling me I look more and more like my father each day. I think maybe I have little understanding of women, but how cliché is that? Maybe I understand them quite well, or sufficiently, but I've only come across women at transitional times.

***

"Your hair is getting long," Tammy says.

"Thank you."

"Maybe it's time," she says.

I watch Tammy maneuver around John like he isn't there. The way she chews gum, working up an excessive amount of saliva, audible even, makes me hungry. She wears a red hoodie with Mickey's face centered with cutoff jean shorts. John watches her from his position on the couch. Outside, the fall rain comes down hard, tapping the rhododendron leaves outside the cracked window.

"You knew Cody was coming, right?" She brushes hair from her face so I can see her anger. "The one day a month I need the place clean like John isn't a sloppy invalid."

Invalid is much better than retard, but it invokes the same cringiness up my spine. John doesn't seem to notice. Tammy continues to pick up sunflower seeds (John's favorite) and can tabs off the rug.

"I just—" Tammy stops herself and holds her hand up to me.

"I'm sorry but there was no note. I had no idea," I say. "You should put it on the calendar or something?"

"What calendar, Chris? Where's this thing you call a calendar around here?"

She licks her finger, bends down, and wipes crud off of John's cheek. He sits still, even sticks his chin up.

"I'm sorry. I know it's a big day for Cody."

"It's fine," she says and wipes her forehead. "Kerryn was

supposed to call you. Text you. Whatever. I should be taking it out on her."

"I think she lost my number."

"Here's the deal, Chris." There's my name again. I only hear my name when someone is going to scold me or levy advice. "You come on too strong. Needy like. When John and I got together, it was all fun. Weeks at the beach, concerts, we drove to Florida and back just for shits. You're young. Loosen up. Cut your damn hair. Maybe try some of the weights when you bring John."

"Sure." I make myself useful and pick up the loose laundry on the floor and behind the couch. John likes to go through ten pairs of socks a day.

"I'm not trying to be mean. I'm trying to help."

She tells me to comb John's hair while she goes to pick-up Cody. I climb on the couch and sit along the top open-legged, my feet at John's sides. I'm straddling his shoulders, but I don't want to think of it that way. I run a comb with a pink handle through his knotted black hair. The bristles catch thick knots and I work through with force, but John doesn't wince. He claps at something on TV and laughs and I can't help but tug a bit harder on the knots.

***

Cody calls John "uncle" and for all of the visits so far I've stepped outside to what little of a backyard John has and picked mini Christmas tree-shaped weeds out of the grass. Long stems and prickly leaves. I usually make a pile of them in the middle of the yard. My fingers would smell like my father's musk aftershave. From how I remember it. The resemblance and memories the weed evokes makes me wonder if retreating out to the yard during the visits are a better choice than staying inside.

But for today's visit, with the rain coming down, I decide to tough it out. Cody gives me a dap and I admire his flat-rimmed Sox hat. It's pristine. Tammy shuts off the TV, and John taps his knee, inviting Cody to sit on it. But Cody is twelve, the age when boys tend to sprout, becoming clumsy in their newfound length, and even under normal circumstances decide to create an emotional bubble around themselves. When a boy discovers his sexuality, understands or tries to understand the workings of his manhood, fear of everyone around him knowing what he's been doing lives largely in the forefront of his mind. It's a terrifying time, and the only time I can think of being worse is when you open up that quiet intimacy to another person and it doesn't work out. But that's putting growing up simply.

Cody doesn't sit on John's lap but finds the cushion next to him.

"I'm going food shopping," Tammy says and wraps her purse strap over her shoulder. "The cabinets are bone dry."

Cody and John nod so in synch, so indistinguishably, that I want to point it out. As soon as Tammy is gone, I realize my presence is making it difficult for Cody and John, probably mostly Cody, but I really do not know what to do with myself. I sit in the recliner. Out of habit, I look to the blank TV. I notice the VHS tapes where John's feats of strength rest.

"You ever seen *Terminator*?" I say.

Cody shakes his head.

"One of my favorites. I love time travel stuff."

Cody reaches across John, grabs the remote, and puts the TV on. We watch a college football game. I go to the kitchen to get some snacks, but after a quick search of the pantry and cabinets I realize Tammy wasn't kidding about John having no food. I scrounge the fridge and find a block of cheddar cheese and some ham. I cut up the cheese on a paper plate and roll up slices of ham. I put the cheese stacked in the center of the plate and line the perimeter with the ham slices. I make it look nice. I sneak a few bites before heading to the living room.

I put the plate on the coffee table. John's asleep. Cody grabs a piece of cheese and chews it.

"He always falls asleep," he says.

"Moving around takes a ton out of him."

"Yeah, well, wasting Saturdays here takes a lot out of me. I hate coming here."

I lean forward and grab some cheese. "I get it. Trust me, I do. But it means a lot to your uncle that you come."

Cody looks up to the ceiling. "Not you, too," he says. He looks back to the football game. "I know he's my dad I'm not an idiot."

"I didn't think you were."

We eat more cheese and watch the game. John is snoring loudly and he's sliding towards Cody. Cody shoves John's shoulder to straighten his large body out.

"Kerryn told me when I was ten. Said she couldn't stand everyone lying."

"I guess it's good then that she broke it to you."

"I would've found out anyways."

John sneezes himself awake. He smiles at Cody and slaps Cody's thigh. "Hey buddy," he says. "You're my buddy."

***

John's legs were getting tight, so we went to the therapist. The muscle-faced man told me to stretch John. He showed me some. Stretches. I took mental notes but knew John wasn't game.

I take John home and we watch *Ren and Stimpy* on DVD and order two pizzas and a large fry. John rocks and wipes his mouth with the purple afghan Tammy draped over the couch.

"How's Kerryn?" I ask.

He chews loudly. There is a moth in the room that steals his attention. I snap my fingers at him.

"How's Kerryn?"

"She chubby now," he says. He pinches his hips. "Big and fat."

"She ever ask about me?'

John laughs his deep laugh. He haw. He haw. "Always," he says. "She don't stop."

I bite into hot cheese and the sauce is hot enough to burn my tongue.

"Say I asked about her."

John swipes a fry through thick ketchup.

"Scaredy cat," he says. "You. You do it."

***

Kerryn draws from her straw and doesn't look at me. I ask about the residential home, and she explains the women there need privacy. HIPPA. Can't talk about it. Sun beats in through the thick glass and my cheeks are hot.

"But how do you like it?"

She slurps. "It's my passion," she says. There's something outside the glass she's intent on watching.

She is a goddess. No, she isn't. She's goddess blonde, sure, but her hips wouldn't draw a thousand ships. I honestly don't care about what she looks like. I gained a few inches myself. I think I love Kerryn. Sure, just being Kerryn is enough to be a goddess.

"I got John crushing weights," I say.

"He needs it."

The fast-food dining room smells so salty I want a juice box. Kerryn looks tired. She's spoken enough—I can tell—more than she intended. At the counter, change slides down the shoot for a waiting customer. I dab a fry into a cup of ketchup. Her mouth is uninterested.

"What was it you wanted to talk about? What is so pressing about Uncle John?"

"Have some of my fries," I say.

"No," she says. "Nope." She looks off and finds a reflection off a windshield. "You love Uncle John. I love that you love him. He needs someone like you. You're perfect for him. But I shouldn't have come. I believe relationships should just end. I don't enjoy this part. You're going to play a game and that's all it'll end up being. A dumb game."

I want to talk about Cody. I think someone should. I look for a long time at an old women's face. She holds it so well. She eats so slowly she's frozen. Like a picture. A face I'll never forget. Someone must care for her. A son. A daughter. There's no way she takes care of herself.

"Stop staring," Kerryn says. "What are you doing?"

David Zoffoli

from *anguish is intimate: a widower's walk*

8

alone i'm traveling to Firenze thru Dublin
to stand on the famous bridge and say
i love you more today than all our yesterdays
and traveling alone i've packed a picture of us
as we did secretly for each other
our wedding ceremony's right after moment
that celebrates equality and i remember
how downright happy you were to be out

to be proud to be married to me and so
optimistic about our future our plans
our downright joy and right to be together
forever. forever. breathe. in and out.
in and out. off and on. the toggle switch
of your last breath will haunt me forever.

11

i can't imagine moving beyond us, you
are riding shotgun and make these moments
interminable. Who am i now after you
before you after our sentient life? Alone
tonight, headlights approach through the trees
and present a snapshot worthy of you
and us, they drive by our home silently
giving me hope and promise and love.

i planted paperwhites before i left and
they're all blooming, fragrance unique
and tonight i devoured them, heady
with passion and promise and love
for the man of my dreams and
the love of my life, kissing you deeply.

12

love of my life hold me
contain me with you
in our little home now tidy
without clutter without you, you.
containers of death: the body bag,
the hearse, the coffin, the urn,
and 12 small Tupperwares of you
distributed among the tulips.

i owe it to him to respect
every feeling, every memory,
every kiss, every icon in our
little home our little home
surrounded by hundreds of
acres nestled with little homes.

Gerry Murphy

On Her Hair

after the Irish, 15th Century

Your dark
intricate curls
would put Absalom's
luxuriant but lethal
hair to shame.
In your dusky tresses
a flock of parrots
could nest unnoticed
with a flock of nightingales.
Your perfumed ringlets
invite the bemused poet
to lose himself
and find himself,
then lose himself again.
I could remain entangled
in your black glossy locks
until Time's,
or my own
sorry end.

Gerry Murphy

Aphrodite Radiant

What if you could go back
to any particular time or place.

Listen again in a tumult of anticipation
for the rumble of her car in the cobbled lane.

The familiar whinge as the rusty gate
scrapes on the concrete path.

The dry squeak of her key in the lock,
her brisk steps clipping up the stairs.

The bustle and flap of discarded clothes
as she undresses on the landing.

And there she is, standing before you,
twenty-three-years-old to the very day.

That glossy black hair, that impish grin,
the *postponer of old age*, incarnate.

Kassie Dickinson Rubico

Church Lady

No one stopped the man with the torn jacket and tangled hair from going up on the altar that day. It was halfway through the 11:30 Mass. The man made it past the woman with the headscarf, who always sits in the front row, and past nine choir members. Father O'Malley continued blessing the gifts as the man stumbled by. Only one person seemed to notice: the small woman with short white hair. Some weeks she collects money; other weeks she reads scripture; this week, she held the man with the dirty hands long after the organ stopped.

Joseph Donahue

The Exhibit

Not until
I see
you seeing
those glowing
squares, those
legendary
splendors,
see you
caught up
lost in looking,
not until I see them
only in your
seeing
them,
will I ever
really see them,
really be
before them,
be in the truth of
those pulsing
colors, those
vibratory
gates
of shade.

Paul Marion

One Night

The good way
Don turned his
head and dropped
three nickels
into the bent
tambourine of
the Salvation
Army-man between
sips of 25-cent draft
and bites of pretzel
at the Old Worthen
in one of the high-
backed booths with
his three friends who
had stopped a cribbage
game when the deaf
Frenchman in a
blue-green overcoat
came to the table
with eyes of a
saint and handsome
brown gloves that
held the jingling
pan so our good
Christmas will
would get us to
push a few coins
his ever-loving way.

Ali Bracken Ziad

from *Place and People Without*

Inshallah

There will be more poets
On this land than there are people—
The lovers left their walk to the lepers
To pay the toll at St. Luke's steeple.
The bells were ringing out in
Scattered shouts,
Exhaling the rain
They drank created by brewery clouds.
Our time is drunk:
Half one in Blackpool
Six o'clock at the Opera House.
Work is the curse of the drinking class,
And Áine and Jimmy
Don't settle for an empty glass.
"I wouldn't mind some eggs—"
The bottom of Summerhill
Served a winter of empty kegs.
"You just finished an egg roll Jim—"
There is always more than one way to sin.
"—Áine. I needs to eat something to calm me nerves."
With the brewery on its last legs
What was once straight once was now in curves.
"—Take a gawk down the Old Tram Line Lane Jim
Before we cross the Boru Bridge."
There's nothing more frightening than an empty fridge.
"All I can see is that lad that can't play his didge."
Arête between the Lee will be Matthew's ridge.
—At least if we don't play our cards right.

The Bridge of St. Patrick

We walked on her for many years
Three culverts of text unfolded
Her faces faced the dam kissed waters
Like words of the oft-time read.
She lay and watched the whole place burning
And watched it grow all over again.
"Sure, she nearly drowned."
All the lads up on the hill
Said they had her in their prayers.
The men in yellow vests came
One day at a time,
They took her down.
Matthew said he saw her being put together again.
They stopped one day,
A ship rose from the deep stench of the Lee,
Brown waters drenched and tickled the reflecting light,
It cut little rapids on the tall ship's wooden body,
Trying to get back to its brown-green home.
Not one Corkonian believed Matthew
When he said he was sure he won a glimpse of its name.
Just a cod they said.
No wonder they undid the knot of the bridge:
To allow room for herself through they thought.
She said he said the name,
Something along the lines of Theseus.
And they laughed.
Sure no wonder we love you Matthew.
They said he was a rogue just like Mr. O'Connor.
He's got more stories than sense.
Sure didn't he say once
The smell of McCurtain Street was better than sex.
All faces frowned at that.
Of course, he'd say that,
He's got no taste.
So that was the day they closed Patrick's Bridge.

If you stand on her midpoint,
Look up at Shandon,
Or gaze down towards Brian Boru,
You know you're at the centre of the universe,
And anything beyond is just a rumour.
Of course, you do,
You're from Cork,
Born and raised arrogant.
The day they opened her up again,
I didn't recognise her Jimmy.
And I wondered why she had a man's name.

Matthew

Echo Echo
Cornered on a stepping-stone and unstuck in time.
Garnished by moments manifesting the line.
Stone thunder on the lips, never eye for an eye.
Call on eclipse, where whispers fall, they must fly.
Master riddler, riddle me this:
What does have lips and still can't kiss?
Stoney man sat beside them despite being stood up.
"I have been drinking since I was this tall—"
The clock can hold his cup. Time was flat and not stuck.
"—Pana always changes yet I lay and luck."
Master riddler riddle me this:
What does have lips and still can't kiss?
Wearing the same jacket since eighteen-sixty-four,
"I had two fathers to be sure to be sure—"
"—If there's food to cook, I won't eat another book."
Someone sneezed; with them his in vain: "Matthew look."
Master riddler, riddle me this:
He still has lips and cannot kiss.

Los Borrachos

And the trumpeting golden angel
Bellowed the sounds of a full-stop
The day that our city's fathers'
Wishes were thought to be brought about.
Clear and blue north and south
No clouds to drink
No mellow mouth.
Flood defences tall and high
Cork a desert
Cobh was dry.
"Come here—"
The tolling of the non-iron-non-bell
Brought the faithless to their drying knees.
"—I heard there's a lad down in Skib
That's got some sauce left under lock and key."
Down here we use religion
And the sauce to keep us free,
Our golden mother bows to
Both a God and a brewery.
"I heard they had the black stuff
Still brewing up in Dublin bay—"
How could a pretender ever believe
The actor in the play?
"—Ah but sure that's about as real as God
Or the Wild Atlantic Way."
Sonia said she wouldn't run
Without something stronger than a firing gun,
And Mother Jones said we were but the same
Miners' children that chisel glass now instead of stone.
We chose Áine to speak to Bacchus the brewer's son.
"She'll twist his arm soon enough."
And that she did and said she'd do again.
She had no reserves
And told him God was the people

And not a father from the sun.
"Poor old Matthew will have to come down—"
No more room for temperance
When they open Iniscarra dam.
"—Sure, we can move him down
To Winthrop Street facing the GPO."
This time the people had no place
For flirting with a no.
Áine stood above yet with,
Now at Pana's vanguard in cradle of her kith.
"We feel sober when we're drunk."
She stood to ward off brewer's funk.
The golden trumpet ceased to play,
The coming of the final day.

SEVEN

Rose Keating

Guide to Hauntings

1. Inherit a house from your aunt Mary.

You were never close to her, but you didn't dislike her. She powdered her face with talcum and shaved her eyebrows and wore bright red lipstick, no other makeup. Her lips were thin, and her slash of mouth looked like an open wound when she smiled. She watched, but rarely spoke.

You will not be surprised to inherit the house, because everyone else is dead.

You won't need the house; you have an apartment of your own in the city. An apartment, roommates, a job. A life. You used to have friends as well, but you haven't seen much of them since Will. They were more his friends.

You used to have a Will.

You don't need the house but decide that you need a break. Pack quickly. Ring work and ask for time off. Put on the hoodie that he left behind and throw your bag into the backseat of the car.

Drive away. Drive faster than you normally would. You'll want to play music, to turn the volume up so high that the bass turns your brains to jelly. You won't do this because the only CD in the car is the mixtape he left in the slot.

Instead, open the windows wide and open your mouth wider. The air hitting the back of your throat like a punch, so hard you choke on it. Let it fill your lungs to bursting point. You would not be able to scream if you wanted to. Try to scream anyway.

When you get there, open the door and be surprised by the amount of dust. Evening sunlight pouring through the open windows of the hall, causing the dust particles to glow. Hovering in the air, like something solid, thick as honey. Breathe in heavy gold. Do not let it escape.

2. Unpack your things.

You won't bring much, just a couple of bags which you drag up the stairs. The steps are a musical instrument, giving off creaks and squeaks and moans with every movement you make.

Place your bags down on the bed of your aunt's room. There are many guest rooms upstairs and you could pick any; it's a country house, large, sprawling. But you want one already claimed. The room will be musty, cluttered with her things, smelling faintly of perfume. Put your things in empty drawers. Feel curious about the ones that are not empty.

Drag your hands across the surfaces, pick up the photo frames. Mary is alone in most of them, or with her sisters. Finger the knickknacks. Postcards and porcelain dogs and jeweled boxes filled with rings and feathers and buttons. Open her drawers: starched blouses, beige bras, socks with holes in the sole. Find a dildo at the very back, hidden inside a sock. You will feel like a voyeur but that won't make you stop.

Root around in her wardrobe. Slip on the black heels that you find, a size too big, sticking out over your tracksuit bottoms. Find a pile of paper at the back, thin and fragile as flower pressings. Letters. You won't understand the handwriting; messy, slanted, hectic. You can make out words at random: purple, mine, lungs, sea, run. They are all signed off "Yours." All from the same person, but you won't be able to make out the name. You catch parts, but never the whole.

Take one of the letters to bed with you, running your fingers back and forth across the paper as your breathing slows. Fall asleep with the lights on, clutching something that does not belong to you.

3. Be woken by a loud noise in the middle of the night.

A deep heavy bang will jolt you from sleep; the shock of it feeling like someone dropping your lungs into snow. Jolt upwards. The room will be black, although you won't remember turning off the lights. Blink into the darkness, dense as molasses.

Slug your way through the treacle dark to the light switch. Flick it on. Jerk back.

Letters plaster the walls, the ceiling. Hundreds of them.

Ink running from most of them, leaking on to the walls. Spin in a circle. The clear words leaping out at you—*purple, mine, lungs, sea, run.*

Be unsure what to do. Feel scared, but uncertain. Should you gasp? Cry? Scream? Watch yourself from a distant cinema screen. Imagine yourself in a billowing white gown, fainting dramatically into the arms of a dark figure.

Do none of these things. Pick up a pillow, a blanket and your phone. Take them with you to the bathroom downstairs. Lock yourself in there. Double lock the door. Climb into the bathtub with your blanket and pillow and try to make yourself comfortable. Go on to Will's Facebook page and scroll through the photos he has been tagged in.

Will, tanned, on the beach. Will at a party, a girl touching his arm, her face blurred. Will lying in the grass in a park, a sliver of stomach showing as he laughs in the direction of a woman with a pixie cut.

Click on her page next. Scroll through her tagged photos. Compare your heights, your waists, the size of her breasts and yours. Her eyes are very blue. Yours are not.

Keep clicking, until the sun comes up. You won't fall back asleep until then.

4. Almost drown in the bathtub.

Roll over in your sleep, breathing in slow and deep. Take liquid into your lungs, wake up spluttering and thrashing.

The bathtub will be full of ink. Soaking through your clothes, into your skin. You will be bruise-blue, stained to the bone.

A figure standing at the foot of the bath, looking at you. The outline of a man plastered in paper.

"Your breasts are about the same size as hers, really," he'll say.

The outline of a man will disappear, letters floating to the floor in his place.

5. Research.

Drag yourself from the bathtub, sopping and heavy. Walk to the kitchen, leaving blue footprints in your wake. Open your laptop and google "ghost."

Find definitions.

An apparition of a dead person which is believed to appear to the living, typically as a nebulous image.

A slight trace or vestige of something.

Vestige; a small trace of something that was once greater.

Did you know that the word ghost finds its origins in the proto-Indo-European root "to rage"? That the old Latin word for ghost, "spiritus," was a synonym for "breath"? That not all ghosts are dead?

Now you do. You click, click. Let the words swirl round in your stomach.

Image, spirit, breath.

Something that was once greater.

Parts, never the whole.

Rage.

6. Talk to the ghost.

Come prepared in battle armour. Spray yourself in your dead aunt's perfume. Rim your lips with red. Put on a white slip from her wardrobe. It clings to you in the wrong places; she was a smaller woman than you.

Light candles in her bedroom, play her old vinyls that scratch and whine in the gloom. Close your eyes and think of the taste of the night sky.

"I mean, you could have just said hello."

Open your eyes. The figure of a man lined with letters at the foot of the bed.

"Hello," you will say.

His head moving up and down, examining you. "You don't look one bit like her, you know. Not one bit."

Think about apologising for this. Do not apologise. "Have you ever heard of a fetch?" you will ask instead.

The ghost will scratch his head. "A fetch? It's a ghost, the ghost of a person who is still alive, to the best of my knowledge."

"Are they real?"

"As real as I am."

"Are you real?"

A smile. "Is the past ever very real?"

"That's a rubbish answer."

He will stop smiling. "Yes, yes it is," he will say.

7. Summon it.

Summoning is a tricky business. It requires procedure, ingredients, intention. But the man lined with letters will give you the recipe when you ask.

Take the mixtape out of the car and play it so loud that you can't hear yourself think.

Open a bottle of wine and drink it from a mug while crooning out the words of his favourite song.

Burn a lock of your hair. Takes the ashes, mix them with honey and the blood of a newborn dove. Smear the paste across your lips, your eyelids. Take a picture of this and put it on your Snapchat story.

Go outside and strip, wearing nothing but his hoodie. Dance until your feet bleed. Let the moon lick your skin. Howl until the wolves come. Let them fuck you in the toilet of a nightclub while their friends take a video.

Crawl from the club to the forest on your hands and knees and rub yourself in the dirt. Eat every rock in the forest until your stomach splits open. Check his Facebook in the forest while lying in a pile of your own entrails.

Bury your entrails in the ground and wait until a crow claws its way out of the earth. There will be a piece of paper in the crow's beak. A number that you deleted from your phone months ago on the paper. Dial the number.

"Hello?" the ghost will say.

"Hey," you will reply. The ghost sighs.

"Jane, please stop doing this. I asked you to stop contacting me. Just, just stop," he will say, and then hang up.

The man lined with paper leads you up to bed, puts the blanket over you.

"Sorry," he'll say, "Sometimes it works, sometimes it doesn't."

8. Banish the ghost.

Gather up all the letters. The words that you can understand sticking into you like blades.

Take all the parts that you understand and scribble them out with a pen until you can't see them anymore.

Take the letters and place them in the bathtub. Go get the mixtape and snap it in half and throw it in there too. Piss on his hoodie and give it to the crow to eat. Slit the crow's throat and drop it in the tub. Delete his messages. Block him on Facebook, Snapchat, Instagram.

Get oil from the kitchen. Pour it over everything in the tub. Set the lot on fire. Watch the whole thing burn.

The man lined with letters watching you doing this, looking at you with something that could be pity, or something that could be tiredness.

"Did you really think that would work?"

"Not really," you will say.

9. Perform a cleansing ritual.

The man lined with letters won't know how to do this and won't be able to advise.

But you will know. You have always known how to do this, even if you weren't always aware.

Go take a shower, not a bath. Turn the temperature so high it hurts. Scrub at your skin until all your blue bleeds away. Watch the ink wash away down the drain.

Put on an oversized t-shirt that is clean, and your softest socks.
Sweep away the ashes and bleach the bathtub until it gleams.
Pour salt around the boundaries of the house.
Throw out the milk that has gone mouldy in the fridge.
Reply to the concerned texts from Susan from work.
Pack your aunt's things into boxes.
Make tea brewed with holy water, mint and the memory of bright light on winter mornings.
Light a white candle in every room.
Let ice melt on your tongue.
Say the word "yes" over and over until it is the only word the walls can remember.
Burn sage.
When it rains, open up all the windows so that the house can remember what the sky tastes like.
Cry until the house floods.
Fall asleep in laundered sheets that smell of fresh linen.
Breathe.

10. Say goodbye to the ghost.

Meet the man lined with letters on the front porch, not in the bedroom of a dead person.

Do not smile at him but take his hand and hold it. Sit down on the porch together. He will put his paper arm around you while you email an estate agent about selling the house.

You will have avoided looking directly at the ghost for the entirety of this trip. You have looked at the outline of him. The shape of the ghost is all you know, because you don't know if you can live through seeing the sum of him. But now is the time to be brave.

Look at the ghost. It will feel like thrusting your hand in a deep fat fryer. Keep your hand in the oil until the pain feels as clean and clear as a crescendo. Look at him for five hundred seconds. Or for five hundred years. However long it takes. However long you need.

215

Do not say goodbye to him in words. Kiss him on the cheek and rise. Walk away.

(Look back, if you need to. You will need to. That is okay.)

Put one foot in front of the other. Do it again. Do this over and over again for the rest of your life.

Climb into your car. Drive away, slower than the way you came.

Take your time coming home. You'll get there, eventually.

Tom Sexton

In Praise of the Graveyard Shift

Whoever named it never walked out of an old brick
building at 6 a.m. to bird song and a sky not blue
but white like a china plate used only on holidays,
or watched the stars overhead during a break,
or saw how mist on an old car's paint could make
it appear almost new, or felt cold chrome on their palm
while opening the driver's door after a good night's work
that paid the bills and left a little over for the ponies.

Whoever named it never stopped at the small diner
down the road, the bullet-shaped one on a riverbank,
where after your face was known, a waitress would
set your mug of coffee with cream and sugar down
on the counter before you then scribble your silent
order on a blue-lined pad, a kind of benediction.

Willy Ramirez

No More Poetry

And let the words remain in silence.
I want to keep quiet.
No more metaphors.
I want to part with what I am.

But I will not speak of music or of sea waves.
Only of flesh and blood,
of bone and dust.
of earth and silence.

The time to invent and to contemplate has ended.
Words have intoxicated the essence of things.
No more poetry.

My body in the dirt:
the word, the poem, and the metaphor.

Willy Ramirez

Unease

There is an open wound,
a cut in the tongue,
a sty,
a broken bone,
a toothache.

There is a sowing of hatred,
the tension of pus ripening on the finger,
an infection,
a rotten lung.

There is a broken tree,
the unease from an incessant migraine,
a colic,
an open burn,
a torture of nerves and broken discs.

There is a wound and a sowing and a broken tree,
something injured between muscle and bone,
a nausea,
a smell of plague and winter.

Alex Hayes

The Mountain

Perched, gleaming, upon a precipice,
Home to colonies of lichen,
The glass mountain defies elements,
Chipped and tarnished, but it remains whole.

The people that made their lives here
at the foot of this shining peak,
Have let the detritus of ages
calcify around their culture,
Forgetting the days when mountains walked.

In time they prayed to the mountain,
To purge the malady from their hearts,
So they could meet each other's gaze,
Feigning reassurance of good health,
But the mountain could not hear them.

They remained marooned in their own minds,
Fumbling with symbols and noises
in futile attempts to pierce the eyes,
Wishing to be as transparent
as the enormity they worshipped.

The people of the mountain fractured
steadily across tribal lines,
And broke each other before their God
to wash away silence with blood.

Silence prevailed, as it always has.

When their thirst for war had been sated
and the time for them to heal had come,
They turned their backs on the mountain,

Proclaiming it to be mere glass,
and so they lost their sense of scale,
Casting their eyes down into the dirt.

Then the mountain moved; the giant awoke,
It obliterated their history
with a single step.

The oblivious titan lurched forward,
Inscrutable in motive, meaning, form,
Until by capriciousness or design,
It keels over and rends the earth apart,
To slumber again,
Be worshipped again,
And teach again the lesson of scale.

Joseph Donahue

Back

Chuang Tzu
asked the skull: What
do you want?
The skull
said: To be
rushing among
all those
who seem
still tumbling
from bed, to shower,
to street, to work,
hair still wet.
The river wind
must feel even fresher
for them,
a cold crown
to their
thoughts,
as they marvel
at the day's news
about minerals
found on meteorites . . .
I want to be,
the skull said,
back in
New York.

Sandra Lim

Remarks on My Sculpture

In 1973, I found myself engaged in a sort of assemblage
of odd pieces of organic material, connected in a series.
I asked the questions, what is a subject?
What are the isolations around what something is?
The shapes and dimensions of my figures, its volumes
of air and light and dew, had a fraught and transient quality.
I used string and wire, the scent of snow and winter dawn,
fanaticism. I hated less than the wholeness of a situation.
Hunger is a conventional metaphor for desire, and here
I use it simply—it is just what the hand does, where the
eye leads. The absent senses of a word on a starless night,
implied and precluded, mediate the tone of a condition.
Not instances of a geometry or some other larger order;
more or less thinkable, it is paid for by existence.

Alex Hayes

Architect and Shadow

Tumble, tumble tumble
into the arms of the Shadow,
Ephemeral cradle,
Purveyor of poisoned delights,
That pilferer of time
who slips a dagger under the
ribcage of best-laid plans.

And from atop the citadel
the Architect watches, weary,
as the darkness engulfs borders,
artfully crafted monuments,
Gleaming fractal designs of glass
implode, warp, and return to dust.

Eye to eye, now, formless smirk and defiant glare.

The Architect raises a hand,
and the great void splinters into
inky rainfall bursting upon
desiccated plane, seeping through
the innumerable gaping
wounds torn open by the Shadow.

Sable droplets travel
through unreal paths alluvial,
In time to coalesce
and, as always, spark life in shade,
While a solitary
figure prepares to birth a world,
Again, the wheel begins to turn,
Samsara of the heart.

Masada Jones

There Are Days When Lint and Hope

There are days when lint and hope are the only items
    in our pockets
We sing songs of encouragement to each other
Do not get it anywhere else
Know that our hearts have to be fuller than any space
    that is meant to rest our hands
Comprised of litter and pressure
Pearls
Stuffed in cycles and circumstance
We walk like overcome is our middle name
Head high
Determination in every step
Sometimes moving forward is not about choice
Just an understanding that there is no other place for us to go
    aside from up
And up we go
Even with there being so much against us
So many things not moving
Up
The ancestors knew all about this
All about struggle trying and repeating
Not everyone is able to recognize their own light
Be a flame
We have to help them wake up
We sing songs of encouragement for them
For those whose light switches don't flick on
For those who have forgotten the power of song
This little light of mine
I'm gonna let it shine
This little light of mine
I'm gonna let it shine
Let it shine
Let it shine

225

Let it shine
We walk like overcome is our middle name
Head high
Determination in every step
Sometimes moving forward is not about choice
Just an understanding that there is no other place for us to go
     aside from up
And up we go
This little light of mine
I'm gonna let it shine
Let it shine
Let it shine
Let it shine

Emilie-Noelle Provost

Death and the Modern Girl

One thing I've learned as I've gotten older—something no one ever tells you about, by the way—is that Death isn't just the thing that happens the moment that someone dies. It took me years to understand it, which is why I'm telling you about it now. Death is a presence, almost like a living person. The Ghost of Christmas Future. Joe Black. La Catrina. Azrael. The people who made those guys up knew what they were talking about.

Death has personality and soul, but if you see it don't get too used to the way it looks because Death changes its appearance all the time. It can show up in the most surprising places, too, when you least expect to see it—in the middle of a dinner party, for example (that happened to your Uncle Ray once), or on the side of the road while you're walking your dog.

It's a good idea to learn to recognize Death so you'll know when it shows up. That way, you can try to come up with some kind of plan. Occasionally, you can tell that Death is hanging around by a scent carried on the breeze, or by the way the light outside looks when you get up in the morning. Sometimes it's by the tone in someone's voice when they say, "Good morning," or when you find something in the pocket of an old coat that you thought you'd lost. Death is tricky, though, because often it doesn't want you to know it's there. It can blend in with its surroundings like one of those lizards that changes color to avoid being eaten.

I'm not telling you anything new. People have known about Death for ages. At least as long as people have been around. But you have to rely on your intuition to pick it out of a crowd. That's what they did before the invention of Google and all this new technology that's supposed to be able to tell you everything. When it comes to Death, your instincts are a lot more accurate than anything you can look up on your phone.

The first time Death showed up at our house, it was late on a Thursday afternoon. You were upstairs doing homework. I was trying to get dinner started in the kitchen, listening to one of

227

those news shows on the radio. I went out to get the mail and I'll be damned if Death wasn't just standing there on the front porch. He was a lanky teenager with a sneering upper lip, a battered skateboard tucked under his arm.

Death had come for your cat, Tish. I knew it was for her—she'd been losing weight for weeks. Poor Tish. I should have taken her to the vet right away and saved us all a lot of pain and heartache. But I just couldn't. I thought about the day we brought her home from the shelter, back when you were in the third grade. I wasn't ready for her to go.

But I learned my lesson. I can assure you of that.

As soon as I opened the door that day, Death marched right in and made himself at home. He stood in front of the refrigerator with the door open, eating leftover lasagna right out of the Tupperware container. For days, Death took over the television remote control and your brother's Xbox. His dirty socks littered the living room floor, making it impossible for us to forget he was there. Death doesn't like to be ignored.

Finally, knowing it was the only way to get Death out of the house, we took Tish to the vet and had her put down. What an awful day. Death stood right beside the vet's stainless-steel examining table the whole time with a snarky look on his face, like he had better places to be.

Tish died on a Monday. Telling you about it when you got home from school was one of the worst things I've had to do as a mother. But still, it was a relief when Death finally clicked off the television, pulled on his grubby denim jacket, hopped on his skateboard and rolled off down the street. After he was gone, we shut off the heat and opened all the windows.

When Death came for my great uncle Charles, she was a debutante in a faded white dress, a limp corsage circling her bony wrist. She sat outside on one of Uncle Charlie's deck chairs for three solid days and nights, even in the rain. Every time I looked out there she was. It was like she was waiting for some handsome young capitalist to come and ask her to dance.

The worst was when Death came for my mother, your *Mémé* Francine. One winter day, Death crept into her house on cat's paws, so quiet and low to the ground that no one ever knew it was there. Death lurked beneath the living room sofa for months, just waiting for the right time to show itself. You've never seen such persistence.

When Death finally emerged, he was a balding middle-aged man with a comb over and rotten breath. He got into the liquor cabinet and drank all of *Pépé*'s Canadian Shield. Drunk every night, Death parked himself right in the middle of the same sofa he'd been hiding under, slurring his speech while he made sarcastic comments about *Mémé*'s breast cancer. He smashed his whiskey glass against the wall and dared any of us to cross him.

Death even followed *Mémé* into the ambulance, Canadian Shield and all, when they finally came to take her to intensive care. She never made it to the hospital, though. Death jumped out the back someplace along Route 495. I don't think he liked the way those paramedics were looking at him.

Once you've seen Death a few times, you get better at spotting it. Sometimes it's the look in Death's eyes that gives it away, but often it's just a feeling you get. I felt it a couple of weeks ago when I was driving home from the grocery store. There was a car accident at the intersection of Clark and Main. Traffic was backed up for a mile. A few of the witnesses said they thought they saw a toddler riding a tricycle near the scene of the accident, but I knew better.

You can be as modern as you want, with your cellphone and Instagram account, your master's degree and high-level job. There's nothing out there that can predict when death will arrive at your door. Even the doctors don't know. They do their best with their chemotherapy and immunizations and triple bypass surgeries— and I'm not saying those things don't throw a few spikes under Death's wheels—but they're only slowing it down.

Now that you're grown up, I hope you can appreciate why I'm telling you all this. Someday, you'll be a mother yourself and you'll want your children to know.

One day, you might find Death sipping an espresso at a table near the back of your favorite café. He'll be wearing an Armani suit, one eye on the clock, the other on the *New York Times*. You should offer to buy him a drink, because you won't know who he's come for, or how long he'll stay.

Richard P. Howe, Jr.

The Marathon Bombing

With the past week's tragic and dramatic events now a part of history, life in Lowell can start edging back to normal. The primary for the special election for the U.S. Senate seat is a week away (Tuesday, April 30) and conflict at the City Council meeting will grab center stage for some. During the crisis, I found it hard to write blog posts: things unrelated to the bombing seemed trivial, and things about the bombing were coming in overwhelming waves from other sources. Best to stay silent. Before moving on, however, I wanted to post some observations from the week past, more for archival purposes than anything else.

News of the Boston Marathon bombing arrived at 3 p.m. last Monday, Patriots' Day. More than a decade after 9/11, my first reaction when told there had been an explosion at the Marathon wasn't "terrorist attack," although that reality set in quickly enough. The death toll was quickly set at three and the injured toll at fifty. My expectation was that the former number would creep upwards, but it did not (from bomb injuries, at least). But the number of persons wounded did rise to a final figure around 170. Given the packed surroundings, it is amazing more were not killed by the two explosions, but that is attributable to the construction of the bombs (at ground level, they propelled shrapnel outward not upward, causing massive injuries to legs but few to vital organs) and the instant availability of top quality medical care at the nearby marathon runners' tent.

As is often the case, connections to Lowell were soon established. The photo of a gravely injured Lowell High School student being treated by two bystanders dominated the Tuesday front pages of both the *Boston Globe* and the *New York Times*. A surprising number of the injured were from Greater Lowell or had close ties to this area, and there was Ed Davis, a calm, authoritative voice throughout the crisis as Boston's police commissioner (and Lowell's former police superintendent).

Wednesday was spent reading of the victims, of those who responded to them first, and speculation about who had done it. One website had pre-explosion crowd photos with every isolated male with a backpack annotated as the possible terrorist. (As someone who routinely carries a backpack, I found this crowd-sourcing exercise creepy and, while possibly of some assistance, a source of potential harm to the reputations of many innocent bystanders).

Thursday was the interfaith memorial service featuring President Obama. As is so often the case (in my view), his public remarks struck the right note of comfort for the injured, defiance towards the perpetrators, and inspiration to everyone else. After the service the President visited victims at Massachusetts General Hospital.

Throughout Thursday, the media spread the word that the FBI had photos of the bombers and would be releasing them to the public soon. That happened in the late afternoon: it was a video loop of two men striding relaxed but purposely down the sidewalk in column, the first with a black baseball cap and a black backpack squarely strapped to both shoulders (Suspect #1), the second with a white ballcap worn backwards, with a grayish colored pack slung casually over his right shoulder. Still photos were grainy but good enough allow the persons to be recognized. I went to bed at about 10:30 p.m. with no further news.

Waking up Friday at 4:30 a.m., I immediately glanced at my phone for overnight news. Two emails from my son, Andrew, who lives near Harvard Square in Cambridge, grabbed my attention. The first was at 11:41 p.m.: "There was just a shooting near MIT. Some injuries. No threat here." The second at 2:06 a.m.: "I'm sure you'll see all the details when you wake up. Eventful night. They're not done sweeping the area of Watertown, but it's a lot less chaotic than it was. I think I'll be going to bed soon." The first thing that popped up on my computer was Facebook. I locked onto Andrew's feed: "There was a shooting around MIT. Then there was a car hijacked in Central Square. Pursued by police. I heard sirens then turned the police radio on. I heard an explosion and gunshots in the distance from my room ... they're now saying grenades and automatic gunfire in Watertown. Second officer down."

After that, news came rapidly from the TV and the computer. The Marathon bombers had been identified as two brothers from Cambridge. One of them was now dead, the other on the run. The news Friday morning was that they had ambushed and killed an MIT police officer, robbed a 7-11 store (an erroneous report), hijacked a car, and been stopped by police in Watertown where a massive firefight ensued. An MBTA transit police officer had been badly wounded in the gunfight, one of the terrorists (Suspect 1) had been killed and Suspect 2 had escaped.

By 6:30 a.m., Governor Patrick had shut down the entire MBTA subway and bus system. The communities of Watertown, Cambridge, Newton, and several others were all locked down, which meant people were to remain at home and businesses were not to open while a massive manhunt was conducted. Within minutes, the lockdown was extended to the entire city of Boston. Here in Lowell, the workday continued uneventfully, but all eyes and ears were trained on whatever "breaking news" source was available. An Amtrak train in Norwalk, Connecticut, had been evacuated, and a bomb squad in Buffalo was searching a car with Massachusetts plates. Nothing came of it.

Twelve hours later, exhausted and disheartened elected officials and police announced at a news conference that the suspect continued to elude them, however, the lockdown would be lifted and the MBTA resume operating. With that announcement, the local TV news morphed into Diane Sawyer and the national news, something I hadn't watched in months. She broke for a commercial at 6:50 p.m. After the ads, the local news anchors on Channel 5 were back on screen, telling of breaking news in Watertown. Suspect #2 had been located hiding in a boat stored in a yard just outside the day's search perimeter. Gunfire broke out and then faded. Wave after wave of police of all types arrived. At 9:00 p.m., they announced that Suspect #2 had been captured, alive but badly wounded.

Since then and continuing there has been a mix of stories about the terrorists and their motivations and actions as well as other stories about the victims, their funerals and their recoveries. For most of us, returning to work today will be a chance to share accounts of consuming the news of Friday night and sharing nuggets of information picked up over the weekend. I suspect that those involved in K-12 education who are returning from a week of vacation will have a different experience. With the news profiles of the younger terrorist all reporting that he was a fine student, an excellent athlete, a good friend, and many other superlatives, those who work with and educate young people must be struggling with the question of what makes someone who by all appearances was a "good kid" morph into a murdering terrorist and how can that transition be identified, diverted, and derailed?

April 22, 2013

Meg Smith

Bram Stoker Bequest

Dublin September 2018

Our blood bloomed
from the land of hunger.
Our songs rose
from the land of winter.
Green, among
your ghosts,
your words from your life.
I'm standing
at your door
on Kildare Street.
A housing protest
is brewing
at the street's end.
Across the way,
Yeats' voice
in bright clouds
rises from the
national library.
Our home
is our fire, ghosts.
Still, still we burn
and they burn
and our songs
cover the clouds
over low-lying hills.

Gerry Murphy

Just Saying

Of Henry Morton Stanley's
many expeditions to Africa,
one in particular stands out.
He was commissioned by King Leopold
to check out the scene in the Congo,
search for ivory and rubber
and determine
whether the local population
were ready for the benefits of slavery.
Amongst his entourage
was the whiskey heir Jameson,
an enthusiastic amateur artist,
who, it is said,
bought an eleven-year-old girl
for six handkerchiefs,
handed her over to some cannibals
and sketched
while they butchered her.

Doireann Ní Ghríofa

At Half Eleven in the Mutton Lane Inn,
I Am Fire, Slaughter, Dead Starlings

Though this pub is packed with bodies,
a shifting mass of limbs and laughter,
I feel your gaze on me. It burns.

I know what you'll say—you've said it before—
that you don't care about my silver ring,
that tomorrow morning, you want us to be

lying together still, in your attic room
up on the tallest city hill, where windows
tilt open and starling song flies in.

We have resisted long enough, you'll say.
No, we can resist some more. If you come
closer, I'll keep my gaze on the floor; I'll say:

In 1622, on the last day of May,
a lightning cloud shadowed this city.
Its sparks flared on thatch and pulsed to flame.

People stumbled over each other
through narrow laneways, clutching children
to their chests, weeping, afraid.

Lightning and fire bloomed
along the paths where they ran,
 and fell, and ran.

After that fire, those who survived
spoke of the omen of a fortnight before,
when two murmurations of starlings

clashed in the sky, flinging
themselves at each other, high
and wild, until small corpses thumped

into gutters by the dozen and ripped wings
cobbled the streets, leaving the paths all
bird-bloodied, all blush and trembling.

For hours, those birds' tiny magnet-hearts
jerked toward each other, as though
they couldn't help themselves

in shiver and grasp and shatter, their bodies
swooning and falling, falling into each other
—a thousand small deaths—

except, listen, in those days,
they didn't call them starlings,
they called them stares.

So, you see, I will say, stares spark fires
that cannot be quenched, stares cause
children to weep, clutched tight to chests.

Turn away,
I will say.
Find someone else.

Kate Hanson Foster

Dear Mugford,

I thought I would try to talk to you in a beautiful, quiet place where I know no one in the world goes: my website.

Look! I'm starting with a joke. Today might be a little easier than yesterday. The truth is, I am just sitting on the couch trying to process these words through some formal gesture—that they might translate into a universal language-less knowing that will accompany you to wherever it is that dead dogs go.

I thought about writing from the porch where we normally sit when I'm working on my computer, but it is still hard to look at the birds that we spent so many summers watching together. There are a lot of "hards" I didn't think of when we knew it was time to say goodbye. I foolishly thought I'd feel some relief. You wouldn't be struggling to get up to walk anymore. No more pain. No more humiliating falls up the porch steps. But you, my enormous English Mastiff, big as you were both in body and spirit, have left a large aching hole in the house. All day I feel like I am tiptoeing around it. Without warning I'll fall in, and there I am on my hands and knees pressing my nose into the hardwood floor of the empty space that was once your dog bed. I run my fingers over the scuff marks in the wood made from your gigantic paw nails. I open the ring box over the sink and smell the bundle of fur I collected after I held and comforted you on the porch for the last time. The fur that fell as you comforted me back and flopped a knowing paw on my shoulder before we took that dreaded drive. And then life pulls me out of the hole again. Maeve needs to be driven to soccer. Dinner needs to be made. Henry has a piano lesson. And time continues to move you further away.

I cleaned the drool off the French doors almost immediately after we put you down. I couldn't bear to see it. Now I can't bear that the doors are still clean. In the over 10 years we've lived in this house that's never happened. Even now, with you 4 days gone, a bundle of your hair will blow across the floor like tumbleweed. It lets loose from some corner no matter how many times I sweep or vacuum. I know I have to accept that I'll be finding remnants of your life with us for many years to come.

Hey, remember that time you shook your head and your drool hit the ceiling? That was incredibly disgusting. Or the time Bert and I were watching a show, and you let out a fart so foul that you raised your heavy head and looked at us like, "Damn, it stinks like shit in here," and you got up and left. I thought I wouldn't miss the ugly things that came with your bigness. Your rhino-sized shits. Slipping on your drool. And the many times I stopped in my tracks as I was rushing around because of something or another and yelled, "Mugford! Why do you always have to be such a fucking mountain in the middle of everything!" I'm sorry for that. I'm sorry you couldn't be the lap dog you always wanted to be. I'm sorry for the many small dogs that would visit and effortlessly leap up onto the couch while you were stuck on the floor letting out a big, "oh fuck that little shit" sigh.

I took our new little shit, Arlo, for a walk this morning. It was the same route we used to take when you were young and enjoyed walks. I ran into a woman who asked if Arlo was friendly. "I think so?" I said, unknowingly. "He's just a puppy." And she replied, "Oh, he seems so calm, so behaved." I told her that he had an elderly Mastiff to show him the ropes. And she immediately knew who I was, where I lived, and the Mastiff I was talking about. "Oh, we always admired that beautiful dog." It's true, you've always been something of a celebrity, and not all dogs get that. When you'd accompany me outside to fill the bird feeders or wait for the kids to get off the bus, cars would often stop just to look in awe at you. Random adults and kids would often smother you with affection without warning. And you would always take it, or rather, you received it. Always thankful for attention however it came. I'll never forget that time we took you to the Lowell Folk Festival and you were treated as one of the main attractions. We couldn't turn a corner without someone wanting to pet you and talk about you. We heard, "Wow! look at that dog!" constantly, and the not-so-clever line we've gotten your entire life, "When are you going to put a saddle on that thing?!"

Yeah, I won't miss that.

When we were grappling with the decision to put you down. I said to Bert, "It feels like a chapter is ending." And Bert said, "Are you kidding? Mugford is the volume that holds so many chapters." And it's true—you were the dream of how we saw our future. A big gentle dog that would guide us through so many monumental milestones. Our first home. Our marriage. Your largeness a faithful and concerned anchor at my feet as I waited through the labor pains of all three of our children. And you always greeted each baby with simple, unequivocal love. You saw us all through so many sleepless nights, the many tears, and so much laughter. You spent more time in the house than any of us. I can count on one hand how many times I have been alone here without you. And just like that, in a terrible instant—you have disappeared, and I am so very lonely with you gone.

Bert and I sat on the porch most of the weekend in what felt like our own private memorial service. The kind of lonely commemoration only animals receive because, well, if it's not your animal no one truly feels it or understands. We talked about all of the things you must have seen from your various vantage points in and around the house. At one point we moved outside and placed two Adirondack chairs in a sunny spot in the yard, and let ourselves soak in the sun, just like you loved to do, no matter how hot it was. "We are enduring that one true thing, aren't we?" Bert said. "The certainty of death. It is never certain that something will be born, but once it's born, it is certain that it will die." We always knew the day would come. I look at Arlo, and I know I am beginning the process again. A new volume with barely one chapter yet to fill it. He's been keeping me company a lot, licking my tears away, ruining shoes, and pissing and shitting on the floor. For a little guy, he's a mighty big distraction. I am thankful for that.

Mugford, you were our closest friend. I wish we could have given you more. It's not fair how much you loved us so unconditionally despite all of our flaws—always taking a back seat to the needs of others. When we were saying goodbye, I rested the entire weight of my body on top of you. You always loved that, to feel the literal weight of someone's affection, no matter how heavy. You had a body built to hold it. I hope that you felt me as the needle entered your vein, and you drifted away from us. Maybe you saw us from above your big beautiful snore, your last breath, my head resting on your head, your head in Bert's hands—and us both not knowing what else to say other than another true thing: "You are such a good boy. Such a good boy. Such a good boy . . . you're Him."

EIGHT

Gerry Murphy

Mozart to His Father

Paris. July 3rd. 1778.
The Symphony was a triumph,
no sooner had the last notes died away,
then I hurried off to the Palais Royal,
where I had a large ice,
said the Rosary, as I'd promised,
and went straight home.

P.S. I suppose you heard that Voltaire,
that arch-rogue, has died like a dog,
a fitting reward.

Jacquelyn Malone

Cheerleader

The bleachers teemed with restless fans,
and arc lamps, ringed in a spangled haze,
threw light down goal to goal,
like a dome over the measured field—
as if it could seal in the ref's shrill *burr*,
the *clank* of helmets head to head, the chant
"Kill 'em. Kill 'em!" as though it could seal out
anything beyond the lights. That fall night
I brought confetti—ribbon chips
from my weekend job at the gift wrap counter
at Cain-Sloan.

Confetti boxes ready, we'd rallied them,
my legs powerful as any boy's,
and when it came—the goal—they followed us,
fistfuls of ribbons bursting in the air,
their throats blown out, the bleachers throbbing.

The ribbons swirled and caught the light
against the blackness above the dome,
and like meteor showers they winked
and fell. I stopped to watch one gold chip
drifting beyond the chain-link fence
where silence sang its reflective song
and asters were blooming in the autumn dark.

Tom Sexton

Lowell's Irish Micky Ward

Round 2. Ward's left eye is already cut,
but he keeps moving around Arturo Gatti.
My wife's gone to bed and turned out the light.
Gatti's left hook sounds like a thunderclap.
I haven't watched a fight in many years,
not since I moved away from Lowell.
A Celtic Cross glistens on Ward's shoulder.
I wince as he shakes off blow after blow.
He has my uncle Leo's fighter's face,
with features almost as flat as a stone.
Staggered by a right, he picks up the pace.
I want to see a hurt Gatti go down.
They fight to a draw. Closed eye for closed eye.
I go to bed shamefaced and stubbornly tribal.

Ryan Gallagher
Good Friday

A hammer comes down on a piggy
bank. Smash. Pink ceramic shards
float like a butterfly and
           lean like
Nefertiti. Mariposa. Sting

  like a bee.   Sing

  like Cleopatra.

                I tremble in

    a soap bubble smashed
                by a hammer—

No I am not
  the Virgin of Guadalupe either.

I am the rain, sweet
Jane, pass me that

    piece of the Pentecost.

Bob Martin

My Father Painted Houses

My father painted houses in the small town where we lived.
When we drove through town, he would point to a house
And say, "That's one that I did."
And the season best was summer for all that it would give.
And it gave us everything we would ever need,
Gave us everything we'd ever need.

So, I worked for the ole man every summer from the age
　　of fourteen years.
Was a big white house, took a six-man crew; we split up
　　to work in pairs.
The ole man and I climbed to the highest peak of a big house
　　on Fort Hill.
As we looked across the city at the sunset on the mill, he said,
"Don't it seem like you're never gonna leave and get out
　　on your own?
Don't it seem like when you're young, the time goes by so slow?
Remember, when you're gone and you're far away, this place
　　where you were born.
You know you're gonna take that with ya everywhere you go,
Gonna take that with you everywhere ya go."

In the back yard, we burnt out the paint pots, scraped off
　　the crust around the rim.
The start of every workday, we filled them up with paint again.
We brushed out the colors of the rainbow from our buckets
　　made of tin,
And the summer sang a song we could believe,
Summer sang a song we could believe.

Don't it seem like you're never gonna leave and get out
　　on your own?
Don't it seem when you're young the time goes by so slow?

249

Remember, when you're gone and you're far away, this place
    where you were born.
You know you're gonna take that with you everywhere you go,
Gonna take that with you everywhere you go.

But it was the worst of all the winters, and the snow
    had closed us in.
The truck was drifted over, and no work was coming in,
So, we try hard not to notice our chances getting slim,
But we made it through that winter still alive,
Made it through that winter still alive.
But the old man was getting tired in the years before I left.
I feel guilty that one day I just up and hit the road to see
    how far that I'd get.
Now, I'm somewhere far away, so desperate to forget,
Passing through a different city with the same sunset.

Don't it seem like you're never gonna leave and get out
    on your own?
Don't it seem when you're young the time goes by so slow?
Remember, when you're gone and you're far away, this place
    where you were born.
You know you're gonna take that with you everywhere you go,
Gonna take that with you everywhere you go.

My father painted houses in the small town where we lived.
When we drove through town, he would point to a house
And say, "That's one that I did."
The season best was summer for all that it would give,
And it gave us everything we would ever need,
Gave us everything we'd ever need.

Gerry Murphy

Temporary Abdication

You wake,
to a cloud of unknowing,
a blizzard of lost connections,
all slates truly wiped clean.
You cannot tell
where you are,
you cannot tell
who you are.
Embalmed in a moment,
without past or future,
name or memory,
need or desire.
Until the panic kicks in
and the accumulation of identity,
the mad pursuit of meaning,
the scramble for signifiers,
promptly return.
The whole shebang
rushing back into place,
fitting you out
with the same stale details,
name, location, time, date,
occupation, social position,
likes, dislikes ...
The sprawling entity,
the tiny ungovernable kingdom:
you.

Bob Hodge

Duck Soup Dream

I was running in the time and mind of King Philip's War, Metacom urging his people on to no avail, and I was running on the route of momentous battles, my curiosity in the roadside markers partially buried by weeds and grass and trash, running this ground three hundred-and-more years later, lost in the wonder of how that might have been, and being spurred on by the lively spirits in them, their concerns for the basic needs of life, and as my mind wandered my pace quickened, any comparison with today's world so close yet so far away.

I hit George Hill and worked it, in my prime again, a mind on fire perfectly exploding, full of raw power but running with grace and elegance, a future Kipchoge, the greatest runner the world has known, crested the hill and continued to the spot of Mary Rowlandson's first night in the captivity of the natives, feeling their presence in the firelight, darkness descending.

It was a run that never ended except for tea and a nap and a dousing or swim in Lake Waushacum and occasional visits with family kept to a minimum, no distractions at this key juncture when I would be tested.

Soundtrack: "Dream #9" by John Lennon

NINE

Daniel Mulhall

Douglas Hyde and W. B. Yeats in America, 1891-1932

For Irish public figures in the latter part of the nineteenth century and in the opening decades of the twentieth, the tour of America was a well-trodden path. Prominent individuals crossed the Atlantic because they knew that the vast Irish American community was a huge resource for Irish political and cultural movements. They were understandably keen to tap into this rich vein of moral and financial support.

Among the Irish politicians to visit the U.S. at that time were Charles Stewart Parnell, John Redmond and Eamon de Valera, who spent eighteen months traveling around America in 1919-1920 garnering support for the newly declared Irish Republic.

America also had its attractions for literary figures. Thomas Moore came to the Americas in 1803/1804, but that was before he acquired an international literary reputation as the author of *Moore's Melodies*. Moore's visit also took place decades before the huge influx of Irish immigrants changed the demography of America, and of Ireland, from the 1840s onwards.

Oscar Wilde was admired by many Irish-Americans on account of his mother's nationalist writings under her pen-name Speranza. According to his biographer, Richard Ellmann, Wilde "rediscovered himself as an Irishman" during his 1892 American tour. George Russell (AE) visited America late in life and met with President Franklin D. Roosevelt who was interested in AE's ideas about how to create a viable rural society.

In this essay, I want to concentrate on two Irish writers, Douglas Hyde and W.B. Yeats, who paid extended visits to America in the decades between the 1890s and the 1930s. Douglas Hyde, co-founder of the Gaelic League in 1893, and later Ireland's first President from 1938 to 1945, spent two extended spells in North America in 1891-92 and again in 1905-06. Unlike most Irish visitors, Hyde published a detailed account of his travels in 1905-06, which provides a valuable picture of Irish America as it was more than a century ago.

Between the five visits he paid between 1903 and 1932, W. B. Yeats spent more than a year of his life in North America. Spurred no doubt by the strength of patriotic sentiment he encountered among Irish-Americans, Yeats made some of his most overtly nationalistic pronouncements while he was in America. This was especially true during his first American tour in 1903-04. His other four visits took place at important moments in the complex evolution of Yeats's up-and-down engagement with nationalist Ireland.

Douglas Hyde in America, 1891-92

The son of a Church of Ireland clergyman, Hyde grew up in Roscommon where he acquired a knowledge of the Irish language from local people there and it became his lifelong passion. After studying Theology at Trinity College, Dublin, he was offered a lecturing post at the University of New Brunswick in Canada and spent the academic year there before travelling to Boston and New York on his way back to Ireland.

In those two heavily Irish cities, he delivered well-attended lectures in which he set out some ideas that would inspire the creation of the Gaelic League in 1893. Speaking in New York, he was keen to highlight the linguistic pedigree of the Irish language. It was not "a poor, mean, limited language," but "a vast, varied, very opulent one" which "stands upon an equal footing with Greek, Latin and Sanskrit." And as far as literature was concerned, there was "an enormous mass of Irish literature ... (which) has not only never been equalled but never been approached either in age, variety, or value by any vernacular language in Europe." It was "the language of the Bards and Brehons, of the Saints and sages."

It is not difficult to imagine how well such sentiments would have gone down with his Irish American audience. Hyde then took aim at those Irish who did not treasure their native language. "It is," he said, "a most frightful shame the way in which Irishmen are brought up, ashamed of their language, institutions and of everything Irish."

Hyde made it plain that he did not envisage Irish ever replacing English in Ireland. What he wanted was to see Irish established "as a living language, for all time, among the million or half a million who still speak it along the west coast, and to ensure that the language will hold a favourable place in teaching institutions and government examination." According to the 1891 Census, there were 680,000 people in Ireland who could speak Irish. This figure was down from 1.5 million forty years earlier.

When Hyde returned to Ireland, he was elected President of the National Literary Society and in that capacity delivered his famous speech on "The Necessity for De-anglicising the Irish Nation," which was perhaps the single most influential public statement made during the two decades before the Easter Rising when a new spirit of Irish idealism was much in evidence. In his speech, Hyde called for the building up of "an Irish nation on Irish lines" so as to "once more become what it was of yore: one of the most original, artistic, literary, and charming peoples of Europe."

Those were inspirational ideas and the Gaelic League grew rapidly under Hyde's stewardship attracting the devotion of a new generation of Irish people, better educated and more restless than their predecessors. By 1903, there were some six hundred Gaelic League branches all over Ireland and up to 250,000 people taking language lessons.

Yeats's 1903-04 tour

In the four months he spent in America in 1903-04, Yeats delivered more than sixty lectures, many at leading American Universities, and amassed $3,200, a substantial sum, especially for someone like Yeats who had up to that time been perennially hard-pressed financially.

Yeats had laboured throughout the 1890s arguing the case for a national literature for Ireland and this was one of his main preoccupations during his time in America. In a lecture entitled "The Intellectual Revival in Ireland," he conjured up a pastoral, egalitarian future for Ireland, which would "preserve an ancient ideal of life" centred on agriculture rather than industry. He enthused about Ireland where "alone among the nations" will be found "away on the western seaboard, under broken roofs, a race of gentlemen, keeping alive the ideals of a great time when men sang the heroic life with drawn swords in their hands."

Yeats's American tour came at an interesting time in his engagement with Irish affairs. In one sense, he was at the height of his renown as an Irish nationalist having the year before produced, in collaboration with Lady Gregory, his most overtly political piece of writing, *Cathleen ní Houlihan*. But Yeats's Irish horizon was not all sweetness and light. In the opening years of the twentieth century, he had come under attack from, for example, Patrick Pearse, who had insisted that a national literature for Ireland could not be in any language other than Irish. Pearse later regretted his dismissal of Yeats as a third-rate poet and invited him to speak at his school, St. Enda's.

The prominent Irish-American lawyer, John Quinn, had worried that Yeats might not go down well with Irish American Catholics on account of his unorthodox religious views, but Yeats quickly won over any doubters. Indeed, he was asked by the Irish American Fenian body, *Clan na Gael*, to deliver a lecture in memory of Robert Emmet. When Yeats spoke at the Academy of Music in New York in February 1904, his talk attracted an attendance of 4,000. It would have been impossible for Yeats to have reached an audience of anything near that size in Dublin or in London. Such was the scale of Irish America.

In this speech, Yeats offered an unbridled nationalist interpretation of Irish history. He lionised Emmet as someone who "showed that there was something in Ireland which not all the wealth of the world could purchase" and predicted that "when Ireland is triumphant and free, there will be something in the character of her people, something lofty and strange, which will have been put there by her years of suffering and by the memory of her many martyrs." None of his critics in Ireland could have taken exception to his American lectures. This was the outlook of an advanced Irish nationalist and his audiences evidently lapped it up. We know from his letters, however, that Yeats was already harbouring doubts about the direction of political developments in Ireland.

Mo thurus go hAmerice, Hyde in America 1905-06

In November 1905, the Gaelic League sent Hyde on a fundraising tour of America which lasted a full seven months. As with Yeats's visit the year before, New York lawyer John Quinn was instrumental in putting Hyde's tour together. Quinn evidently did a very good job for, according to Hyde's account of the visit, *Mo thurus go hAmerice* (My American Tour), he spoke in some fifty-five cities on the Eastern seaboard, throughout the mid-West and on the West Coast. His visit attracted considerable media attention wherever he went.

His first appearances were in two of America's most prestigious universities, Harvard and Yale. In New York, he spoke for ninety minutes to a capacity audience at Carnegie Hall telling them how, in the twelve years of its existence, the Gaelic League had transformed Ireland from a miserable province into a proper nation. In Boston, he met with Mayor John F. Fitzgerald, grandfather of President John F. Kennedy.

Everywhere he went he was well received and drew significant audiences for his lectures, which generated considerable financial support for the Gaelic League. In Pittsburgh, he addressed two events with attendances of 1,800 and 2,500. In Philadelphia, 2,600 turned up to hear him speak and this yielded a collection of $400. An appearance at San Francisco's newly built Tivoli Opera House produced a return of $1,200 although the money he collected there was sent back to California for the relief of victims of the earthquake which hit the city shortly after Hyde's visit. His tour was not without opposition and he suspected supporters of the United Irish League (the support organisation for the Irish Parliamentary Party) of trying to spike his fund-raising efforts.

As he made his journey across America, he met plenty of people who spoke Irish and whose company he relished, but there were others among the more well-to-do Irish who appalled Hyde because they seemed to be ashamed of their heritage.

On one of his two visits to Washington, the Professor of Irish at the Catholic University, a Dr. Ó Duínn, accompanied him to the White House where President Theodore Roosevelt hosted him lunch during which the President revealed that he had recently published an essay comparing the old Irish stories with the Norse sagas! For his part, Hyde spent the long train journey through Wyoming and Utah translating one of Dante's cantos into Irish! He was especially impressed by America's west coast and Seattle was the place that most reminded him of home.

Hyde's account of his American sojourn, which has recently been published in a new edition, reveals a number of things about Irish America in the early twentieth century.

First, it highlights the scale and prominence of the Irish-America community as well as its passionate commitment to Ireland. Delegations of leading Irish Americans often came to welcome him at train stations around the country.

Second, the fact that he was able to make frequent use of Irish in his public appearances confirms that many of the immigrant Irish who arrived in the decades after the Famine had come from Irish-speaking backgrounds.

Third, Hyde showed phenomenal energy levels during his U.S. tour, travelling incessantly and often finishing his days at convivial social functions that sometimes lasted into the smallhours.HewasintriguedbyAmericancocktails,including"Mint Julep" to which he was introduced in Washington's Willard Hotel.

Finally, the manner in which he was fêted at the country's major universities illustrates the extent to which the Irish literary revival, of which Hyde was part, had by that time captured an international following.

Yeats's 1911 Tour

By the time Yeats returned to America in 1911, his view of Ireland had darkened markedly. The prime cause of his disenchantment had been the negative public response to Synge's *Playboy of the Western World*, and when the playwright died in 1909 Yeats turned him into a symbol of artistic integrity ground down by what he considered to be philistine notions of Irish identity.

This visit was part of the Abbey Theatre's first tour of America and Yeats accompanied them for about six weeks. He believed that Irish America could become a vital source of support for his theatre, although he observed that "The Irish imagination keeps certain of its qualities wherever it is, and if we are to give it, as we hope, a new voice, and a new memory, we shall have to make many journeys."

Inevitably the controversy that had surrounded Synge's *Playboy* in Ireland followed Yeats and his troupe to America. One Irish American body described the *Playboy* as "the foulest libel that has ever been perpetrated on the Irish character." Yeats, never one to shirk a verbal battle, went into bat for Synge's genius. "He took his types from reality indeed, but he exaggerated them and arranged them according to his fancy until he created something as strange as the wandering knight and the Sancho Panza of Cervantes."

Yeats in America, 1914

By the time of his 1914 visit, Yeats's disenchantment with Ireland had reached new depths and this was reflected in the poems that appeared in *Responsibilities*, some of which have a bitter, unattractive tone. The most refined statement of Yeats's disillusionment came in "September 1913."

Was it for this the wild geese spread
The grey wing on every tide;
For this that all that blood was shed,
For this Edward Fitzgerald died,
And Robert Emmet and Wolfe,
All that delirium of the brave?

This reads like a farewell to Irish affairs and, during his 1914 tour, Yeats largely steered clear of Irish America. His visit took place in the teeth of the raging controversy about Irish Home Rule, and Yeats expressed guarded optimism about the prospects for an agreement that would preserve the unity of Ireland. This visit was a lucrative one, raising £500, a figure that can be put into perspective by the fact that his total income in the previous year was £522.

Yeats's 1920 visit

By the time Yeats returned to the United States in 1920, everything in Ireland had, as he put it in "Easter 1916," "changed utterly" and the country was in the throes of revolutionary turmoil. The Easter Rising had revived Yeats's interest in Irish affairs and encouraged him to move back to Ireland from London where he had lived for most of the previous three decades.

There was, inevitably, considerable American interest in Yeats's analysis of developments in Ireland. Although his lecture topics studiously avoided current Irish affairs, in his response to questions from reporters he tended to be more strongly nationalistic than he would have been had he been speaking in Ireland or in Britain. On one occasion, he described Ireland as "a country of oppression" and expressed his desire for some form of self-government for his strife-torn country. While he acknowledged Sinn Féin's mandate, he decried political fanaticism as "a bitter acid that destroyed the soul."

Yeats's final visit to America

Yeats's last American tour in 1932-33 was undertaken for familiar reasons, to boost his own finances and to raise money for his latest project, the Irish Academy of Letters, which he set up in September 1932. This was Yeats's rejoinder to the literary censorship that had been introduced during the 1920s, and to what he saw as a narrowing of the new State's intellectual horizons.

During this visit, Yeats, who had spent a number of years in the 1920s serving as a member of the Irish Senate, was often described as "Ireland's cultural Ambassador." His own aim was "to substitute a cultural link" between Ireland and Irish America for the political one. The lecture he delivered most often was entitled "The New Ireland" in which he divided Irish history into four eras, the fourth beginning with the death of Parnell in 1891. This was very much in line with the thesis he advanced in his Nobel Prize acceptance speech in 1923 in which he sought to claim some of the credit for Ireland's political transformation.

Conclusion

W. B. Yeats was a considerable success in America. He worked hard, travelling widely and lecturing frequently. He left a positive impression wherever he went and was invariably seen by the American press as someone who ought to have an opinion on every current topic to do with Ireland. And he did not disappoint them. While some in Irish America might have had doubts about the integrity of his nationalism, they could not help being impressed by the fact that he was so well received in America. He played to the gallery of Irish-American sentiment, suppressing his various reservations about developments in Ireland.

For his part, Douglas Hyde helped bring into being the most influential movement that emerged during the decades preceding the Easter Rising of 1916. The Gaelic League energised a generation of Irish people, many of whom took leading roles in our independence struggle. W .B. Yeats was somewhat ambivalent about Hyde, whose stringent advocacy of de-Anglicisation threatened his own position as an Irish poet. Yet in his Nobel Prize speech in 1923, Yeats gave Hyde due credit:

"Dr. Hyde founded the Gaelic League, which was for many years to substitute for political argument a Gaelic grammar, and for political meetings village gatherings, where songs were sung and stories told in the Gaelic language."

Hyde's travels in America, and the enthusiastic reception he received, suggest that many in Irish America bought into Hyde's vision of linguistic and cultural regeneration, even as they were busy Americanising themselves and becoming an integral part of the fabric of twentieth century-America.

The highly positive experiences of Douglas Hyde and W. B. Yeats in America highlight just how much of an asset it was for the Ireland of their time to have America as a welcoming beacon and a supportive backstop.

Thomas McCarthy

White Egrets by Derek Walcott, a Verse Review

This I was thinking as I read Walcott's *White Egrets*:
A poet's life is lived more with love than regrets,
Passion out of proportion. (Out of menus, sonnets).
What can you say in prose about a perfect book?
If you want to know what poetry is take a look
Inside this box of Cartagena and bougainvillea nooks,

And all the fantasy that goes with art—
Consider even how advertising plays its part:

"and vanilla-coloured girls rub cream on their thighs
in an advertisement Italy, a plastic happiness
that brought actual content."

Poets burn at close quarters to fantasy's asphalt
As Walcott always shows. Indeed, there are few
Concessions to any restricted, Puritan overview
When Walcott says what he knows to be true

About life's imperfections. In this perfect farewell
To all on earth who shared the mineral water bottle
With him in prose and poems: those who stand still –

"You have seen Umbria, admired Tuscany,
And gaped at the width of the harbour at Genoa,
now I show you an open secret . . ."

He shows how much truth is in the act of being alive,
For, let's be honest, every poet's life is a dive
Into an indigo sea. This world is where poets thrive

And poets love the sea a lot more than fame;
They want to be in Capri to watch the light frame
Itself in little squares, or on a Spanish train
As it catapults across blood-crusted earth,
"the cape-shade of cork trees," a rebirth
On the bell tower in Alcalá, a third or fourth

Neat whiskey and a free-flowing fountain pen.
What more could be wanted by woman or man
In search of a perfect phrase, warmed by the sun:

>   "I hear the snorting stallions
> of Córdoba in heat, I hear my bones'
> castanets, and a rattle of heels like machine guns,"

Walcott writes as he enumerates joyous days,
Joyous friendships, all the joyous ways
A man may be loved or moved. Of friends, he says;

> "Jesus, the beauty he contains, a beauty of soul,
> no less than that, a wit, an intelligence, the degrading
> indifference he has had to endure; some of the best already
> gone, Wilbert Holder, Claude Reid, Ermine Wright.
> Against the wind for a long time they kept a steady
> flame of devotion, they had to do what was right . . ."

This is how *White Egrets*, the book, coheres:
The *Examiner* reader could spend years
Learning from "Sicilian Suite" or "The Lost Empire"
With its deadly opening couplet
That puts the illusory power of a ruling set
And all its flags into a world as liberation sees it:

> "And then there was no more Empire all of a sudden,
> Its victories were air, its dominions dirt."

266

Such complete truths in little canisters of art
Are found everywhere in *White Egrets*.
It is a *Star-Apple Kingdom* blown apart
By age and travel. A far cry it is, dear
Examiner reader, from the Commonwealth scholar
Of Caribbean studies: instead, Nobel gold is here.

As some were destined to be minor and obscure,
One poet alone was forensically sure
Of post-colonial being and its imaginative ether:

"your island is always in the haze of my mind
with the blown-about sea-birds
in their creole clatter of vowels, *maître* among makers,
whom the reef recites when the copper sea-almonds blaze,
beacons to distant Dakar, and the dolphin's acres."
Yet happy with the beauty of Europe, still taking pigments
From the azure sea, friend of Heaney and august elements
In world poetry, here he has made a lamp from fragments;

And no book this year or the next will be as grand,
As noble in outlook, or as easy to understand.
Walcott, a great poet born on lovely St. Lucia island,
A Paganini in verse now far too ill to go on tour:
He has heard the horseman passing by, for sure –
But red sails in the sunset also, and egrets flying over.

Janet Egan

Saturday Morning, Reading "Howl"

If everybody takes one page from "Howl"
and you all read it aloud at the same time
in front of the *Kerouac Commemorative*
at Bridge and French streets,
it sounds like a Buddhist chant.
It feels like a prayer in the mouth.
Vibrating. Urgent. Impassioned. Cacophonous.
If you look up from the *Commemorative*,
you can see the outline of the old Keith's Theater
in the red brick wall.
In true New England fashion,
You can see what "used to be."

If you listen, you can hear Allen Ginsberg
reading by candlelight
at the dedication
of this monument to his good friend Jack.
And you're glad somebody taped it.
You're glad to be here now
in the cold morning dampness
among granite columns
etched with prose and poetry.

If you drop a stone into the still water of the canal,
you can see the ripples go out and out and out,
wrinkling the reflections of the warehouse,
the mill, the fence, the pipes, the bridge . . . outward and outward
until you can't see it anymore,
but it's still rippling all the way to the Merrimack River,
down river to Newburyport,
and out to sea.

Janet Egan

October Americana

South Campus smells like fried potatoes.
Freshmen sprawl before game consoles,
immersed in other worlds.

At O'Leary Library, scholars and poets,
but few students,
gather to hear the voice of another era.
A professor brought his six-year-old daughter
to see an American icon.
What is a six-year-old to make of this man,
these words,
this time and place?

Amiri Baraka in Lowell.
The freshmen at their games
have no context for this.
The angry poet of the '70s
still angry in his seventies
reminds us
poetry is political.
Always was.
Always will be
whether gamers wake to
smell potatoes or not.

Do they know the Beats weren't beaten
And the Silent Generation wasn't silent?

Christine P. O'Connor

Road Trips: "Where Strange Things Pass"

On a hot July day, away from the crowds and stickiness of O'Connell Street, I tucked into the old Bank of Ireland building for a Seamus Heaney exhibit called "Listen Now Again." Inside was Heaney's desk, plain and simple; and under glass, the many written pages of his poems. I saw his sometimes-hurried handwriting, the strikeouts and arrows redirecting readers from misplaced words. Sitting on a shelf was a lamp once owned by Yeats and later purchased by Heaney. What writing its light must have reached!

On a chalkboard were the last words he ever wrote. It was a message to his wife, although I like to think it was meant for a wider audience. Translated from Latin, it means: "Don't be afraid." And here and there were reminders that the words he used to describe the struggles of his day remain relevant to our own: *once in a lifetime/ The longed-for tidal wave/ Of justice can rise up/ And hope and history rhyme.*

But it was his poem "Postscript," reprinted on a wall of the exhibit, where I lingered most, reading it over several times; listening to it, again and again:

And some time make the time to drive out west it begins. The poem was written after a drive the Heaneys took along the Flaggy Shore of Clare with the playwright, Brian Friel and his wife. The poem came to him a few days later, and although working on another project, he stopped and gave in to it. After completing it, he sent it to the *Irish Times.* Included in the exhibit was Heaney's own cut-out copy of its printing, along with the marginal edits he wished he made. Regardless of his desire to tinker further, it would become regarded as one of his most loved poems.

In recent years, this poem has tugged at me with a deep sense of familiarity. Perhaps it reminded me of my own flaggy shore, not in the west, but the north: the rocky coast of Maine; and of my aunts, Eileen, Edna, and Mary, and the many times we took a ride to the shore in the off-season; bundled up in sweaters, hands deep in pockets, we'd walk from one rocky outcrop to the next, leaning, red-faced, into a stiff Atlantic headwind.

In the exhibit, as people passed, I stood, reading the poem until I ached with a dull sadness.

"Are we set, Chris?" my cousin Marie asked.

"Yes," I said, "just another minute or two."

I had been thinking of Mary, Marie's friend with cancer, and how often they have talked of going to the Aran Islands. I left the exhibit with a few books and my head filled with many reasons as to why poetry is good for the heart and soul.

The next morning, I was leaving on an extended road trip to Scotland with Marie and another cousin, David. Together we packed the car, positioned the map between us, and left for Northern Ireland. At the P & O ferry port in Larne we joined the ranks of trucks, camper vans, and between each, it seemed, was a Fiat. There were children holding their mother's hands; men in Ray-Bans and shorts; books left open on dashboards; random BBC broadcasts coming from open windows; bikes strapped to the backs of vehicles, and even a salt and pepper Standard Schnauzer named Fritz who appeared to know that he too was about to begin an adventure.

It was summer after all. The big exhale. It takes all year to get here, to this moment that promises to last forever, but is shortest of all. Like moths to the back-porch light, we were gathered in the collective energy that accompanies travel. There's an old black and white photograph that I love. It is of my grandparents, and an aunt and uncle. On the back of the photo, the stamp—1951—is barely visible. Their car is pulled over, tilting on the side of the road, and they are sitting around a picnic table having lunch. They were on a road trip. It didn't matter where they were going or for how long. I understood the photo and instinctively knew what it must have felt like that day to eat in the open air, beneath the green shade of a tree, on a day as pure as the white clouds above.

I suppose our earliest road trips were pilgrimages. On foot, by donkey, in wagons, people traveled to reach sacred places. But maybe the spiritual experience comes not from the destination, but from the journey. Steinbeck claimed people don't take a trip, "the trip takes us." In the ever-changing light of day, we are transformed on such journeys. With open windows and a good stretch of road, time doesn't matter; there's no early or late, and midnight's as dear as noon.

We stood outside Marie's Hyundai with its Wexford plates and looked upon an unusually calm Irish sea. *And some time make the time to drive out west*, I thought. Whether in Ireland or Scotland, the West is where life is wild and rich. It is a place of fairy forts and fairy pools; of deep-seated spirituality felt by pagan and priest alike; a place often associated with the Otherworld, it's where the living and the dead can again connect, and where *strange things pass.*

In the shadow and spirit of those who took the time, we traveled through Northern Ireland, the Inner Hebrides and the Scottish Highlands. There was a trip to the island of Iona, where it's said all who visit do so three times; the Bealach na Bà drive, the steepest ascent of any road climb in the UK; the viaduct in Glenfinnan (another minute more and we would have seen the Hogwarts Express); the mountains at Glencoe; the Dark Hedges, nature's most mystical passageway; the mathematical symmetry of Giant's Causeway; and hiking on the Isle of Skye to magical places like Old Man of Storrs, the Quiraing, and the Fairy Glen.

But, in between such wonders are those moments, brief and fleeting, yet dearly treasured: drinking tea from paper cups while waiting for the ferry; sitting on the same patch of ground, high on a hill, where St. Columba did much of his writing; the outdoor lunch on the edge of the ocean; running my finger along a cut in a grave slab made thousands of years ago; a strawberry Cornetto cone in the middle of the day; discussing the Beatles and Johnny Cash 'til two in the morning; walking in the shadows of standing stones as they capture nature's most sacred light; a full moon; a cold cider; and the synchronized movement of grass in the wind. It's often not those things we travel to see that move us, but the experiences found along the way; *it's useless to park and try to capture it.*

At the end of our stay we dropped David at the train station in Bowling, he was heading on to Glasgow, Marie and I were heading back to Ireland. *You are neither here nor there.* On the side door was our well-worn map. Its folds were so familiar now. It was a drizzly day of foggy windows and windshield wipers. And then the dampest part of the day: saying goodbye.

"It's going to take a while to process all this," said David wearing the backpack that sat in the trunk for the past couple of weeks.

Nodding, we hugged goodbye. With my arms still around him, I knew it would be sometime, maybe not until Christmas, until I would see David, and longer still until I would again experience the freedom of a road trip. The day we crossed the Irish sea now seemed so far away. In the lingering smell of train diesel, my surroundings became blurry from a sudden welling from within. Walking away *a soft buffeting came at* me and caught me off guard.

It was that beautiful poem, bright and glittery on its surface; but like the geese with their heads busy beneath the water, it takes you to another place, to that other side of life. I will never again walk the beach on stiff October days with my aunts, and that's why this beautiful poem hurts, because it cannot remind us to take the time, without reminding us that time is limited, that life is limited.

Getting back into the car, I turn to Marie: "You and Mary must really get out to Inishmore."

"Yes, yes, I know," she replied, "we must."

TEN

Rogers Muyanja

My Story

It is July 2007, and I have just entered my office where I work as a reporter. As I approach my desk, I see a letter sitting by my phone. It is from the United States Consular Section, a response to my Green Card visa application through the Diversity Visa Lottery Program. I have mixed feelings.

You see, my friends and family have encouraged me to go to the United States, epicenter of media, saying I would do well there. And, of course, everyone else is fascinated by the United States, which I believe is due to the great job Hollywood has done selling America to the rest of the world.

At this point, I take a moment to think about the great successes I've attained in my career and start to wonder whether I should give up all this and just go. I have family and friends, and so I'm torn, not sure how I feel.

A year later, I board a plane heading to the U.S., to the unknown, with hope and dreams like any immigrant. Landing in Boston, I wonder why I see the sun but feel cold. You see, it's October, the fall season has kicked in. I move in with my brother who has been in the city a few years. My first reaction to America is mixed. Why is everyone inside their homes all the time?

My number one priority is to find work. I'm excited to be a reporter again, to get a good job with a good newspaper or a television station. I go online and start sending resumes, googling and looking for different positions. I talk to people and submit resumes and keep sending them. No responses. Weeks go by. I get my Social Security card and driver's license, but not a job. I'm nervous because I have expenses, rent and food.

After six months, and still feeling strong, I'm ready to take any job. I get excited one day when I finally get a response. A media outlet tells me that I can cover stories for them. I feel awake again. It's the same feeling as when I used to get assignments back in Kampala, Uganda. I find out that I am going to cover Governor Deval Patrick's re-election campaign, in Worcester, Massachusetts.

I don't even know where Worcester is, but I am going there. And I show up and meet people, but it's totally different. I come back and write what I think is a really good article, feeling alive again. I pass it in and write another story about Ugandan politics. I start to see things and feel excited and proud. My excitement, however, is cut short because I don't get paid. I follow up and learn that the media outlet doesn't have money to pay me. I don't have a choice now. I need a job that pays.

One of my friends tells me about a company that assists elders, and the work sounds easy enough. You show up, put someone to bed, and you wake them up in the morning, making sure they get something to eat. What he didn't tell me is that in the middle of the night I will be changing someone's bed sheets or pacing in the hallway, trying to be as patient as I can with someone in the midst of an Alzheimer's attack. I used to work on a deadline. Things used to happen so quickly, but now I have to slow down and be with patients and try to give them peace and comfort. While I'm glad to be there, this is very far from what I studied. I decide to stay even though the money is not enough to make ends meet. I need another job. My family in Uganda counts on me to send money to help them.

A friend tells me about a dishwasher job at a local grocery store. I expect to be hand-washing dishes. Instead, I stand in front of a big dishwashing machine as the steam flushes my face. I remember my time in Uganda with my friends telling me that my life is going to be so good in America, so good! Now, I'm not so sure. People in other places often think that life in America is easy and glamorous, as portrayed in the movies. And here I am, standing at the dishwasher, not what I imagined. It's what I have to do. Everyone thought my time in America would be amazing. Even worse, they are writing, asking about my new life, and getting mad at me for not writing back fast enough to tell them about my adventures. I don't have time. Because in America, immigrants work all the time.

Standing in front of the automatic dishwasher, I consider that my path to journalism in Uganda was education, and perhaps my only path to a professional career in the U.S. has to be through education again. So, despite having my two degrees from Uganda, I pursue three degrees: an associate's, bachelor's, and a master's degree. During this time, I go to my job at the senior home from 7 p.m. to 7 a.m. I then rush home, change my clothes, eat, and drive across town to my dishwasher job. Then, in the evening, I get back and start school. I fit in my homework before and after classes the best I can. With all this happening, and not being able to contribute as a reporter right now, I decide to work with organizations that support immigrants. I will use my experience to make it easier for those coming after me.

Through my community work, I learned about tremendous organizations that work day-to-day to assist immigrants and refugees resettling in Lowell. These groups teach newcomers English, help them apply for a work permit or Green Card and health insurance, or locate the nearest food pantry. They can go to the Lowell Community Health Center without having to worry about bringing someone to translate because there are interpreters available. This is a life-changing experience for many people I have worked with as a case management intern at the International Institute or as a community volunteer with the Africa America Alliance of Lowell.

In 2019, I was a member of the Public Matters leadership development program sponsored by the Lowell Plan economic development group and the National Park Service. Participants in this civic engagement initiative are trained as upcoming community leaders to contribute effectively in a forward-moving, diverse, and partnership-oriented city. Despite challenges immigrants face when they resettle in Lowell, there is a support system that helps to create a welcoming environment for newcomers. The fact that their (our, really) concerns are core to daily conversations in the community makes me hopeful as I look ahead.

Thomas McCarthy

The Day Warms Up

for Catherine

When we feel the first heat of the afternoon sun,
A victory of the galaxy over a winter of four years,

I want to give thanks to our Holy Father in Rome,
You want to thank your Holy Father from Tibet.

The sun, it must be said, demands not even

Our least attention. Instead, it moves to the one handclap,
Warming everything in its path. On an atheistic run.

Thomas McCarthy

Camping in Snow

All canvas needs to be challenged the way art is:
February came roaring into my *Hilleberg* studio,
Saying we're all fools.
February had learned something we didn't know.
Late winter would not share its sovenance
With anyone: indifferent snow falling in pools

Of blue, perished trees awaiting redress,
The wind with its down-stroke and flourish—
All had been winter-taught, critically formed,
All placed their mark upon the flapping canvas.
In my tiny vestibule I tried the churlish
Stove but it wouldn't be primed

Into a warm response. Wind invigilated the tent,
Finding the ground hard, but the snow too moist.
Guy-lines had tell-tale exhalations of dew,
There was a leakage of colour in the suffrutescent
Hedgerows. I found shelter in the critical device
Of one sleeping-bag. In art, at least, this is true.

Thomas McCarthy

Translucent

A white squall adds its wet mantissa
To the mountain's snowy argument:

A camphor of snow, its translucent
Droplets gliding to a dry area;
Drops as indifferent as telephonists

In the olden days. The pure gold
Of comfort is chalked with

The basonite of such Melleray winds
As must have made each poet cold

In the nights before rescue:
A flying column of Inniskillens

Is abroad in cold drifts, the wings
Are white, the night-march is snow.

This tent, though red and beautiful
In winter light, is outrecuidance

Personified, spitting at centuries
As they fall upon me. I am away

With the snow and nothing is near,
Though somewhere, I am sure,

My snowed-in ancestors call for
A troop of horse, a bold Rittmeister.

Resi Ibañez

The Canyon

I'm no geologist, but
it is a miracle on earth

How liberating it is to see a border

made of water and air
two rock forms on either side
left without words
and gasping

How many canyons do I have
under my skin
beneath the surface

how many canyons
eroding at what I thought I knew

I am 28 years old
and 7400 feet above sea level

Beneath my feet
are millions of years of history
containing lifeforms
older than I can comprehend

I am at elevation
and when I go into the canyon
I am just as inconsequential

Someday too
I will be these bones
I will be in this earth
and water may expose me,

but I will fade into the dark
nightly

I went climbing down
after dark
and saw my shadow
cast by moonlight

It followed me back to the rim
where it disappeared

It must have returned back
into the canyon

carrying a piece of me
back into the stone
back into the earth

Breaking
teleological
geological time
breaking
back into the earth
with every step
breaking in
my soles

what does it mean
to be in this body
in this skin
in this space

the layers of sandstone and limestone are smooth
yet all layers come to points:
sharp angles lookouts
and switchbacks

like the pangs
of a gender heartache
I can feel geography shifting

the first time I wanted to be a boy
was on the edge of Plateau Point
where I needed to carve
new places in this earth and impress my soul in it
and you did

next time I see you, shadow
I won't ask how you are
I will ask you
saan ka pupunta
where are you going?

though I feel like I know.
You went farther back
than I could hike
to a place called Skeleton Point:

I want to hear what you have to say
of life and bones
below the surface

Alex Hayes

Altars

Man sat making minute gestures onto an altar composed of glass
and metal,
He was not alone;
Altars stretched to the horizon,
each attended by a willing supplicant,
His movements were as deft and subtle as those who had made
the altar,
Though his were made out of indolence and comfort,
Theirs a cruel necessity of a particular system of economics.

At regular intervals, he opened his wrist to feed the altar;
out spilled time and motivation and dreams,
A thousand stories poured onto the floor and seeped through the
cracked stone,
never to be heard,
Though he gleefully captured the moment, that it might adorn
the altars of others,
Buying him a precious second of attention.

Man mistakenly believed that the altar nourished him in kind,
He convinced himself he was full,
The altar belonged to him and he belonged to it,
Upon it he had inscribed all he needs know,
And nothing was written upon it but what he willed,
And yet, Man felt a gradual chill spreading throughout his chest,
and that is when he noticed the fog begin to envelop him.

He could no longer see the others,
His fingers stiffened and quivered and he could not move,
Courage was needed now,
but when it came time to step away from the altar and look upon
the face of the frost
he could do nothing but feel the rumble in his stomach and the

self-imposed lethargy of his veins,
As Man moved from whimpers of agony to sepulchral silence,
    the altar made no protestations;
it was, after all, only a thing.

Kate Hanson Foster

Reincarnate

I open the backdoor and baptize
myself in a clean rush of garden air.

The crows announce themselves—
a sub-song of quick, downward cuts

from tall pines. *Have we met?*

A child buries her head
into the warmth of my waist. I look

down and my own face is looking back,
like the dull glow of moon in earthlight.

I am amazed by my own body.
The assembly of cells building and rebuilding

without incident, or song, or ceremony.
I comb skeins of hair, brush clipped

fingernails into a dustpan—slivers
of life I simply collect and throw

away. I sink my knife deep into the skin
of vegetables—eat the light hidden

in the tomato. The slow horse of my heart
clopping as if it has nothing better to do.

Paul Marion

Names of Barges

After Donald Hall and his horses

Theodela, Vianen, Maersk, Werner Reich, Votesse, Synthesis 6,
Rhinekrone, Andrea II, Inversa, AnneRose, Mejora, Rhemus.

Like Mark Twain in his Heidelberg cap at the controls,
Captain Greta guides the ship with the current seaward,
Her vessel overloaded with the fraught freight of all of us,
Pushing past Twain's quaint Rhine Gorge of castles and traces
Of pirate toll-takers, past the ramparts and princess spires,
Just not funny these days, not a distraction that Greta
Can abide, all business as she strikes forward, using nature
To reveal Nature and yelling at us from the bridge,
"The house is on fire!" (unsaid, You stupid old fools!).

Marcona, Kohl-Düsseldorfer, Hyundai, Tramp, Inga II, Valetta,
Oscar Wilde Basel, Amakristina, Ella Rotterdam, Evident, Till.

And the barges line up behind her lead, heading away
From the highlands and towards open water where hot cargo
Can be cooled and cleaned by windmills and salt-tides,
The lock-tenders alerted to the convoy, the river levels enough
This summer to satisfy the pilots, not like last July when boys
Played football in the dry bed, the expensive tours cancelled,
The burning air killing the weak and poor in Strasbourg,
Before the Yellow Vests in Paris streets said, "We can't worry that
The world's ending—we try to live to the end of the month."

Lorely Elegance, Marktheidenfeld, Chateau Chalon, Stolt Maas,
Terra Nova, Virginia, Springer, Gerhard Schmitter, Ina, Damina-K.

Chath pierSath

Bamboo Bush/Kapok Tree

Returning,
Sixteen years of smells and sounds.
A Cambodia/Kampuchea of a different time.
No, neither guns nor exploding bombs.
They tell me
Phnom Penh is full of people.
I've forgotten. I've read of emptiness.
Weddings and deaths.
They tell me
I could never understand the destruction wrought
They tell me.
I left
On foot,
Hunted in Thailand on the way to America.
We were all fleeing, making safety and fame,
For war and genocide.
Nothing is familiar
About my home—the river drove on.
The kapok tree my mother had planted.
My sister had told me to look for a bush of bamboo,
But they are everywhere, and how could she remember
If I couldn't—I asked an old man Grandfather if he
Knew my sister Sareen, and, shaking, he didn't know
My Father Uy Lam. Everyone knows him, and I am
His youngest son, but fingers point north farther on
Toward a woman squatting under a kapok tree not asking
Questions about mangoes or bamboo.
The missing fence and house not embraceable,
But my mother's voice echoes back from the market
Past a broken bridge where a machine gun was searching
For an idyllic view.
No house. No pond. No bamboo.
No lemongrass.

Dave Robinson

from *Sweeney in Effable, Book V, Sweeney In-Clear-Light*

Chapter 10

After a "wicked bad winter," as we say, spring sometimes doesn't know what it's doing. Really none of us do.

On the flat, raw days when I can't bodysurf, think, meditate or write, I reread "For Once, Then, Something"—Frost's response to the critics who wrote of his supposed limitations as a poet-thinker. It is funny and sad that an artist of his caliber could spend a lifetime looking deeply into things to create works of art only to be told by strangers that his way of looking was all wrong.

In the end, criticism is just one flawed diamond trembling in an in-finite web of connected jewels (to use the Buddhist metaphor). You can't get trapped staring at one shiny facet for too long when the flawed *and* flawless are all the same pulsing thing. Frost knew that. After all, "For Once, Then, Something" is about wondering at the well's mouth *while* hauling the water (probably just before wondering *while* chopping some wood). The practical Buddhist point of view helps connect with the practical Frost.

When I read the poem, I'm reminded that I've spent too much of my life afraid that my blindness and ignorance would be revealed to everyone at some time. If, I feared, it hadn't shown itself plainly already. Doubts are ordinary and expected, but I suppose I had phases when I let them trouble me too much.

One of my favorite living poets taps into the futility of fearing our own blindness. As Basho and Walt Whitman wrote of fields and graves and grass, so does Denis Johnson:

... the grass becoming green

does not remember the last year,
or the year before, or the centuries
that kept passing over.
        —from the poem "Spring"
                by Denis Johnson

The grip of winter weakens by the Atlantic as spring slips north along the coast. Dozens of condemned mills in Seawell remain gutted, miles of mills, but the bars and restaurants brim with formerly cooped-up locals.

The first mild days of May and early June wrench open ten thousand stuck windows. Cherry blossoms, bluff willows and crocuses have opened their soft doors.

June leafshadow freckles
Yellow smokestacks—laughs spill from bars
Across wet cobblestones.

I used to crave the return of calmer weather, but I know now it means long spells of flatness. And I want to bodysurf when it is warm out, not stare at Lake Atlantic. I wait until after the summer solstice to fly to South or Central America for the Pacific's southern hemisphere swells.

In the northeast, spring dusks lean into long twilit evenings while the cold water repels the fair-weather surfers for a few more weeks. The bulk of cottages and beachfront homes remain vacant till school's out. There are moments of balance and solitude to be found at this time of year—when the sun slides far enough north to set behind the Sun Valley neighborhood:

Lone surfer waits to watch
May's sunlight igniting distant
Insides of empty homes.

And once these quiet beaches brim with sunburned families—everyone trying to get outside all day, to unwind, to forget about work for a week or two, then I look for a few other signs that I should go. My favorite is catching sight of my namesake bird on the hunt again down from the Arctic. The Irish poet Trevor Joyce translated the story I modeled my life after in his 1975 book, *The Poems of Sweeney Peregrine*. And I'm fortunate enough to see migrating peregrines perched on the tallest smokestacks or stooping in the skies above Seawell's downtown streets and canals:

> Springtime's great wanderer
> Wears a bluegray cloak and dark hood—
> Peregrine shits then flies.

Paul Hudon

Context Rules

Somewhere in the past George Burns and Gracie Allen are talking politics. George is asking Gracie to name her favorite party, and in one of her timeless non-sequiturs Gracie answers, "The surprise party." There's only one way to parse that, as a joke. So we laughed.

That was then.

As if to prove that context rules, the same joke was recently played-out as farce. Farce is not a joke. Farce is performed, it needs a cast. Farce works on forged identities and deliberate misdirection, on doors opening and closing. There's a fair amount of shouting.

Farce takes time. Where George and Gracie got it done in well under twelve seconds, not long ago we watched Sanders (stage left) and Trump (stage right) take a full twelve months to play it out. Stamina became a civic virtue, and not many of us laughed all the way through.

Context

When Burns and Allen began their career (1922), Harding was in the White House, and when Gracie retired (1958), Eisenhower was midway through his second term. In that time, they graduated from vaudeville to radio to movies to television; but though the venue changed, the schtick stayed pretty much in place. A patient husband and his "Dumb Dora" wife come to an understanding with complacent amiability. No slamming doors. And never, never, never was contempt or humiliation any part of George's input. That could explain their longevity. Ralph and Alice Kramden may be more honest in their sketch of married life, but who given a choice would spend thirty-six years with the Kramdens?

Context

There's no telling, even as a guess, where or when Gracie first hit that punchline. It could have been on Bridge Street, here in Lowell, where vaudevillians on the Keith circuit came to road-test their material. But I'd be willing to bet the line got a laugh every time, and I'd be willing to argue that's because no audience ever took Gracie's Surprise Party for a threat. There was never any chance in the four decades of their career that a Democrat or a Republican would be ousted by a third-party candidate, not in a national election. Not even in the volatile '30s.

Context

The volatile '90s, the 1790s, that's another story. In the opening decade of the New Republic, Madison and Jefferson surprised new-made *national* voters with a party. It was called "republican" (mainly in the South) or "democratic" (mainly in the North). It may have started as a break-out event in the intramural wrangle of Virginia politics, or as an incident on James Madison's learning curve. Either way, the party found a national context.

In fact, it built one. When Jefferson was elected president, he called it The Revolution of 1800. He referred to his achievement and his administration together as The Republic. Like it was a Done Thing. (Memo to Francis Fukuyama.) He carried-on as though he'd resolved the built-in challenge all revolutions can't avoid: Knowing when it's over. My election, Jefferson was saying, is the endgame. My republic is *The* Republic. We're done.

On the other front of the Atlantic Revolution, in France, a string of actors said the same thing. Only they said it over and over, for a quarter-century. In France, they got to the endgame more than once. And it got weird. The first article in the Constitution of the Year XII (1804) reads, "The government of the Republic is confided to an Emperor."

Context

Actors, those who act. Those who get it done. We seldom use the word that way nowadays. For us, "actors" most often means those who pretend to be someone else. They make-believe. Stage or screen, comedy or tragedy, actors put drama in the action, usually about some real and present danger. And successful acting always involves an audience. Somerset Maugham, box-office boss in his day, said that unless the audience is among the players, there is no play.

Context

For decades, Jefferson's name dominated national politics. As long as a candidate claimed allegiance to Jefferson, voters took him at his word. A handful of outliers—John Taylor and John Randolph among them—made a fuss about the primacy of states over the federal government and a strict interpretation of the Constitution of 1787, twin hallmarks of Jefferson's original creed. But the majority of Jeffersonians drifted toward a more relaxed attitude, especially after 1815. By the election of 1824, five contenders with varied, even contradictory, policies all claimed the Jeffersonian succession. Two of them—John Quincy Adams and Henry Clay—even claimed to be National Republicans. In 1800, yoking "National" with "Republican" in the same party was like putting "republic" and "emperor" in the same constitution; but by 1824, the surprise had been washed out of it.

Context

John Adams, with his usual exasperation, once complained that Washington could "out-Garrick Garrick." This was a reference to David Garrick, a leading stage-actor, an international star of the era. Many who knew our first president in the flesh, noted how dignified he was. His speech, how he "carried himself," set him apart from the general run of mankind. Once in a great while, in private, during the war with his staff for instance, he "lost it." Exploded in a fit of violent temper. But in public he was always "on."

Context

Some of us remember when Ronald Reagan was put down as the "Acting President." Reagan was pegged a star on the B-list of Hollywood actors of the '40s and early '50s. The B-listing, the down-market status, was italicized. And if you really disliked Reagan, or just wanted to take a shot at the Grand Old Party, you made loud reference to *Bedtime for Bonzo*. Bonzo is the chimp Reagan shared top billing with in a film released in April 1951. Thirty years later, Reagan was president. His voters applauded. The GOP offered prayers of thanksgiving to The Great Casting Director in the Sky.

Context

Gracie's non-sequiturs are in fact alternate sequiturs. She takes in the question and drives it around her universe, then lets it out where there's a different question waiting, and she answers that one. And could that be the whole magic of Donald Trump's make-believe? Giving constant surprise, often by way of self-contradiction, seems to be Trump's way of being in the world. A cloud of unknowing, a voice in the whirlwind: maybe it's his impersonation of God.

Trump graduated from the pretense of reality TV to a performance with actual, real-world consequences. From freelance vaudevillian to the mother of all headliners. Along the way he boosted the Grand Old Party across the finish line. The GOP is now that rare thing in American politics, a New Organization. In effect, a third party. (Surprise!) The revolution of 2016 runs apace, promising an alternate context where Americans can handle alternate facts without ever giving them a thought.

Jennifer Myers

Former Irish President Visits Lowell

Mary McAleese and her family were forced to leave their home in Ardoyne, north Belfast in the face of "The Troubles," the sectarian violence of the 1970s that plagued Northern Ireland. She saw, first-hand, the pain of a divided nation; the tragedy and paralysis of progress that comes with a lack of understanding and tolerance and an unwillingness to compromise. In 1997, she was elected the second female president of Ireland, the first to hail from Northern Ireland, in an election where, because of her British citizenship, she and 1.8 million of her countrymen were not allowed to vote. She served as President of the Irish Republic until 2011.

"When I got to the U.S, I was quite gratified to find out Ireland isn't the only place people are sniping at each other," McAleese told an audience Friday afternoon at St. Patrick's Church, in a program presented by the Lowell Irish Cultural Committee and UMass Lowell. "Where there are people there are problems; and good people work to fix the problems." The theme of her Presidency was "Building Bridges," and that she did.

"We simply need to learn to accept each other's point of view," she said, telling the story of St. Patrick, a slave in Ireland who did the unthinkable—loved his aggressor.

As President, McAleese celebrated both the Protestant Twelfth of July and the Catholic St. Patrick's Day at her official residence. She brokered the Good Friday Agreement of 1998, which made institutional changes within the government of Northern Ireland, as well as changes to the relationship between Northern Ireland and the Republic of Ireland and the Republic and Great Britain in an effort to heal old wounds and work towards peace. In 2011, Dr. McAleese hosted Queen Elizabeth II, the first official state visit of a British monarch to the Republic of Ireland.

Mayor Patrick Murphy proclaimed Friday, November 8, "Building Bridges Day" in the City of Lowell in honor of Dr. McAleese and presented her with the Key to the City. Prior to the speaking program, McAleese, who is spending the semester at

Boston College as the Burns Chair of Irish Studies and pursuing a doctorate in canon law at the Gregorian University of Rome, was taken on a tour of the Acre by St. Patrick's Church historian Dave McKean.

In the spring of 1822, industrialist Kirk Boott realized he needed a work force to dig what would become the five miles of canals that would power the textile mills for which Lowell has a place in history books. He contacted Charlestown, Massachusetts, labor leader Hugh Cummiskey, an Irish immigrant from County Tyrone. The two men met in Lowell, and over a pint of ale, decided they could work together. Cummiskey led hundreds of Irish laborers from Charlestown to Lowell on foot. They dug the canals using simple hand tools and gunpowder.

The early Irish formed scattered settlements, some behind what is now City Hall, others just beyond the North Common and along the Western Canal. As the Irish population rose, so did the mayhem. Boott was frustrated by the weekly territorial fights breaking out among the Irish immigrants. It is rumored that he asked his Irish maid, Mrs. Winters, how to calm the masses. "Get a priest," she is said to have responded.

Boott met with Boston Bishop Benedict Fenwick, and in 1827 the Rev. John Mahoney arrived, saying the city's first Catholic Mass, in Gaelic, at the site of what is now the Lowell Adult Education Center on Merrimack Street. The first Mass was said at St. Patrick's Church on July 3, 1831. At that time the church was a small wooden structure, too small for the population even before its doors opened. The existing thirteenth-century Gothic-style stone structure was built around the wooden church, with the wooden building removed in pieces as the stone church was erected in 1854.

McAleese said after having spent two minutes in Lowell she felt a "great familiarity with the place." It reminded her of Adoyne, the mill village where she grew up. She recalled the sacrifices her parents made to guarantee she would not spend her life working in the mills.

"It was good work for many people, but also a trap for many people," McAleese recalled. "To get their children out of the mills they would sacrifice anything and everything and they did."

That experience mirrors that of Lowell's Irish, who through hard work and education moved beyond factory work and into law, medicine, education and politics. They left the Acre, but not St. Patrick's. The church has embraced and been embraced by the immigrant groups that have called the Acre their first American home: Cambodians, Burmese, Vietnamese, and those from Central America.

"People who have come here to the same place the Irish came are stronger and here have become family," said McAleese.

"St. Patrick's doesn't leave you," said Lowell Irish Cultural Committee Co-Chair Erin Caples. "It's more than a neighborhood, it's more than a building—it's a family."

"Today the bells toll for you," Caples told McAleese. "Welcome to the family."

November 9, 2013

Onotse Omoyeni

An American Account of Black Magic & the Green Thumb

I. Down here, we don't use cash. Currency is the skin underneath your fingernails. There are no cash registers, no *cha-ching*! The only sound is the cracking of branches being snapped over and over and over. Trees cannot hold bodies, they come with too much weight, never mean to take children, with every final inhale comes the tree's exuberant exhale. *Cha-ching*. When they snap, we count the rings in the middle. *How much of their history have we taken?* Ours is not a sweet one; the deep south, this was printed on Tommy's tree. Down here, coming of age means you don't walk alone. There is no comfort in silence, so at night we all howl at the moon. During the day we eat peaches, pits litter the ground. My Grandmother tells us we're planting trees, the birth of a new generation. I ask her, Why do we plant something that's going to? . . . *Why do we learn how to knot sugarcane when we know it sits so nicely around our necks?* She smiles and puts more sugar in my coffee, bites her peach, and lets the sweet juice dribble down her chin, stain her blouse. She looks into the sun without squinting and howls.

II. Up north the summers are humid. People grin really wide, show me all their teeth. There are forests here, thick and never ending. They pay in cash, and nothing snaps. Someone smiles at me, wide, sharp canines and red tongues. Sometimes in the summer it gets really humid, the air turns all thick and sweet, hangs around my neck like a candy necklace. I dig and dig, but I don't find any peach pits. When the moon comes up, I howl loudly. Car alarms go off in the distance, and somewhere a tree snaps. In the forest they send the dogs out to dig until they hit the black earth, rich with worms and armadillo bugs. When the sun comes up, the car alarm is blaring. We're mighty underground, like seeds or a time capsule. Flesh rots in the forest, but roots, roots learn to tangle themselves with ancestors.

III. When you visit your mother at St. John's do not bring her a bouquet of roses, slowly rotting in their plastic casing. (*Do not bring your teeth to a gunfight or death to a graveyard.*) Bring her a peach tree, sit there, and pick them off their stems when they're the sweetest, on the verge of rotting, eat them all. Spit out the flesh and swallow the pit, let the sweet juices dribble down your chin. *They cannot tie you to something that grows inside of you.*

Eve Donohue

Coming Home

As our plane comes in to land at Cork Airport, I'm full of different emotions. A mixture of excitement and nervous butterflies flutter in my stomach as we get our first glimpse of green through the clouds. Have we made the right decision? Is this the best for our family life? Will the winter ahead be too miserable for us? What in God's name will we do with our toddler when it rains? All these questions are running through my head as we start our descent. From up here, Cork looks like a giant patchwork quilt of green fields, its seams dotted with trees and tiny houses. It couldn't be more different from the dry brown landscape we have left behind in Australia.

Home has been a lot of places for me over the years. I left Cork in 2009 and have never been back permanently, until now that is. Until recently, I had lived in so many different places that I couldn't have answered the question, "Where is home?" Since meeting my husband Chris while living in Sydney in 2012, we have moved to Melbourne, London, Dublin, then back to Melbourne, home to Cork for a while, then to Melbourne again, and most recently to a beachside town in Queensland.

In between our jobs we like to travel and have been to Indonesia, Sri Lanka, Spain, France, Portugal, Dubai, and Qatar in the past few years. We jokingly call ourselves modern-day gypsies, travelling from job to job, staying in Airbnbs, holiday homes, housesitting and sleeping in our family's spare rooms along the way. We are experts at getting up and going, of packing a lifetime of stuff into a few suitcases, of knowing what to bring and what to leave behind. But we have a little boy now and the travelling is much harder. We have grown tired of moving around.

We long for normality and routine. We have been dreaming of our little cottage in East Cork for months now. We can't wait to light the fire, to pack our clothes away neatly on racks, to hang up our wedding photos, to put all the books we have read on a bookshelf, to start organising the trinkets we've collected on our travels, and I long to cook with my own saucepans. No matter where we are in the world, wherever the exotic location, we long for these simple things.

Cork to us is 99s* on a sunny day, not having to lock our front door, and knowing the postman will drop our packages through the window if our car isn't there. It is daily chats with the neighbours about a weather forecast that rarely changes. It's getting stuck behind Mary as she says hello to half the town in Supervalu. It's dealing with local bureaucracy to get the simplest things done. It's windswept walks on stunning beaches, it's hearing "Sure it will be grand" when people are chancing their luck, it's the offer of directions that will go on for so long you'd wish you never asked. It is the nod of the head as you pass a complete stranger on a footpath, or the lift of the driver's finger on a steering wheel in front of you, so subtle you may just miss it, to indicate their gratitude for your patience. It was no surprise to me that Cork was voted one of the friendliest places in the world some years ago by some posh lifestyle magazine. It really is.

My husband often recounts one of his first experiences in Cork when his Australian family ask him what living in Ireland is really like. He had only been here for a day or two when we decided to take the local bus into a town near my mother's village where we were staying. We spent a few nice hours wandering around, had a dreadful coffee in a Styrofoam cup which we still to this day joke about, and as it started to pour rain we decided to catch the next bus back. As the bus pulls up to the bus stop in my mother's village and we get up off our seats, the rain is now torrential. We have no umbrellas or rain jackets. Seeing our problem, the driver asks where we are going. "Oh, just down the road there, we'll be grand, we'll run," I say. "Oh, sure sit back down there and I'll drop you off a bit closer," he says, turning the bus completely off his route to go down my mother's road. "Thanks a million," I say, delighted we won't get soaked. Chris was open-mouthed. He couldn't believe this man, who was a complete stranger, would go out of his way and off his scheduled route to drop us home because of the rain. I shrugged my shoulders at him. "It's the norm here." That bus journey is just one example of the warmth and community that exists in Cork. It is something we haven't found as easily elsewhere.

For months before we travel back from Australia I will think about our homecoming. I know people will jokingly ask us are we mad. And we will smile and laugh, and I'll give my standard answer: "Sure there's more to life than good weather." Cork does not have good coffee like Melbourne does, and forget about finding decent sushi anywhere. Blarney Castle may give you the gift of the gab, but it will not make your heart sing the way your first look at Sydney Harbour will. And Cork most certainly does not have weather like Queensland. But after years of not knowing what or where home really is, Cork feels as close to it as we will ever know.

*99s are ice cream cones made with soft-serve vanilla ice cream into which a Cadbury chocolate Flake bar is inserted.

Tom Sexton

For Sean Sexton of Coolmeen

While visiting Limerick, I read in the paper
how you discovered nine of your cows
dead in the high pasture when you went
to gather them for the evening's milking,
how you led the singed and blind survivor
down to the barn where it bawled all night.
Why lightning from a quickly clearing sky?
Why the heifer bought with all your savings?

If I had driven out to Coolmeen, we could
have watched the western sky for comets,
celestial debris our ancestors called
the tears of saints. And naked, painted
like two ancient Gaels, we could have walked
the hills reciting the misfortunes of our name—
the cattle stolen and the ancient tower sacked,
until the heaving sea itself was wet with tears.

David Daniel

Poet Laureate

There's a pub I go to called the Old Court. It's named for a castle somewhere in the Emerald Isle. Afternoons I like to sit in there over a pint and write in my notebook, or just think about things. Recently I've had the thought that the Old Court needs a poet laureate.

I'm not the only writer who drinks there. The city is loaded with poets and painters, musicians, photographers, and theater people, too. Also, teachers and after-work bankers and lawyers and laborers. Many of them are Old Court regulars. But as far as I know, I'm the only one who has this ambition to be poet laureate of the Old Court.

Years ago, the spot, at the intersection of Central and Middle Streets (can a place get more essential than that?), was a tavern called the Press Club. A block away was the *Lowell Sun* newspaper building, and after the late edition had been put to bed for the night a lot of newspaper people used to go there. A lot of cops, too.

Now I don't see any of either in there. The *Sun* has moved its offices across town, so if newspaper people (and cops) are still the hard-drinking figures of popular lore, they must do it elsewhere. The Old Court is run by Jerry and Finbarr, a pair of convivial Irishmen, one from County Clare, I think, the other from County Cork, or as they say, "cawrrkk," making the sound raw and deep in the throat.

I think the pub needs a poet laureate, someone who'll more than just drink and eat there, but who'll set pen to paper and rightly celebrate the place and the important role it plays in the emotional and artistic life of the city, someone to pull words and phrases and music from the smithy of his soul, such as it is, and give voice to the collective conscience of the race, etc.

I hereby announce my candidacy for the post. I don't need a laurel wreath; a wee taste o' the pure now and again will do nicely, t'anks. So please pick up the phone and call. Ask for Jerry or Finbarr, or one of the friendly waitresses, Megan or Jess, and let them hear from you. Better yet, pull up a glass and sit down.

Contributors

Stephan Anstey is a poet and artist who lives, works, and creates in Lowell with his wife and two cats. For several years he edited and published the small literary magazine *Shakespeare's Monkey Review*. He is deeply inspired by his two children and large extended family, his many travels, and his roots, including his great grandmother's family who came to Boston from Cork, Ireland.

Raised in Lowell by immigrant parents displaced by the Vietnam War, **Joey Banh** earned a dual bachelor's degree in management and marketing from the University of Massachusetts, Lowell. He then co-founded FreeVerse! and spent time as a traveling spoken-word artist, outdoor youth counselor, community organizer, and public-school teacher. A business consultant and career coach now, Joey is a former program manager for EforAll (Entrepreneurship for All) and also cofounded Lowell's Sizzling Kitchen restaurant with his brother and sister-in-law.

With his collection of poems titled *Obscenities* (Yale University Press/Warner Paperback Library), **Michael Casey** won the Yale Younger Poets competition in 1972, a work that judge Stanley Kunitz called "the first significant book of poems written by an American to spring from the war in Vietnam." His later books include *There It Is: New & Selected Poems* (2017), *Check Points,* and *Millrat.* Born in Lowell, he lives nearby in Andover.

Patrick Cook of Lowell is the author of a history of Middlesex Community College, where he is executive director of public affairs, and co-author of *Sully: The Words and Wisdom of Paul Sullivan.* He has been a newspaper reporter, spokesman for the city police department, and district director in the region's congressional office. Beyond his wife and two children, his passions include running, Bruce Springsteen, and comic books.

Cónal Creedon is a novelist, playwright, and documentary filmmaker; and adjunct professor of Creative Writing at University College Cork (2016-2020). His books include: *Pancho and Lefty Ride Out* (1995), *Second City Trilogy* (2007), and *Begotten Not Made* (2018). Cónal's plays include: *The Trial of Jesus* (2000), and *The Cure* (2005). His plays received critical acclaim at World Expo Shanghai (2010) and The JUE International Arts Festival Shanghai (2011). U.S. premieres were produced at The Irish Repertory Theatre, New York, in 2009 and 2013. He has written more than sixty hours of radio drama—broadcast on RTÉ, BBC World Service, and other media services. His film documentaries including *Flynnie: The Man Who Walked Like Shakespeare* (2008), which was shortlisted for Focal International Documentary Awards UK London.

John Daly has been a freelance writer for over thirty years, working mainly in the areas of business, film, and politics. He divides his time between Cork and Kerry, with regular jaunts to Barcelona, Spain. His ideal day has warm sun, an endless beach, and a stiff gin and tonic any time after 4 p.m.

David Daniel was born in Boston and now makes his home in the Merrimack Valley. He is the author of fifteen novels and story collections, including the prize-winning Alex Rasmussen private eye series set in Lowell (*The Heaven Stone, The Skelly Man, Goofy Foot,* and *The Marble Kite,* all from St. Martin's Press); *White Rabbit,* a novel of the 1960s; *Reunion;* and *Six Off 66* and *Coffin Dust* (both short fiction). His most recent book is *Inflections & Innuendos,* a collection of flash fiction from Storyside Press.

Victoria Denoon writes fiction and poetry, her work often influenced by stories her grandmother told her as a child. For several years, she was codirector of the Center for Irish Partnerships at the University of Massachusetts, Lowell. After calling Lowell home for fifteen years, she recently returned to Northern Ireland where she resides with her partner, Stephen, and dog, Jameson.

Kassie Dickinson Rubico is an essayist currently working on a memoir. She received a master's degree in creative writing and literature at Rivier University and an MFA in creative nonfiction at Pine Manor College. She teaches writing at Northern Essex Community College in Haverhill, Mass., and in the Changing Lives Through Literature bibliotherapy program.

Maggie Dietz is the author of *That Kind of Happy* (University of Chicago Press, 2016) and *Perennial Fall* (University of Chicago, 2006), which won the 2007 Jane Kenyon Award for Outstanding Book of Poetry and a Wisconsin Library Association Literary Award for Outstanding Achievement. For several years, she directed the Favorite Poem Project, a national undertaking founded by Robert Pinsky during his time as United States Poet Laureate. She is Associate Professor of English at the University of Massachusetts, Lowell.

Joseph Donahue's poetry collections include *Wind Maps I-VII* (Talisman House, 2019) and *Red Flash on a Black Field* (Black Square Editions, 2015), as well as *Musica Callada* (forthcoming 2019), *Dark Church, Dissolves*, and *Terra Lucida*, which are sections of the ongoing poem "Terra Lucida." His Lowell family roots reach back to the nineteenth century. He lives in Durham, North Carolina and teaches at Duke University, where he is a Professor of the Practice in the English Department.

Eve Donohue is a Cork native who has lived on and off in Australia since her twenties. After graduating with a BA from University College Cork, she studied for a master's degree in Melbourne in 2011. Since then she has worked in television in Australia, Britain, and Ireland. She met her Australian husband while working together on a breakfast show in Sydney. They moved back to Cork permanently (they hope) with their toddler son in 2019.

D-Tension is a Lowell-based poet, actor, hip hop artist and producer. He has performed around the world for almost three decades and has appeared on HBO, at the Apollo Theater, and Nuyorican Poets Café, and he's won two Boston music awards. D is known for disguising heavy topics as light-hearted humor. He says his top albums are *Rap Music Sucks, Contacts and Contracts*, and *The Violence of Zen*.

Trish Edelstein lived in the Middle East for ten years, where she worked as a scriptwriter and producer of films in Jordan. She recently returned to live in Ireland.

Janet Egan has been writing and taking photos since getting her first typewriter and camera in second grade. Her poetry is inspired by the rich literary tradition of the Merrimack Valley, nature, and baseball. For the past twelve years Janet has been a regular at the Untitled Open Mic at Brew'd Awakening Coffeehaus in Lowell.

Emily Ferrara is author of the poetry collection *The Alchemy of Grief*, which won the Bordighera Poetry Prize and was published in a bilingual edition (English and Italian) in 2007. She is on the faculty at University of Massachusetts Medical School where she teaches medical students creative writing as a form of reflective practice. Her poetry appears in literary and medical journals, magazines, anthologies, and on a stone pillar in Cabot Woods in Newton, Mass. She lives in Lowell.

John FitzGerald's poetry appears regularly in journals and anthologies. A chapbook of his poems, *First Cut*, was published in 2017 by *Southword*, in their New Irish Voices Series. *Darklight*, a fine press edition of his poems with etchings by artist Dorothy Cross, was published by The Salvage Press in 2019. He was awarded the Patrick Kavanagh Poetry Prize for 2014 and his poetry was shortlisted for the Hennessy New Irish Writing Award in 2015. He is a recipient of a Key West Literary Bursary and the Busolo

Prize. John lives with his family on a farm in rural County Cork and works by day as University Librarian at University College Cork.

Robert Forrant is a professor of history at the University of Massachusetts Lowell. teaching courses on global labor issues, labor history, immigration, and international development. He has been a consultant to the United Nations Industrial Development Organization, the International Labour Organization, the Organization for Economic Cooperation and Development, the International Metalworkers Federation, and several trade unions. His books include *Metal Fatigue: American Bosch and the Decline of Metalworking in the Connecticut River Valley, Lawrence and the 1912 Bread and Roses Strike,* and *The Big Move: Immigrant Voices from a Mill City* (edited with Christoph Strobel).

Ryan Gallagher is an artist, writer, and publisher who teaches high school journalism and literature. He is the author of *Plum Smash and Other Flashbulbs* (poems); *Red Book of Blues* (poems); and *The Complete Works of Catullus* (translations). A co-founder of Bootstrap Press, he lives in Lowell with his family.

Charles Gargiulo grew up in Lowell public housing, joined the military, went to the University of Massachusetts, Lowell on the GI Bill, and graduated summa cum laude with a bachelor's degree in sociology. He founded the Coalition for a Better Acre, a nationally recognized community development group and was honored by the Lowell International Institute as one of the one hundred most important leaders in Lowell history who have worked on behalf of the city's immigrants. His writing has appeared in the *New Lowell Offering, Spare Change, Merrimack Valley Magazine* and is forthcoming in *Résonance,* an online journal about Franco-American culture at the University of Maine, Orono. He is the author of an unpublished memoir about Lowell's Little Canada in its final years, *Farewell, Little Canada.*

Brendan Goggin is the former Academic Registrar of Cork Institute of Technology (CIT), a position he held from 1993 to 2008. In that capacity he had wide ranging functions in relation to the operation and development of the academic programmes of the Institute and for student affairs. Previously, he was Head of the Chemistry Department in CIT and a Lecturer in Chemistry. External to CIT, he has been extensively involved for many years with educational initiatives, including the Cork Lifelong Learning Festival, and with schools and colleges at all levels in Cork.

Kate Hanson Foster's first book of poems, *Mid Drift* (Loom Press), was a Must-Read choice for the Massachusetts Book Awards in 2012. She is the founder and editor of the popular Lowell-based lit-mag *Renovation Journal.* Her work has appeared in *Birmingham Poetry Review, Salamander,* and *Tupelo Quarterly*. In 2017, she was awarded the NEA Parent Fellowship through the Vermont Studio Center. She has a bachelor's degree from the University of Massachusetts, Lowell, and an MFA in poetry from Bennington College. She lives and writes in Groton, Mass.

Declan Hassett was an award-winning journalist with *The Irish Examiner* for forty-two years; he has written five books and five plays; one of his productions, *Sisters,* played Edinburgh and New York, as well as Cork.

Alex Hayes is a writer whose work deals with the intersection of technology, alienation, and meaning in modern life. He was awarded University College Cork's Patricia Coughlan Award for his writing in 2017. He attained first class honours in English and Philosophy at University College Cork. He lives in Waterford with his fiancée Tina and their perennially bratty cat Luna.

Bob Hodge sent this message to the editors of this book last fall: "I woke up on the right side of the dirt and my cat winked at me, so I knew it was a sign, and sure enough I got notified that my writings had been selected for this fine anthology. I have been a writer always, but for a long time I never wrote anything down, only saved it, and now mysteriously it is all coming out." Bob's first book, *Tales of the Times: A Runner's Story*, will be launched in time for the 2020 Boston Marathon. He says, "The book has a lot of Lowell in it, where I spent my formative years, and probably by way of genealogy, Cork as well." As a runner, Bob finished third in the Boston Marathon in 1979 and won the 1982 Beppu-Oita Marathon in Japan.

Alannah Hopkin is a journalist, travel writer and critic, and has published eight books, including two novels. Her story collection *The Dogs of Inishere* was published in 2017 by Dalkey Archive Press. She is the editor of the popular anthology *On the Banks, Cork City in Poem and Song*. She writes regularly for the *Irish Examiner* and the *Irish Times*.

Richard P. Howe, Jr. created *RichardHowe.com*, a hyperlocal blog about Lowell, and founded Lowell Walks, a series of guided tours plus related heritage activities. The author of several books on aspects of Lowell, including a new history about veterans' organizations, he has served as the Register of Deeds of the Middlesex Northern District since 1995. With Paul Marion, he co-edited *History as It Happens: Citizen Bloggers in Lowell, Mass.* (Loom Press, 2017), selected writings from the first ten years of his blog.

Paul Hudon is the author of *The Valley & Its Peoples: An Illustrated History of the Lower Merrimack* (1982, 2004) and the poetry collection *All in Good Time* (2011). Born in Lowell, he is back living near the Pawtucket Falls on the Merrimack River. After earning a Ph.D. at Georgetown University, he taught history at several colleges and was a museum curator for a time. He founded the Relevance Company (research and writing services) and is developing "Time and the River," an online concept to "build a brain to manage the watershed of the Merrimack."

Resi Ibañez is a genderqueer Filipinx writer and community storyteller in Lowell. They are the founder and emcee of the LGBTQ+ Lowell Open Mic series and have been published in bklyn boihood's anthology *Outside the XY: Queer Black and Brown Masculinity* and in *LOAM* magazine. Originally from the northern New Jersey/New York City metro area, they have made Lowell and the New England region their adopted home.

Masada Jones (she/her/her) is an artist, community builder, and youth worker. She is a Lowell native dedicated to investing in her people and community. A graduate of Lesley University, she is a cofounder of FreeVerse! in Lowell, which was formed to teach poetry and performance to young people. *Becoming Broken* (Bootstrap Press, 2016) is her first full-length collection of poetry.

Rose Keating is a undergraduate studying at University College Cork on a Quercus writing scholarship. She has been published in *Banshee* journal, *Southword* journal and *Hot Press* magazine. She was a recipient of the Marian Keyes Young Writer Award and the Eoin Murray Memorial Scholarship in 2019. She is a columnist for the *Waterford News and Star*.

Anthony Lawrence has published fifteen books of poems and a novel. His collection *Headwaters* (Pitt Street Poetry, 2016) won the 2017 Prime Minister's Literary Award for Poetry. A senior lecturer at Griffith University, where he teaches Creative Writing, Anthony lives on Moreton Bay, Queensland, Australia.

Sandra Lim is the author of *The Wilderness* (W.W. Norton, 2014) and *Loveliest Grotesque* (Kore Press, 2006). Her poems and essays have been published in anthologies including *The Echoing Green: Poems of Fields, Meadows, and Grasses* (Knopf, 2016) and *The Poem's Country: Place & Poetic Practice* (Pleaides Press, 2017). A recipient of fellowships from the MacDowell Colony and the Getty Research Institute, she is Associate Professor of English at the University of Massachusetts, Lowell.

Elinor Lipman, born in Lowell, writes novels, stories, essays, and poetry, for which she has received the New England Book Award for fiction, a lifetime achievement award from the New England Library and Information Network, and the Paterson Fiction Prize of the Poetry Center. Her recent books include *Good Riddance, On Turpentine Lane,* and *The View from Penthouse B.* In 2008, her novel *Then She Found Me* was made into a film starring Helen Hunt and Bette Midler. Her essay reprinted here is from *I Can't Complain: (All Too) Personal Essays* and originally appeared in the *Boston Globe.* She lives in New York.

Thomas McCarthy was educated at University College Cork and worked for many years at Cork City Libraries. His published collections include *The First Convention, The Sorrow Garden, Lost Province, Merchant Prince* and *The Last Geraldine Officer.* His *Pandemonium,* 2016, was short-listed for the Irish Times/Poetry Now Award, and his latest collection, *Prophecy,* was published in April 2019. He has won the Patrick Kavanagh Award, the Alice Hunt Bartlett Prize, and the O'Shaughnessy Prize for Poetry as well as the American-Ireland Funds Annual Literary Award. A selection of his work is included in the new *Harvard Anthology of Irish Poetry* (Belknap: Harvard University Press).

David D. McKean is an educator and historian focusing on Lowell's Irish community. He recounts the tales of those who came to a foreign land where they were often not accepted for who they were or for their faith, worked at the most menial and often dangerous jobs, and yet became integral to the culture of the city. He writes because their stories need to be told. McKean is the author of *The Cross and the Shamrock, From Erin to the Acre,* and *Lowell Irish.*

Jacquelyn Malone's work has appeared in *Poetry, Beloit Poetry Journal, Salamander,* and *Poetry Northwest.* Two of her poems were nominated for the Pushcart Prize. One appeared on the website *Poetry Daily.* She recently won the Tupelo Press Broadside Prize. Her chapbook *All Waters Run to Lethe* was published by Finishing Line Press. A former editor of www.masspoetry.org, she lives in Lowell.

Bob Martin is a singer-songwriter from Lowell whose albums include *The River Turns the Wheel, Next to Nothin', Last Chance Rider,* and *Midwest Farm Disaster,* his first album, which was recorded in Nashville, Tennessee, in 1972. He left the music business for a time and managed the Mountain Heritage School for traditional music and crafts in West Virginia before returning to Lowell. He has toured across the U.S. as well as in Europe, performing and recording with artists like Bill Morrissey, Cormac McCarthy, Merle Haggard, and drummer Kenny Buttrey, who played on *Blonde on Blonde* by Bob Dylan. A graduate of Suffolk University, he lives in Lowell with his wife, Anne Marie.

Born and raised in Lowell, **Matt W. Miller** is the author of *The Wounded for the Water* (Salmon Poetry); *Club Icarus* (University of North Texas Press), selected by Major Jackson as the winner of the 2012 Vassar Miller Poetry Prize; and *Cameo Diner: Poems* (Loom Press). Winner of *Nimrod International*'s Pablo Neruda Prize for Poetry and the *River Styx*'s Microfiction Prize, Miller received poetry fellowships from Stanford University and the Sewanee Writers' Conference. He teaches English at Phillips Exeter Academy in New Hampshire.

David Moloney received a bachelor's degree in English and creative writing from the University of Massachusetts, Lowell, and an MFA degree from Southern New Hampshire University's Mountainview low-residency program, where he won the Lynn Safford Memorial Prize. His fiction can be found in *Guernica,* and his debut novel, *Barker House*, will be released by Bloomsbury in April 2020. He lives with his family in Lowell.

Daniel Mulhall is currently Ireland's Ambassador to the United States. Educated at University College Cork, he has spent four decades with Ireland's Department of Foreign Affairs. He has previously been Ireland's Ambassador in Malaysia, Germany, and the United Kingdom. He has maintained a lifelong interest in Irish history and literature and is the author of *A New Day Dawning: A Portrait of Ireland in 1900* (Cork, 1999) and the co-editor of *The Shaping of Modern Ireland: A Centenary Assessment* (Dublin, 2016). A keen user of social media, he posts some lines of Irish poetry daily on his Twitter account, @DanMulhall

Born in Cork, **Gerry Murphy**'s recent publications include *Muse* (Dedalus Press, 2015), *My Life as a Stalinist* (*Southword* Editions, 2018), *A Complaint to the Muse*, a bilingual selection (PNV Macedonia, 2019) and *Kissing Maura O'Keeffe* (*Southword* Editions, 2019).

Rogers Muyanja immigrated to America in 2009 and settled in Lowell. He was a journalist for Vision Group in his native country, Uganda, and a reporter in the U.S. for *Ajabu Africa News*. Recently, he has been a community relations manager at the International Institute of Lowell, an organization that resettles refugees in New England. He runs a business in financial literacy through the World Financial Group. Rogers is a graduate of the Law Development Center in Uganda, Middlesex Community College, and the University of Massachusetts, Lowell. He is on the board of directors of the Africa America Alliance, which brings together people who identify as black in Lowell and nearby communities.

Jennifer Myers reported news for the *Lowell Sun* for more than a decade, during which time she won nine awards for her work and was the first journalist to receive the New England Society of Newspaper Editors "Newsroom Rising Star" award. A former aide to Lowell Mayor Patrick Murphy, where she launched the popular *Room 50* blog, chronicling events in the city, she is communications director for State Senator Ed Kennedy of Lowell. As a freelance writer and photographer, she has worked for Harvard Business School, *Merrimack Valley Magazine*, Phillips Academy, and *Howl* magazine.

Doireann Ní Ghríofa is a bilingual writer whose books explore birth, death, desire and domesticity. A Book of the Year in both *The Irish Times* and *The Irish Independent*, her most recent book *Lies* draws on a decade of her Irish language poems in translation. Awards for her work include a Lannan Literary Fellowship (USA, 2018), a Seamus Heaney Fellowship (Queen's University, 2018), the Ostana Prize (Italy, 2018), and The Rooney Prize for Irish Literature (2016), among others. Her prose debut, *A Ghost in the Throat*, will be published by Tramp Press in Spring 2020.

LZ Nunn is executive director of Project LEARN, Inc., collaborating with the Lowell Public Schools to help ensure that all students receive a world-class education. A former Loeb Fellow at the Harvard University Graduate School of Design, LZ is also a former director of the Lowell Office of Cultural Affairs. She has taught at Harvard's iLab and at Emerson College. Her writing has appeared in *Renovation Journal*, the anthology *Where the Road Begins*, and other publications.

Christine P. O'Connor is a practicing attorney who serves as chief counsel for the City of Lowell. She holds a master's degree in American Studies from Boston College and a JD from Suffolk University. She is completing a memoir about her grandmother and the RMS *Titanic* and was recently shortlisted in the RTÉ *Write by the Sea* competition.

Stephen O'Connor of Lowell, where much of his work is set, has family connections in Youghal in County Cork. He is the author of the novels *The Spy in the City of Books*, *The Witch at Rivermouth*, and *This Is No Time to Quit Drinking or Teacher Burnout and the Irish Powers* as well as a story collection, *Smokestack Lightning*. He has a master's degree in Anglo-Irish Literature from University College Dublin.

Frank O'Donovan was born in Cork and still lives there. He teaches Journalism and Communications at Cork Institute of Technology. He was runner-up in the Fish International Short Story Prize on two occasions and was a prize winner in the Maurice Walsh Memorial Short Story Competition. He had two stories published in the annual *Fish* anthology and another in *Phoenix Irish Short Stories* (Phoenix House, London).

Onotse Omoyeni is a political science and philosophy student studying the language and charisma behind dynamic political movements at Howard University. She is attempting to master the art of storytelling in its many mediums. Onotse is excited about a future in which she builds narratives that inspire action and encourage others to be brave and see their dreams through.

James Ostis, a lifelong Lowellian who has worked in Lowell City Hall and the State House, is a PhD candidate in Public Policy at the McCormack Graduate School of Policy Studies of the University of Massachusetts, Boston. In 2018, he launched the *Return to Room 50* blog with posts about the city and mayor's activities. He works for State Senator Ed Kennedy of Lowell.

David Perry owns Vinyl Destination, an all-vinyl record store in Mill No. 5, in Lowell, with his son Dan. He's a veteran newspaperman and was nominated for a Grammy Award in the Album Notes category for his essay accompanying the *Jack Kerouac Collection* box set.

Chath pierSath lives and works on a small family farm in Bolton, Mass. He writes, "I contemplate writing as a form of escape, but can't just rid myself of human ties. I paint the American sky thinking of Cambodia's tyranny and blood. Alone, but not lonely, I try living to the fullest, however long it will take me to acquire true freedom on the road, with nothing but the clothes on my back." Chath is the author of two collections of poetry, *After* and *This Body Mystery* (with his paintings).

Emilie-Noelle Provost is a Franco-American writer, author, hiker, traveler, history geek, and open-space advocate. A former magazine editor, she has published hundreds of articles and essays on a wide variety of subjects and is the author of the middle-grade novel *The Blue Bottle* (North Country Press, 2018). Her second novel, *The River is Everywhere*, will be published in 2021. She lives in Lowell.

Willy Ramirez is an educator, poet, and cultural advocate residing in Massachusetts. He is the founder and director of La Guagua Reading Group, as well as of the annual La Guagua Poetry Festival, hosted by Middlesex Community College in Lowell, where Ramirez is an Associate Professor of English.

Dave Robinson grew up in Lowell, where he met his wife, Anna Isaak-Ross, and where their two children, Griffin and Oona, were born. He has published five books with Loom Press (in two volumes): *Sweeney on-the-Fringe* and *Sweeney in Effable*. He's shopping around a collection of poems, "Nocturne in 'White' or 'Yellow,'" while working on a photography book about Famel motorcycles with Anna, whom he says is a far better photographer than he'll ever be.

Liam Ronayne, Cork City Librarian, manages seven libraries and develops new services such as the Cork World Book Fest and the website www.corkpastandpresent.ie. He chaired the Triskel Arts Centre board until 2016 and is a past President of the

Cork Historical & Archaeological Society. Born in Ballinacurra on the eastern shore of Cork Harbour, Liam has a law degree from University College Cork and a postgraduate qualification in library science from the University of Strathclyde in Scotland. He has written and edited many books on local history.

Tom Sexton was born in Lowell, and, while he lives on the other side of the continent, he has never really left. A former Poet Laureate of Alaska and member in good standing in the Lowell High School Alumni Hall of Fame, he's the author of several collections of poetry including *Li Bai Rides a Celestial Dolphin Home* (University of Alaska Press, 2018), *I Think Again of Those Ancient Chinese Poets* (2011), and *For the Sake of the Light* (2009). His *Cummiskey Alley: New and Selected Lowell Poems* is forthcoming from Loom Press.

Colette Sheridan is a Cork-based freelance arts and features journalist who reviewed plays for the *Irish Examiner* since the 1990s. She now writes occasional theatre and book reviews for the paper and a weekly column for the *Echo* newspaper. A graduate of University College Cork, she never thought her degree in philosophy (and English) would lead to gainful employment!

Brian Simoneau is the author of the poetry collection *River Bound* (C&R Press, 2014), which was chosen by Arthur Smith for the 2013 De Novo Prize. His poems have appeared in *Boston Review*, *Colorado Review*, *Crazyhorse*, *The Georgia Review*, and *Salamander*. Originally from Lowell, he lives near Boston with his family. His book *No Small Comfort* is due in 2021.

Meg Smith is a writer, journalist, dancer, and events-organizer living in Lowell, as well as a former member of the board of directors of Lowell Celebrates Kerouac! Inc. Her poems have been in *The Cafe Review*, *Poetry Bay*, and *The Dwarf Stars Anthology of the Science Fiction and Fantasy Poetry Association*. Meg's recent poetry books are *Dear Deepest Ghost* and *This Scarlet Dancing*.

Marie Sweeney of Tewksbury, Mass., is a long-time activist in local community, civic, political, historical, and cultural affairs and an advocate for education, human services, and volunteerism. With deep family roots in Lowell's Irish Acre, she promotes Irish culture, heritage, and history through her writing and commentary. A retired educator, she is an alumna of Lowell State College, now the University of Massachusetts, Lowell.

Sean Thibodeau was born and raised in Lowell. After spending ten or so years away for college and such, he and his wife settled back in Lowell to raise their two children. He's had a few poems published here and there, but no book yet. You can find him in Lowell's public library, where he works.

Peuo Tuy is a Khmer American award-winning spoken word poet and literary arts workshop educator, storyteller, and community organizer. The author of the poetry collection *Khmer Girl* and co-founder of the Cambodian American Literary Arts Association, she is studying for her master's degree in Special Education at the University of St. Thomas in Minneapolis/St. Paul, Minn., and co-teaching elementary special education academic and behavior/social skills classes. In her spare time, she loves to write, hike, swim, and eat delicious dark chocolate cakes.

William Wall has published six novels, most recently *Suzy Suzy* (2019) and *Grace's Day* (2018), three collections of short fiction including *Hearing Voices Seeing Things* (2016) and *The Islands* (2017), and four collections of poetry including *Ghost Estate* (2011) and *The Yellow House* (2017). He was the first European to win the Drue Heinz Literature Prize, and he has won numerous other awards including the Virginia Faulkner Prize, The Sean O'Faolain Prize, and The Patrick Kavanagh Award. His 2005 novel *This Is the Country* was longlisted for the Man Booker Prize. He holds a PhD in creative writing from University College Cork.

Ali Bracken Ziad is working on a debut chapbook entitled *Place and People Without.* He has been published in *Feasta, Ó Bhéal's Five Word Anthology, Spoken Worlds: Exhaling Ink*, the *Evening Echo*, and *The Quarryman.* He was the 2017 Munster Slam Champion, finishing fourth in the National Slam Poetry Championship final of the same year. He was awarded a Quercus College Scholarship for his work at University College Cork in 2016 and the Eoin Murray Memorial Scholarship in Creative Writing in 2018. He holds a BA (Honors) in English and is now studying Law at University College Cork. In November 2018, Ziad represented Cork in the Cork-Coventry Poetry Exchange.

David Zoffoli's selections are excerpted from a crown of sonnets titled *anguish is intimate: a widower's walk*, self-published in December 2018. Limited-edition copies are available at zhandmadefashion.com. His long involvement in Lowell included award-winning work at Merrimack Repertory Theatre as an actor and managing education and outreach activities, as well as teaching at Middlesex Community College and the University of Massachusetts, Lowell.

Editors

Paul Marion is the author of *Haiku Sky* (superlargeprint.com, 2019), *Union River: Poems and Sketches* (Bootstrap Press, 2017), and *Mill Power: The Origin and Impact of Lowell National Historical Park* (Rowman & Littlefield, 2014), as well as the editor of Jack Kerouac's early writing, *Atop an Underwood* (Viking/Penguin, 1999). With Richard P. Howe, Jr., he co-edited *History as It Happens: Citizen Bloggers in Lowell, Mass.* (Loom Press, 2017). His work experience includes overseeing community relations at the University of Massachusetts, Lowell, and directing cultural affairs for the Lowell Historic Preservation Commission, U.S. Dept. of the Interior. He lives with his wife, Rosemary, in Amesbury, Mass.

Tina Neylon coordinated the Cork Lifelong Learning Festival at Cork City in Ireland for fourteen years from its inception in 2004. Under her leadership, the festival expanded from sixty events to six hundred in 2017, the same year that Cork hosted the third UNESCO International Conference on Learning Cities. She is a former Books Editor at the *Irish Examiner* and arts journalist, which included presenting a live show on RTÉ, the national broadcaster. Born in County Clare, she grew up in England and attended University College Cork (UCC) as a mature student. Her master's thesis is on writer Francis Stuart. In the 1990s, she worked on the Volunteer Project for the Department of Modern History, UCC, interviewing Irish veterans of World War II. Tina was Parliamentary Assistant to the Chair of Ireland's Banking Inquiry (2014-2016). She is the author of *The Hunter Adventure Guide to Ireland* (Hunter, 2004).

John Wooding is professor emeritus in the Department of Political Science at the University of Massachusetts, Lowell, where he served as Provost for four years. On campus, he advanced interdisciplinary study and research on regional economic and social development. With Kristin G. Esterberg, he co-authored *Divided Conversations: Identities, Leadership, and Change in Public Universities* (Vanderbilt University Press, 2012), and with Charles Levenstein co-authored *The Point of Production: Work Environment in Advanced Industrial Societies* (The Guilford Press, 1999). He has written a biography about a leading thinker on nonviolence and peacemaking, as yet unpublished: *Gandhi's American Friend: The Untold Story of Richard Gregg.* He is very active in the Lowell community, including leading the Lowell: City of Learning campaign.

Acknowledgements

"Downtown" from *That Kind of Happy* by Maggie Dietz (University of Chicago Press), © 2016 by Maggie Dietz, is used by permission of the author; "Back" and "The Exhibit" from *Red Flash on a Black Field* by Joseph Donahue (Black Square Editions), © 2014 by Joseph Donahue, are used by permission of the author; "Saturday Morning, Reading 'Howl'" and "October Americana" from *Content for a Creative Revolution* by Janet Egan, Vol. 1, No. 1, © 2018 by Janet Egan, are used by permission of the author; "Good Friday" from *Red Book of Blues* by Ryan Gallagher (Bootstrap Press), © 2014 by Ryan Gallagher, is used by permission of the author; "Marathon Bombing" by Richard P. Howe, Jr., from *History as It Happens: Citizen Bloggers in Lowell, Mass.*, edited by Paul Marion and Richard P. Howe, Jr., (Loom Press), © 2017 by Richard P. Howe, Jr., is used by permission of the author; "Port Authority" and "The Canyon" by Resi Ibañez, which appeared in *Undone: A Legacy of Queer (Re)imaginings,*" Issue 1, 2019, are used by permission of the author; "Guide to Hauntings" by Rose Keating, which appeared in *Banshee* literary journal, Issue #8, 2019, is used by permission of the author; "Remarks on My Sculpture" from *The Wilderness: Poems* by Sandra Lim, © 2014 by Sandra Lim, is used by permission of W. W. Norton & Co., Inc.; "A Tip of the Hat to the Old Block" from *I Can't Complain: (All Too) Personal Essays* by Elinor Lipman, © 2013 by Elinor Lipman, is reprinted by permission of Houghton Mifflin Co., All Rights Reserved; "*White Egrets* by Derek Walcott: A Verse Review" by Thomas McCarthy, which appeared in the *Irish Examiner*, May 2011, is used by permission of the author; "One Night" from *Union River: Poems and Sketches* (Bootstrap Press, 2017), © 2017 by Paul Marion, is used by permission of the author; "Names of Barges" by Paul Marion, © 2019 by Paul Marion, which appeared in *Poets Reading the News*, is used by permission of the author; "My Father Painted Houses" from the music album *Next to Nothin* by Bob Martin (Riversong Records), © 2000 by Bob Martin, is used by permission of the author; "Invocation at the Merrimack" by

Index